PRAISE FOR *THE 20 PS OF MARKETING*

"David Pearson is one of the most experienced and talented marketing professionals I have ever met. I read and enjoyed every word of this book, which is an absorbing and exciting exposé of marketing best practice. The mini case histories are brilliant and the lessons David Pearson spells out will be of enormous value to practising marketing executives. Students of marketing would also learn a lot about the application of marketing theory. It was great to read such and unusual, interesting and useful book." **Professor Malcolm McDonald MA(Oxon) MSc PhD DLitt DSc Emeritus Professor of Marketing, Cranfield University School of Management**

"This original yet highly practical book will not only help Marketers do a better job next Monday morning, but also, properly applied, enable them to advance their capabilities over the next five years.

David Pearson's successful experience at a senior management level in consumer goods, hi tech, and business to business, for first rate American, European, and Japanese companies, give him a unique perspective.

Those who wonder why Marketers often lack a strong voice in the Boardroom, how they can radically raise their productivity in this digital age, and whether they are following the right priorities, will find the answers in this book. This is a 'Must Read' for all Marketers, in companies big and small, especially for ambitious people who wish to move up into senior management. It re-positions and expands the key principles of Marketing in a readable and actionable way." **Professor Hugh Davidson, co-founder of Oxford Strategic Marketing, author of *Even More Offensive Marketing* and *The Committed Enterprise***

"A rare man is David: possessed of a remarkable intellect, an insatiable curiosity about customers and a gift for seeing what really matters commercially. I've known David for many years as colleague at Mars, Inc., and through the Marketing Society where I was Chairman. Here he has helped us all by grasping the central truths of marketing – never accept that marketing is all about 'gut feel' – and vividly demonstrated how this understanding turns into success. His light touch and powerful examples make this the perfect book for practitioner and student alike. Everyone needs to know a marketing guru like David – now you can." **Stephen Robertson, former Marketing Director of Mattel, B&Q, Woolworth and WH Smith, and Director General of the British Retail Consortium**

"A brilliant read from a great marketing practitioner. David tells it as it is. A crystal clear exposé of marketing practice rather than just the theory. A wealth of knowledge and experience distilled into simple rules for application. From the blue chip marketeer to the entrepreneur there is sound advice for everyone." **Alan McWalter, former Marketing Director of Comet and Marks and Spencer**

The 20 Ps of Marketing

The 20 Ps of Marketing

A complete guide to marketing strategy

David Pearson

LONDON PHILADELPHIA NEW DELHI

First published in Great Britain and the United States in 2014 by Kogan Page Limited

2nd Floor, 45 Gee Street
London EC1V 3RS
United Kingdom
www.koganpage.com

1518 Walnut Street, Suite 1100
Philadelphia PA 19102
USA

4737/23 Ansari Road
Daryaganj
New Delhi 110002
India

ISBN 978 0 7494 7106 4
E-ISBN 978 0 7494 7107 1

British Library Cataloguing-in-Publication Data

A CIP record for this book is available from the British Library.

Library of Congress Cataloging-in-Publication Data

Pearson, David, 1950-
The 20 Ps of marketing : a complete guide to marketing strategy / David Pearson.
pages cm
ISBN 978-0-7494-7106-4 (pbk.) – ISBN 978-0-7494-7107-1 (pbk.) 1. Marketing – Management.
2. Marketing. I. Title.
HF5415.13.P36 2014
658.8'02–dc23

2013033896

Typeset by Amnet
Print production managed by Jellyfish
Printed and bound by CPI Group (UK) Ltd, Croydon CR0 4YY

To my father Eric Pearson (1920–2010) who taught me that the secret of business was to earn the trust of your customers.

And to my wife Carmen, who taught me that there is so much more to life than business.

CONTENTS

FOREWORD

Human history is shaped by ideas. People die but ideas live on. Forty years ago I graduated with my MBA from the Wharton Business School. The revelations in the books *Basic Marketing* (1960) by E Jerome McCarthy and *Marketing Management* (1967) by Philip Kotler were the state of the art and science of marketing. They proposed the four Ps of Product, Price, Place and Promotion. Since then, other authors have added a few more random Ps but David Pearson's new book has brought marketing theory into the modern age by identifying 16 relevant and systematic further Ps, which describe marketing actions, measurements and behaviours.

Nelson Mandela said: 'Education is the most powerful weapon you can use to change the world.' The education of marketers has become even more vital as they can now have such a crucial impact on their organization and on the communities in which they operate. I believe that marketing should be seen as a sector where there are four key elements, as in the traditional professions. These require that professionals learn both a *theoretical framework* and useful *practical techniques*, live by a *moral code* and experience a proper programme of *continuing education*.

In relation to a *theoretical framework* and *practical techniques*, David Pearson is an ideal person to provide this, given his long experience both as a practitioner and as a commentator. Marketers have to understand what customers need or want; they have to stimulate activity, create growth and instil confidence. This is true whether you are an entrepreneur or work for a major corporate, a small or medium-size company, a charity or a public sector organization.

The *moral code* for all professionals requires them to operate for the good of society. They must have a code of ethics like the doctor's Hippocratic Oath. It is vital that marketers know the legal and regulatory framework within which they operate. However, an ethical marketer does not only follow the letter of the law. You must make sure that your activities are not only legal but that they are also ones that you would be quite happy to read about on the front page of a newspaper. Unless they can pass that test then they are almost certainly best avoided.

Continuing education is required if you are to stay at the forefront of your profession. Marketing people should not blame market conditions for failures but seek to learn more about their profession in order that their organizations can prosper. The economic and technological landscape alters almost daily, which leads to huge changes in the way that consumers engage with and purchase brands. Marketers who are in tune with these developments can be the difference between business success and failure.

The global economy is currently patchy with some countries doing very much better than others. However, in all countries it is business that will provide the basis for the upturn. It is free enterprise that generates the wealth that pays for schools, health care and social services. Marketers are therefore a vital element of the turnaround.

The five Ps in Part 4 of this book relating to the human behaviours in marketing – People, Positiveness, Professionalism, Passion, Personality – are very important. Marketers should be conceptual and practical leaders. As life becomes more global we have to compete against populations around the world. We all know that people are the greatest asset for any organization. Whether for a country or a company, whether fighting a war or trying to gain market share, competition is in the end between workforces.

Leading these employees is increasingly important as organizations must be led to overcome their own inertia and to adapt to changing conditions. People do not want to be managed: they want to be led. Marketing should be providing the lead. It is that leadership that gives an organization its vision and translates that vision into reality. It reconciles the wood and the trees. It gives the heartbeat to the organization.

Marketing leadership is about communicating the vision and motivating people. The key quality is inspiration. And the lesson of countless case studies in this book is clear: if you want to inspire your team then first inspire yourself. Case studies in the book on the Sony Betamax and Mars in Chile show what can go wrong. Leadership increasingly links with entrepreneurship. They both require taking a view of the future, generating a vision around an idea, and then mobilizing resources to achieve it.

The world is changing fast, the impact of which is felt immediately and directly through the media. The financial system acts as a lightning conductor in taking money to the safest haven. Technological change is bringing the death of distance as ideas and money move instantaneously. It is also bringing the collapsing of time as competitive reactions become ever faster. As in nature, the sharks have to keep swimming or they die.

The invisible hand of Adam Smith will arrange that the greatest good is achieved by the greatest numbers. It will make sure that resources flow to where they can be best utilized. Jobs and technology will follow those changes. If you believe in marketing and free enterprise then you should expect it to work across countries and continents as well as within countries or regions.

Even Picasso, that most creative of people, felt the need for ever greater improvement. He said: 'Success is dangerous, one begins to copy oneself. It is more dangerous than to copy others, it leads to sterility.'

University is something you complete. Life is something you experience. We all know that life is not a dress rehearsal. We only get one chance to have a life so we should all make as much of it as we can. I am sure that each of you will find messages in this book that help you to achieve your potential.

Sir Paul Judge
President, Chartered Institute of Marketing

ACKNOWLEDGEMENTS

This year I celebrated my 21st birthday for the third time. In a sense I have been writing this book over the last two because that is how long I have been learning about sales, marketing and general marketing. My teachers have been countless. There have been dozens of bosses and I have learnt something from all of them, even if in a few cases it was what not to do. The majority have been terrific. A few of them are referred to in the book but I am grateful to them all. Then there have been hundreds of peers; thousands of subordinates, which the better companies call colleagues or associates; hundreds of thousands of customers; and millions of consumers or end users. I have learnt something from all these contacts and endeavoured to distil that into these pages. If LinkedIn had existed when I set out as a salesman in 1971, by now I estimate I would have connected with at least 10,000 people, and that would only be those with whom I had worked directly, never mind casual acquaintances, compared with the 1,000 or so I have today.

There have been a few academic teachers too. From time to time I have found it helpful to check into a business school or other professional establishment and learn in a classroom. I have been fortunate in finding excellent teachers at the Chartered Institute of Marketing, and at three of the world's top business schools: the world's first collegiate business school, the Wharton School of the University of Pennsylvania, USA; the Institute of Management Development in Switzerland; and at the Ashridge Business School in the UK. These are all excellent but I still think the most valuable lessons are learnt on the front line.

On the journey of actually putting pen to paper I have been fortunate to receive advice and encouragement from several successful published authors including Rita Clifton, Professor Hugh Davidson, Professor Paul Burns, Ardi Kolah, the late Laurie Young, who was discussing with me an endorsement for this book when he so tragically died in September this year, and particularly Professor Malcolm McDonald, who gave freely of his time with several invaluable pointers.

I am grateful to my friends and colleagues at Criticaleye – Matthew Blagg, Charlie Wagstaff and Andrew Minton – who, always keen to encourage thought leadership in their community, encouraged me to share some of my insights with the membership.

Kogan Page has been immensely supportive while guiding me gently through the forest of publishing an author for the first time. My thanks go to Helen Kogan, Matthew Smith, Paul Milner, Kasia Figiel, Ashley Simon, Madeline Voke, Nancy Wallace, and Amanda Dackombe, but these are just the people with whom I have had direct contact; there will be many others behind the scenes.

And lastly I am especially grateful to my family for their love and support. I could not have managed a whelk stall without them.

David Pearson
September 2013

Introduction

As long as I can remember I have always been interested in brands. As a teenager I started to smoke cigarettes surreptitiously, initially in a perverse attempt to prove that I was growing up. Before I started smoking I was fascinated by the different brands on the market and used to spend time gazing at them in the windows of newsagents' shops. The television in our house didn't transmit ITV, not until BBC launched 625-line broadcasting in 1965 and so my father upgraded our rented TV for one that would receive BBC2 – which also meant that the unholy ITV was admitted to our house for the first time and with it the advertising for cigarettes such as 'Consulate – Cool as a mountain stream'.

Once I started smoking I collected the empty packets and always bought different brands so that I could build up the collection kept hidden in my bedroom, in a broken desk that had lost its legs. When the desk was replaced with a purpose-built desktop that extended the width of my room, amazingly my mother did not discover the cache of empty cigarette packets, although I now realize that she must have known of my illicit habit from the start – just as I, a reformed non-smoker, can smell a smoker at 40 paces.

At 16 I was lucky enough to win a place at New College, Oxford University but was too young to take it up until I turned 18. I spent a year in the United States on an exchange programme and for a few months worked in a supermarket filling shelves. I started as a part-timer, three hours on a Friday evening and eight on Saturdays and then, when I was free to leave my grammar school, converted this to full-time. The store was owned by Victor Value, long since swallowed up by the giant Tesco organization, but then an aggressive supermarket chain in its own right. It had its own brand, Dairyglen, which was offered on a wide variety of food Products. My job was to fill shelves, build displays and anything else that the store manager thought necessary. He was a 24-year-old Canadian, and sharp. I am sure he went far in the world of retail, although his ethics might have caught him out. On Sundays he would invite a few of us to earn extra overtime at double rates, getting ahead for the week on filling the shelves and building key displays, which I suspect he was bribed by manufacturers' sales representatives to build. Typically these would be of newer brands of soap powder, featuring special offers of free plastic daffodils or other inducements. By the end of the afternoon I would see the manager filling up his own grocery trolley but I am not sure if I saw him taking it through the checkout.

One day we came in to a flooded warehouse. The warehouse was upstairs above the store and the rain had got in through the flat roof. The manager obviously did not think there had been enough damage so before the loss adjuster arrived from the insurance company he had two of us piling up all the stock damaged before the flood and hosing it down to make sure it was good and wet.

This was my introduction to the world of commerce. I loved it. The work was boring, I suppose, and the pay, which for me was pocket money, cannot have been a living wage. For my full-time work I received £7 per week. Nevertheless, I gained early experience, which was priceless later on in understanding merchandising and other techniques.

But at the time I had no concept that this had anything to do with my future career. I was going to go to university to read Law, or Jurisprudence as it was known in Oxford. I then intended to go to the bar, become a barrister and follow that familiar furrow.

Four years later, as I neared the end of my time at university, I realized that this was not what I wanted. I had wanderlust in me fuelled by an exciting year spent in the United States. I was not ready to commit to a life in London, which seemed to me the lot of the lawyer, and to spend much of the rest of my life in libraries staying on top of the ever-changing laws. I started to cast my net around more widely in a belated attempt to start an alternative career.

I applied to various corporations in various roles. Most of these seemed to offer a Thomas Cook tour of the company over two years or so, at the end of which you would start your career in earnest having decided what it was you really wanted to do. No doubt this was very wise but it held no attraction for me, as it seemed to me that at the end of these two years you still would not have any real experience.

Procter & Gamble (P&G) offered a much more practical career path. Early training would be followed by full business responsibility if the training was successful. In a very professional way P&G sold me on a career in sales. Successful role models were wheeled out to prove that the model worked. (One of these, Henry Jackson, had graduated from Imperial College, London and made management in less than two years. Henry later moved to Pedigree Petfoods, a subsidiary of the Mars Corporation, where, as sales manager about to transfer into brand management, he was instrumental in my own move from P&G to Pedigree Petfoods.) Tests were completed. I even had the opportunity to work for a day in the field with someone who had followed this path a year earlier. Noel Huitson would later be a colleague in Pedigree Petfoods, as Product Manager, but he was then a sales representative in his first year, managing a territory in Bradford. He demonstrated a couple of calls on Greengate supermarket branches, another long-lost name. This did not put me off but reminded me of my time in Victor Value and seemed to complete a circle for me. I could see now where the brands came from.

What I did not know was that Procter & Gamble had invented the concept of brand management back in the 1930s. Neil McElroy changed marketing for ever when he wrote the classic McElroy memo at P&G, which led to the creation of the discipline of brand management. The shift to brand management began on 13 May 1931, with an internal memorandum from Neil McElroy (1904–72), an athletic young man who had come to P&G in 1925 right after his graduation from Harvard College. While working on the advertising campaign for Camay soap, McElroy became frustrated with having to compete not only with soaps from Lever Brothers and Palmolive, but also with Ivory, P&G's own flagship Product (Fairy Toilet Soap in the UK). In a now-famous memo, he argued that more concentrated attention should be paid to Camay, and by extension to other P&G brands as well. In addition to having a person in charge of each brand, there should be a substantial team of People devoted to thinking about every aspect of marketing it. This dedicated group should attend to one brand only. The new unit should include a brand assistant, several 'check-up People', and others with very specific tasks.

The concern of these managers would be the brand, which would be marketed as if it were a separate business. In this way the qualities of every brand would be distinguished from those of every other. In advertising campaigns, Camay and Ivory would be targeted to different consumer markets, and therefore would become less competitive with each other. Over the years, 'Product differentiation', as business People came to call it, would develop into a key element of marketing.

McElroy's memo ran to a terse three pages, in violation of President Deupree's model of the 'one-page memo', a P&G custom that had become well known in management circles. But the content of the memo made good sense, and its proposals were approved up the corporate hierarchy and endorsed with enthusiasm by Deupree.

Thus was born the modern system of brand management. It was widely emulated, and in one form or another was still followed in the early 21st century by many consumer-Products companies throughout the world. Typically, brand managers were energetic young executives marked for bright futures within a company. All of Procter & Gamble's own chief executive officers (CEOs) after Deupree had brand-management experience. This group included Neil McElroy himself, who headed the company after Deupree retired in 1948, and who in 1957 became Secretary of Defense under President Eisenhower.

Brand management as a business technique was one of the signal innovations in US marketing during the 20th century. It epitomized the persistent theme of balancing centralized oversight with decentralized decision-making based on who in the company had the best information about the decision at hand.

What I also did not fully appreciate was that the career of brand management was also open to me and was generally considered as a better path for bright graduates to tread. Indeed, while the sales path I was to tread offered no guarantees of advancement as a graduate – I was to compete with any other colleague for management advancement – only graduates were admitted to the ranks of trainee brand assistants.

But what I felt instinctively was that this was where I belonged. I would learn my brand management on the front line. I would sweat blood and tears building displays, carrying out stock to the front of the store so that I could Persuade the manager that it needed replacing at the back.

Within two months of starting my training I was given responsibility for a section of the company's business and within six months was winning prizes in sales competitions. I was also fortunate in that I had landed in an experimental part of the company's business. At that time, 1971, Procter & Gamble was going head-to-head with its traditional competitor, Lever Brothers, part of Unilever, in the soaps and detergents business, but had a much less developed position in toiletries. Today, thanks to both organic developments and acquisitions of Chesebrough-Pond's, Richardson-Vicks, Clairol, Wella and Gillette, P&G is the world leader in toiletries. Back in 1971 it had much less development and in the UK was barely starting.

Two Products – Head & Shoulders shampoo and Tempo deodorant – were being test marketed in four regions of the country: Tyne-Tees, Yorkshire, Southern and Ulster. A separate sales force had been created for this purpose. To give the sales force more credibility with the trade, Camay and Fairy Toilet Soap had been added. These were the first brands I handled not as the manager but as one of the 30 or so sales representatives charged with keeping them alive in the test markets.

I was not to take personal responsibility as a Product manager for another seven years, when in 1978 after two successful years as a sales manager with Pedigree Petfoods I transferred to marketing as Brand Manager for some of the company's non-canned brands. I was now reporting to Chris Bradshaw, a highly talented marketing manager who had cut his teeth on the launch of Ariel detergent at P&G and had followed the well-worn track from Gosforth (the then UK HQ of P&G) to Melton Mowbray (the then UK HQ of Pedigree Petfoods). He had written the hugely successful strategy that led to the development of the company's most Profitable brand, Whiskas cat food, but was now charged with making a success of the company's investment in technology for dry and semi-moist pet foods. I initially took over Bounce Minced Dinner; a 'me-too' version of Quaker's Chunky Minced Morsels; Munchies; a me-too version of Carnation's Go-Cat; and Trill, a highly Profitable seed mix for caged birds: 'Trill makes budgies bounce with health!'

Unlike P&G, Mars offered very little in the way of training at that time, it was mainly by direct responsibility on the job. However, I Persuaded Chris that I should attend a course in marketing and went on a one-week course at Moor Hall in Cookham run by the Chartered Institute of Marketing.

Here for the first time I came across the concept of the 'Four Ps of Marketing'. First developed in the 1960s by E. Jerome McCarthy in his classic *Basic Marketing*, and Philip Kotler in his equally classic *Marketing Management*, I suppose that in 1978 this was still relatively new in the teaching. It states that there are always four elements in the marketing mix, and for ease of recollection each began with a P.

First, of course, was *Product*. There has to be a Product to sell. Then there is *Price*. We must Price our Product. Then there is *Place*. We must make the Product available for sale at a Place. And finally there is *Promotion*: for the first three are not enough – we must make the potential consumer aware of our Product and Promote it to her/him.

Thousands of students have absorbed this simple lesson of the marketplace. Many business Plans have been written on the basis of this definition of the marketing mix. But for me, as someone whose experience of business was practical before it was theoretical, I was always uneasy about this message. Surely there was more to it than that. And there was. And there is. In fact, senior managers around the world trained in Kotler's famous 'Four Ps of Marketing' still construct strategy around it, whereas Kotler himself sees the 'Four Ps' as too rigid for 21st-century marketing.

Over the last 30 years the marketing profession has struggled to be taken seriously. Within the profession there is a lot of angst about its presence or lack of it in the boardroom. Many observers present analysis that decries British industry because there is no one charged with the role of Marketing Director at board level in the vast majority of large-scale businesses. For me, it would be surprising if there were. If I was on a board where someone had the role of Marketing Director and tried to claim responsibility for these four Ps but not others I would be seriously concerned about the direction of the business.

After spells at Mars in the United States and Chile I returned to the UK initially to work for an embryonic food brokerage named Crombie Eustace. The founder, John Eustace, was yet another who had trained at Procter & Gamble and then traded in his training for a more senior sales role at Pedigree Petfoods, where we worked together. He then gained brand management experience with Revlon before setting out on his own. The business model was to represent brands that had traditional distribution but now needed to expand into the multiple grocery outlets. We acted as a bridge between the brand owner and the distribution channel and, as such, certainly exercised influence over the four Ps in a great variety of brands from reputable houses such as Mars, Akzo, Gillette, Bic and others. This was my first experience as an agent for a brand owner and, unlike advertising agencies that primarily concentrate on just one of the Ps – Promotion – we exercised influence over all four and several more in addition, and which I shall introduce later.

From there I returned to the more formal corporate world and joined Pillsbury. At the time it had enjoyed great success on Wall Street delivering 13 years of continuous growth in earnings per quarter, an admirable record if balanced by reinvestment in brand equity but that was not the case. Nevertheless, Pillsbury was a great brand owner in its own right. Famous for the eponymous Pillsbury Dough and its easily recognizable cartoon character, through acquisition it had added Green Giant, with another famous character, the Jolly Green Giant. Both of these were the creation of Leo Burnett. Then Burger King had been added, thus marking an entrance into the restaurant business, a brand probably second in that sector only to McDonald's. Later during my time it was to acquire and start to expand Häagen-Dazs, a brilliantly conceived upmarket brand of ice cream that took that sector right back upmarket from its dismal past as a cheap imitation of the real thing.

In the UK, Pillsbury, a supplier of cake mixes in the United States, had acquired the leader in that market, Green's of Brighton, and I was hired as General Manager of the business. For the first time I had full responsibility for research and development (R&D) and manufacturing as well as marketing and so could genuinely drive Product development as well as manage a Profitable portfolio. As a Wall Street-driven company, my task was to deliver a Profit contribution in cash terms.

From there I was headhunted to a dream job: Managing Director of Sony UK Consumer Products Company. Here I was responsible for the marketing of the famous range of Sony consumer Products, a business then worth £150 million in the UK. I was to retain this responsibility for over 10 years and, with the help of a wonderful team, grew the business to £523 million. Of course, Sony sold other Products: a range of tapes and batteries and some highly sophisticated Products for Professional use such as cameras for broadcasting. Later I was to become responsible for these too, but as most People would identify the company by its televisions and hi-fi Products I was effectively the UK brand manager for Sony, which was then one of the most Powerful brands in the world as measured by various agencies on reputation, quality, innovation and several other key criteria.

Sony's sub-brands were almost as Powerful. Walkman was of course a category in its own right; and Trinitron defined quality in TV pictures and reliability. I will examine later the reasons why such sub-brands are important as part of the Positioning of a Product and go well beyond the simplistic lessons of the four Ps.

After 10 most enjoyable years I decided to get experience of the world of the public company and so joined Pentland plc, a great brand owner in its own right. Pentland had come to the fore in the 1980s by acquiring a majority interest in the US distributor of Reebok, a comparatively unknown sports brand. Reebok was actually of British origin but the US distributor under the leadership of Paul Firestone drove the brand hard to compete with Nike and Adidas. In the process, Pentland's initial investment of US $77,000 was parlayed into a sale of $777 million, one of the great deals of all time.

With the proceeds Pentland acquired interests in a number of other brands in the sports and fashion markets including Speedo, Ellesse, Berghaus, Reusch, Mitre and several others. It had developed particular expertise in sourcing footwear from the Far East, it was one of the first companies to go offshore, and had also been licensed for footwear by the great Lacoste brand. All of these came under my direction as Managing Director of International Brands and I was able to gain considerable experience and knowledge of global branding and licensing.

I then moved to become Chief Executive of a British plc, NXT, which had developed an innovative method of making loudspeakers out of flat panels, thus delivering obvious design advantages with different acoustic properties and potential cost savings. The chosen business model was to license the technology and simultaneously build an ingredient brand such as Dolby in audio or Gore-Tex in textiles. NXT had licensed over 250 companies and thus we became an intimate player in the development of other major corporations in their marketing, including Toyota, NEC, Philips, Samsung, TDK, Brookstone, Hitachi, Toshiba and many others.

It is not an original thought to propose more than four Ps. Professor Hugh Davidson in his seminal works *Offensive Marketing* and *Even More Offensive Marketing* proposed a different acronym, POISE. Hugh also began his business career in marketing at Procter & Gamble, before developing senior management experience with Playtex. He then established a highly successful consulting business and gained his chair at Cranfield University. He thus meets my definition of a worthy academic in that he learned his first lessons in the marketplace.

Conor Dignam in an article in *Marketing* in January 2000 added the '5th P' in his terms of *Perception*, and I have certainly included that in my list although for different reasons. A very impressive French executive Christian Malissard whom I met in the 1990s had his own list of Ps – profile, People, prospect, portfolio (sales proposition), Partnership (through and with), Promotion, process and politics – but that was more in the context of managing a sales team than the more comprehensive definition that I want to use for marketing. I have included *Partnership* (as well as *promotion* and *people*) but in a wider context.

And in an article in *Journal of Brand Management* (JBM), on whose editorial board I served for its first 18 years, Papasolomou and Vrontis (JBM Sep–Nov 2006) proposed six additional Ps: Philosophy, Personality, People, Performance, Perception and Positioning. Of these I use four, but it is interesting that Papasolomou and Vrontis give reasons based on changes in the marketing method and the context of marketing such as the greater importance of service brands, whereas for me these differences have always been with us. The need to consider *Positioning* was at the core of McElroy's memo back in 1931. The need to consider the distinctive nature of your *Product* was in Rosser Reeves's development of the Unique Selling Proposition (USP) back in the 1940s.

From my limited beginnings as a sales representative in 1971 selling the very brand that Neil McElroy had managed in 1931, and that had given him the concept that led to brand management, I have since managed, directed or in some way interacted with literally hundreds of brands, from the strong and famous to the weak and discontinued. While I have read many business books, and indeed been inspired by some, I offer this book as an analysis of marketing from my practical experience on the front line.

I have been running businesses for over 40 years. I have managed everything from start-ups to cash cows. I have worked in privately held businesses as well as publicly quoted companies. I have worked in fast-moving consumer goods, in durables and in business-to-business. I have worked for British-run companies as well as US, Japanese and Iranian.

I have also run my own business. I have transacted business in over 50 territories all over the world. And I have always done that with a deep-rooted foundation in marketing.

In developing the idea of *The 20 Ps of Marketing* I have not simply raided Roget's *Thesaurus*. I have drawn as much as possible on my own experience and the unique insights that working for and with some of the greatest brand owners in the world has given me. I have divided the book into four parts. In each part there are five chapters and each chapter describes one 'P' – a fundamental plank in marketing. In some cases I have added other relevant Ps but, as I say, this is not an exercise in digesting the dictionary but rather using my practical experience to help the less experienced practitioner.

The first group of Ps, Part One, I call the core. They are the original four, to which I have added *Packaging*. In some versions this is included in *Product* and it also can be confused with *Promotion*. They are distinctive exercises. Of course, Packaging can contribute to the design and thus the identity of the Product – think of Coca-Cola – but first it has to deliver the Product to the *Place* of sale and thence to the place of consumption. A capped bottle does this very well and that is why Coca-Cola and all its imitators are still using it over 100 years later. The Packaging is a very distinctive part of the marketing mix.

Part Two covers the actions taken by the Product manager. These start with *Planning*, an important subject in its own right. I believe that Planning is the start of success and failure. *Persuasion* follows, the subject both of internal championing and external salesmanship. Without it most projects will also fail. *Publicity* is next, for me a separate action from *Promotion* (as it is envisaged in the core five Ps in Part One) as it encompasses Public relations, an exercise that can be passive in nature but still fundamental to success. Two joined 'Ps' follow: the *Push-Pull* of marketing – good marketing, that is – has a rhythm to it that is not well understood. To be successful in business we have to get our timing right. And last in this group is the all-important subject of *Positioning*, arguably at the core of Neil McElroy's original memo on brand management.

Part Three covers the measurements of success. Starting with *Profit*, which many in the financial community will regard as the most important of all the Ps; then considering *Productivity*, a key responsibility of all in management but particularly those in marketing as they must understand the balance of resources required to bring a Product to market. *Partnership* comes next. It is unlikely that we will achieve success without entering into relations of mutual reward with a series of Partners, and this skill is not well covered in the textbooks. After that comes *Power*. Good marketing managers are trying to create and then exercise Power over distribution channels, and then over consumer choices. Finally in this section comes *Perception* as advocated by Conor Dignam. We need to be Perceptive in the appreciation of what is happening in our market. I would expect the marketing manager in a classically organized company to have that insight. I will explain why the sales force can only be a source of information and will not have that understanding.

The final section, Part Four, covers the behaviours of those involved. I start with an obvious P that seems to be missing from most more conventional lists; *People*. People make the difference and we must consider their needs in any analysis of the fundamentals of any human activity. We want our People to be *Positive*, even proactive. We want them to act as *Professionals*, meaning they will work to standards. One of the tragedies of the marketing Profession is that it is not one of conventional standards. If you want to be an accountant or lawyer or doctor you have to pass certain examinations in order to be considered as a Professional. Thus these Professions guard the numbers of their membership. They act as a closed shop as much as any trade union. Marketing has failed to establish these standards and has suffered in consequence. There are many ways to enter the Profession, as my own career proves. But we can still demand that practitioners work to Professional standards. But we also want our People to have *Passion* and pride in what they do. If they are cold and robotic in their dealings they will not inspire and will not get the dramatic results. And my last P? Well, my final P is *Personality*. I think it is extremely important that in business we express ourselves. By exhibiting some Personality we will encourage the creativity in our teams and in those we are seeking to influence.

A note on the definitions in this book

The four Ps were developed in the context of FMCG – fast-moving consumer goods. Companies such as Procter & Gamble and its direct competitors, Lever Brothers, Colgate Palmolive, and Beecham were the first to use these techniques. Their skills were then adopted by an increasingly wide variety of businesses and today are ubiquitous.

The job titles Brand Manager and Product Manager are virtually interchangeable and will vary mainly according to the branding policy of the corporation. Thus Procter & Gamble uses a range of different brand names for its products, none of which indicate the company from which the Product is sourced. Sony, on the other hand, usually uses its Powerful corporate brand as an umbrella over the vast majority of its thousands of Products. Thus P&G employs brand managers whereas Sony employs Product managers – but the job is broadly the same.

A marketing manager performs similar functions at a more senior level. He or she may manage markets and have a number of Product/brand managers reporting to him/her. These definitions also cover services that are not strictly *Products*. One of the largest service businesses in the world, Microsoft, sells software – a not always tangible concept – but in its approach to the 4 Ps or the 20 Ps of marketing it shows little difference from its hardware cousins who carry its software on their computers.

The same might be said for service businesses such as airlines or hotels. Their Product has a short shelf life and thus is just as fast moving as a food Product – indeed faster, as some food Products have value after their sell-by date but the flight has flown with its empty seats.

These techniques came much later to business-to-business (B2B) sectors but are just as valid. I have extensive experience in B2B and regard it to be just as fascinating and demanding as business-to-consumer (B2C). There are subtle differences in the managing of the market, in the area of research for example or in the role of trade shows, but the techniques of analysis are fundamentally the same.

PART ONE
Core

Product

01

There are only three Ps in marketing: Product, Product, Product.

LORD SUGAR TO THE AUTHOR, 1995

Lord Sugar once told me that there were just three Ps of marketing: Product, Product, Product. He was of course echoing the motto of the estate agent – 'location, location, location' – or indeed Tony Blair's soundbite of his three priorities in government: 'education, education, education'. It's a nice line and certainly Lord Sugar has had more than his fair share of product successes. He has built from nothing a billion-pound enterprise and is one of Britain's best-known businessmen, known more now for his television appearances on Britain's version of Donald Trump's *The Apprentice* than for the fact that he did as much as anyone to popularize the personal computer in the UK and later was one of the founders of the satellite television industry.

But for all that, he is wrong on at least one count that I am sure he would acknowledge. What he means is that you have to get the Product right in order to have a chance in the game. But for Lord Sugar getting the Product right is, more than anything, getting the *Price* right. *Price* will be addressed in the next chapter, but for now let us assume that the Price point is right. How do we go about developing the *Product*?

Product development

There are various ways, and you will not be surprised that I will begin with the Procter & Gamble method. P&G bases its Product development firmly on research. It spends huge sums on research and development (R&D) in both the sense of science and also in research into consumer attitudes. It conducts extensive surveys in its chosen field of expertise in order to ensure that it is keeping up to date. For example, as new forms of washing machine are developed it works closely with the manufacturers (an example of the Partnerships that we will consider in Chapter 13), to ensure that it has formulations that will work effectively in the new machines. It also looks at new fields to conquer. Increasingly these are hard to find, which is why, in the recent past, its expansion has come more through acquisition rather than organically.

Many years ago, however, it was a weak player in the shampoo market and decided to become a strong one. P&G's research into shampoo usage and the washing of hair in general showed it that fully two-thirds of mankind, at least in the developed world, suffer from dandruff some of the time, while one-third suffer from it all the time. Dandruff is both uncomfortable to the sufferer and, unless it is controlled or prevented, is very obvious to everyone as it shows on the shoulders. P&G set out to discover a cure. Over a period of many years it researched some 20,000 different compounds before discovering the one that seemed to give the best results. This was zinc pyrithione. P&G then set about establishing a delivery method and researched further into its usage. I was involved in a small way in the test market of this Product, Head & Shoulders, in the UK. It was already an established success in the United States – I used it there myself as a student in the late 1960s – but P&G did not make the classic mistake of assuming that the same Product marketed in the same way would necessarily succeed in the UK. So the Product was tested in different regions with different types of water, hard and soft. Different formulations and Pack sizes were also tried. And, of course, different Promotions were also tried.

Finally, in 1975, the Product was launched nationally in the UK. It had been in test market for seven years (Boots complained that it should be entered in *The Guinness Book of Records*). The Product was successful and became brand leader. It still is. *That* is a Product. Of course, many things have changed; the formulations have been varied with many innovative varieties added. The Packs have changed; the Pricing has changed. But the fundamental Product and its core Positioning (of which more in Chapter 10) have not changed. This research-based method of Product development is no doubt carried out in many other businesses. But it is not the only way.

Sony spends vast sums on research and development, but spends comparatively little on consumer research. Instead its engineers tend to develop their own ideas for Products, based on insights and, of course, a much greater knowledge than the consumer can have in terms of technological capabilities.

Sony is famous for creating markets. Procter & Gamble did not create the shampoo market, it did not even create the dandruff shampoo segment – but it came to dominate it through rigorous commitment to research-based marketing. Sony created the Walkman market, the forerunner of today's iPod, through a combination of genius and dedicated engineering.

The idea of Producing a tape player without loudspeakers and with no recording capability seemed absurd even to the engineers in Sony. It was not in fact an invention, given that it used existing technologies, although it took painstaking development of those technologies to Produce it. Akio Morita, one of the co-founders of Sony, is credited with the 'invention' of the Walkman. But the team of engineers who delivered it was led by Kozo Ohsone, himself a charismatic engineer. He carried around a wooden model of the target Product with the dimensions already decided. To achieve this Shizuo Takashino, his principal assistant engineer, had to Produce a cassette mechanism considerably smaller than those on the market, although the dimensions of the cassette were already fixed. He puzzled over this for months and then one day on his long commute into Shibaura factory he solved it and, displaying a typical example of Sony lateral thinking, bent the angle of the motor to fit the target dimensions.

The Product could now be made but still there were many sceptics, some of whom demanded research into consumer attitudes to the new concept. Akio Morita rejected these calls and argued that no research could predict what would happen. It was Sony's task to propose to the market and for the market to decide. A worldwide launch then followed, and again scepticism was met in the distribution companies around the world. The Japanese-coined name Walkman was originally rejected, as were other names used in the United States (Soundabout) and the UK (Stowaway). However, with imaginative Promotion, the Product was a huge success and spawned a new lifestyle. Within two years the Americans and the British came round to accept the name Walkman, which is now in the dictionary.

Throughout history inventors have been ahead of their time in predicting market demand for a new kind of Product. Yet although the fundamental need might exist within us for such new Products, conventional research will not identify this need – the reason being that because the consumer does not appreciate that the new Product is a real possibility they will not articulate the demand. But put the Product in front of them and they will say, 'All my life I wanted one of those!'

Look more closely, however, and you may find evidence of the need. Take manned flight as an example. Throughout most of history, if someone had proposed manned flight he or she would probably have been burnt at the stake as a sorcerer. Yet there is evidence in Greek mythology, in the story of Daedalus who constructs wings for his son Icarus; while in the *Arabian Nights* there is the story of 'The Magic Carpet'. Once the first powered aircraft had been demonstrated by the Wright Brothers at Kitty Hawk in 1903, it became a new industry within a few years, and within a couple of generations was an entirely normal activity for millions of travellers.

The enormous success of the telephone industry is another example. Even Alexander Graham Bell saw limited potential for his invention, but it has become ubiquitous. The mobile telephone is leapfrogging in terms of new usage and there is now one mobile telephone for every person on Earth. We have always wanted to communicate, not least across vast distances and to loved ones far away. The mobile phone enables us to do so, yet before the event of the mobile telephone, research would not have provided much insight into its feasibility as a Product.

Quality

Another factor in the success of a Product is quality. Quality is a very difficult concept, for it has both relative and absolute status; quality can be subjective. Football commentators describe a player as 'quality' when they mean he is of good quality, not poor quality. A Product must meet a quality standard to be successful and a good manufacturing, or sourcing, company will have quality control procedures to ensure this. These procedures will vary enormously according to the risk of unacceptable quality. A medicinal drug manufacturer, for example, will have an extremely high standard as the risk of failure is too great and unacceptable to society. However, the quality standard has to be built into the Product as it is impossible to test 100 per cent of the Production. In consequence, this Product has a very high Price, which in most developed countries is subsidized by the state and in undeveloped countries is largely unaffordable.

Marginally down from that standard is the food industry, at least with perishable foods that have a risk of salmonella, E. coli or other bacterial risk. Sometimes disproportionately high standards are applied, even though a small degree of salmonella will be present in many foodstuffs and most People are tolerant of that. Nevertheless, the manufacturer cannot take undue risks and so when I was in charge of a food processing factory for Pillsbury, the quality assurance management reported separately from the Production management and had the Power to stop Production and dispatch, pending tests of a suspect batch.

Such standards are not held in the manufacturing of electronics where the Price competition is very high and the customer would not be prepared to pay for the cost of achieving perfection. Nevertheless, standards of quality are considerably higher today than they used to be. Engineers attempt to 'design out' the risk of defect.

In the British television industry of the 1950s and 1960s quality was so poor that the majority of customers preferred to rent rather than buy their television and thus paid for a constant service of maintenance. The dealers who effectively sold the same television set many times over became very rich. However, as the Japanese gradually took over the industry in the 1970s and 1980s with their vastly superior products, the rental industry slowly died out as the cost of acquisition came down in relative terms and the risk of acquisition also came down. As Managing Director of Sony UK I used to receive a number of consumer complaints from people who had bought their Sony television 20 years before, had watched it on average for 50 weeks per year, 35 hours per week, had never had to spend a penny on maintenance or service, and now found that it was beginning to give up the ghost. Their complaint was that they thought they had bought a 'quality' Product and were disappointed that after 35,000 hours of maintenance-free use the Product needed replacing!

Quality in food does not just mean safety, though that is paramount. It also means enjoyment. Successful food and drink companies will have developed research techniques that identify the degree to which their Products, present and future, satisfy consumers on a hedonic scale, and they will have established benchmarks that new Products must meet before expensive resources are committed to launch. In my time at Mars such hedonic scales were sacred and the company then had an excellent record in developing major new Products with fewer failures than the norm. It is an astonishing fact that most new Product development (NPD) fails, and while the reasons are not always about standards I am prepared to wager that a considerable proportion are.

When I joined Pillsbury to run its very Profitable Green's of Brighton subsidiary I found that similar hedonic scales had been established but had been overlooked by the previous management who, charged with an imperative to maintain an active NPD programme, had cut corners and launched Products that did not meet their own internal benchmarks.

I reviewed all the recent history of Product introductions and compared them with well-established and Profitable lines. It was clear that for some time we had failed to launch any new Products that lived up to the long-term reputation of the company. I then set in motion a new programme of research and development, supported by a strict rule that new Products would only be launched if they came up to the benchmark. Our subsequent launches were all much more successful and indeed one new Product quickly broke into our top five selling lines.

Such practices would not be tolerated in industries with sophisticated Product development processes, like those pioneered by Toyota in the car industry. Sophisticated processes such as the Toyota model are, of course, now generic and thus not really a source of competitive advantage as all major companies follow them. Companies that ignored them have largely gone to the wall. Toyota, however, has had the foresight and discipline to customize tools and technology to fit within a broader framework, one that includes People and processes.

Notwithstanding Toyota's recent financial difficulties because of a worldwide collapse in demand for new vehicles, over the long term it can lay claim to be the world's outstanding large company. Its philosophy is to constantly seek improvement, even if of a small nature. This process of *Kaizen* is not unique to Toyota, or indeed to Japanese industry any more, but it was perfected by Toyota who set the standard.

Toyota, until 2008–09, had enjoyed uninterrupted sales and Profit growth for many years. But each year, rather than indulging in excessive celebration, its top management ask what went wrong and what could be improved. The workforce is fully involved in making a contribution to this effort.

In 1984 the New United Motor Manufacturing Inc. (NUMMI) automobile manufacturing plant was opened in Fremont, California. The factory had been a General Motors plant, first opened in 1962. It was now a joint venture between General Motors (GM) and Toyota. GM saw this as an opportunity to gain knowledge about the ideas of lean manufacturing from Toyota and, in return, Toyota gained a manufacturing foothold in North America and a chance to introduce its Production system in a US labour environment.

The Power of Toyota's reputation over time meant that identical models were sold under both company's marques, yet while Toyota was able to maintain its full selling Price, GM dealers were forced to discount heavily (more on this territory is discussed under Price in Chapter 2).

Sadly it was announced on 29 July 2009 that NUMMI would be closed and so this fascinating experiment is over. In its time it showed starkly to the world the differences that had opened up between the Product development and manufacturing techniques of the leading Japanese companies over their North American counterparts. More recently Toyota has had to conduct several recalls involving millions of cars in most of its major markets. Its new CEO, the grandson of the founder, has been forced to go to the United States and apologize. So what has gone wrong? Hubris may have set in with Toyota. With the benefit of hindsight the warning signs were there when the company set out to be the number one and dislodge General Motors from its perch. That is a meaningless objective. We should aim to be the best as measured by customer satisfaction. We should aim to be the most Profitable. We should never aim to be the biggest per se. Perhaps too many compromises will be made in the pursuit of volume.

Too much complexity has entered into the world of car production just as it did in consumer electronics in which I worked for many years. Engineers seem obsessed with more and more gimmicky gismos being added to the specification, most of which now require semiconductors to manage them – and we know how unreliable the engineering in information technology can be. On the other side of the coin, the media love to pull down a giant, and US politicians love to indulge in protectionism. Recalls in the car industry are common and are managed by national bodies. The decision to recall is not made by the car manufacturer independently but by the national organization (ie VOSA in the UK, an association set up in agreement between the Department for Transport and the motoring trade associations) once the manufacturer reports the fault. This has not been well explained by the media.

Portfolio management

In this chapter I have described some of the different techniques that are used by outstanding companies to develop new Products. I have not yet referred to the Product life cycle, which is explored in Chapter 9 in relation to the *Push-Pull* of marketing, but at this stage let me say that for every programme of new Product development there ought to be a corresponding one of 'old Product development'. It is true that forward-looking companies commit themselves to aggressive programmes of innovation that will lead to replacement of a significant part of their Product range over time. However, it is important to remember that much of your Profit will come from established Products; the job of the Product manager is to manage all elements of the process, not to get wholly tied up in new Product development.

The concept of portfolio management was popularized as the 'Growth-Share Matrix' by the Boston Consulting Group in the 1970s. Like all good matrices this is a simple 2 × 2, as shown in Figure 1.1.

The idea was to assist large corporations in deciding how to allocate cash among their business units. The corporation would categorize its business units as 'stars', 'cash cows', 'question marks' and 'dogs', and then allocate cash accordingly, moving money from 'cash cows' towards 'stars' and 'question marks' that had higher market growth rates, and hence higher upside

FIGURE 1.1 Growth share matrix

Market Growth Rate	Relative Market Share: High	Relative Market Share: Low
High	Stars	Question Marks
Low	Cash Cows	Dogs

potential. 'Dogs' would inevitably be discontinued. The approach served very well for at least two decades and is still taught in business schools. However, there are dangers in it. If insufficient cash is allocated to the so-called cash cows then the cow stops producing milk.

Product comparisons

At Mars Confectionery the famous Mars Bar was targeted to track the Retail Price Index. Although the Product was manufactured from ingredients that could vary dramatically in Price, such as cocoa beans, Mars Product managers would vary the size of the bar or the thickness of the chocolate coating in order to maintain Price competitiveness.

Of course, they would do this only after checking its acceptability in the market. This was done by measuring acceptance among a sample of consumers chosen to represent the target market. Recipe A, the current formulation, would be tested against recipe B, the proposed formulation. Consumers would be asked to taste both Products and express their views. The results were then analysed and the recommendation made. Typically, recipe A might get a slight preference, perhaps 48–52 per cent, but on the size of sample this preference was judged as not statistically significant. And so recipe B was authorized for introduction. Some time later, probably after a new Product manager was in post, similar circumstances arose and now recipe C was proposed to be compared with recipe B in order to maintain competitiveness in the market. A similar result was obtained and so recipe C was introduced. Over time, perhaps all the letters in the alphabet were used but each time there was no statistical difference between the two recipes that were tested.

Then after some years a very bright marketing man asked if recipe Z, the current recipe, could be checked against recipe A, lost in the annals of time. The test was done and recipe A was overwhelmingly preferred to recipe Z. This was not surprising because the bar was about 10 per cent bigger: that is how much had been shaved off the bars over time. Then the very bright marketing man, quite within the law, was able to recommend the relaunch of recipe A under the guise of the '10% bigger bar' – and huge share gains were made.

Research of this kind can trap the unwary in all sorts of ways. Coca-Cola has had a long-standing fight for many years with its rival Pepsi-Cola. Overall, in most markets in the world Coca-Cola has a distinct market share lead. You might think that is because it has a preference in taste to that degree. You would be wrong. In blind tests Pepsi-Cola is slightly preferred to Coca-Cola. This is because the recipe for Pepsi-Cola is slightly sweeter than Coca-Cola and so a slight majority of the general population has a preference for sweetness. The difference is marginal, perhaps 49–51 per cent, but over the massive volumes that are drunk that ought to make a difference.

Coca-Cola thought so too, and in a famous move in 1985 it reformulated its Product to be sweeter and launched it as New Coke. It was preferred in blind tests to both traditional Coca-Cola and Pepsi-Cola. But it bombed. Why? Its traditional users liked the original Product but, more importantly, did not go around making blind comparisons. They bought the whole proposition – a can of Coke is part of the American way of life, the 'Real Thing', whereas Pepsi is a younger version. Coca-Cola, having got it badly wrong, then rectified the mistake very quickly and brought out Classic Coke, the traditional recipe in the traditional bottle or can, and regained all its lost share – and a bit more – because it had listened to its loyal customers.

While we're on the subject of blind tests I must just tell you the truth behind the famous advertising campaign that was run by Unilever for many years from after the end of rationing in the 1950s to the 1970s, when the late comedian Leslie Crowther fronted the campaign claiming that 7 out of 10 consumers could not tell the difference between Stork (a margarine made from vegetable oils) and butter. This was demonstrated in tests that were filmed up and down the UK, but which never told you what kind of butter. In those days butter was a much more regional Product with few nationally established brands. Its taste was therefore heterogeneous. The Product manager would choose a type of butter that was completely unfamiliar to the consumers participating in the trial and so it was not surprising that being neither familiar with Stork nor this strange butter they could not tell the difference!

Summary

In this chapter we have:

- discussed various methods of researching new Products and maintaining old ones;
- considered some of the many pitfalls that await even the best companies in these processes;
- compared some of the processes in fast-moving consumer goods with the processes in durable goods such as cars and consumer electronics;
- set up the first P in marketing: there has to be a *Product* or service for there to be a transaction and thence a business.

But there are many Ps yet to go before we can say we have understood marketing.

Price

02

Cecil Graham: What is a cynic? Lord Darlington: A man who knows the Price of everything and the value of nothing.

LADY WINDERMERE'S FAN, OSCAR WILDE

A gorilla walks into a deli in New York and orders a pastrami on rye with a pickle on the side to go. The guy behind the counter puts the sandwich together and when it's ready says: 'That'll be 12 dollars.' He realizes though that he's been staring, and apologizes... 'Uh, I'm sorry, sir, but to be honest with you, I've never seen a gorilla in here before.' 'You keep charging twelve bucks for a sandwich,' says the gorilla, 'and you never will again.'

Pricing is one of the most important elements of the marketing mix. It is also one of the most difficult. Get it right and you may make a lot of Profit. Get it wrong and you may have a huge failure on your hands. There are several different Pricing strategies and there is no one that is always right. However, there are some principles that should always be applied.

Typically companies will calculate their costs and add a suitable mark-up, thus producing a Price at which if the market accepts it they know they will make a Profit. Of course, they will have failed to capture the total potential Profit from the market but will have the security of knowing that the business is Profitable from day one, assuming their calculations are accurate.

A better method is to understand the market Pricing structure and Price the Product accordingly. In this sense it is impossible to separate Pricing from *Positioning*, which we will consider in Chapter 10. If we believe we can obtain a premium for our Product because it is superior to the competitors, then it ought to follow that our Price will be higher. Alternatively, we might decide that our cost base is the lowest possible and so we will squeeze our competitors by undercutting their Price, confident that they won't be able to follow us without significant pain.

For me, the best method is to understand the value to the customer and Price accordingly. Such value Pricing bears little relationship to costs or competitors but to the utility of the Product or service to the customer.

Take ice cream as an example. For years ice cream was sold as little more than a commodity in the UK. Two very large companies dominated the market, with a vast number of smaller players delivering their ice cream in vans. The Product was largely aimed at children and was based on low-cost ingredients with a bland taste. Adults accepted it because they didn't know it could taste any better, although as they began to travel more – and taste superior Products in Italy, for example – some dissatisfaction set in.

Then a brand called Häagen-Dazs was created in the United States, acquired by Pillsbury, and in the late 1980s it was imported for the first time to the UK. Häagen-Dazs was positioned as ice cream for adults, made from high-quality ingredients. The advertising by Bartle Bogle Hegarty was distinctly risqué and the Product was highly successful. And the Price? I was close to the People in Pillsbury who launched the Product and there was a lot of discussion about the Price premium. Should it be 50 per cent, 100 per cent, even 200 per cent above the standard Products in the marketplace? We launched it with a premium of 700 per cent. Yes, it was sold for eight times the Price of standard ice cream. But it was such a different Product. It was not just a little bit better, or even twice as good. It was a completely different experience. It transformed the ice cream market and huge numbers of new entrants came in with sophisticated Products; Häagen-Dazs no longer gets a premium of 700 per cent above the rest of the market but it is still sold as a premium Product and is no doubt very Profitable.

Premiums are desirable but can also be dangerous. For decades Kodak dominated the market for photographic film, based on traditional silver halide technology. Its marketing was Powerful and it demanded a Price premium, first over local competitors such as Ilford in the UK, then over the Japanese imitators who followed them around the world led by Fuji, and finally over own-label offerings sold by all the leading chain stores and usually supplied by 3M. Kodak management were incentivized on the premium they were able to attract over these competitors. It is unlikely that the Product was significantly superior though it may have had different characteristics, but the Powerful Kodak brand with its outstanding distribution management was enough to justify this.

The danger was that this was not the competition. Kodak clearly dominated its own traditional market but as a result it was too focused on its own field to move quickly enough when electronic imaging and digital photography arrived. Now, sales of silver halide have all but vanished and Kodak is an 'also ran' in the new world of digital photography.

On Friday 2 April 1993, Philip Morris cut the Price of Marlboro cigarettes by 20 per cent in order to compete with generic cigarette manufacturers selling budget and supermarket own-label brands at low Prices. The marketing and financial media immediately ran hysterical headlines announcing the death of the Marlboro brand specifically, and premium branding in general. Philip Morris's share Price dropped by 26 per cent in one day, reducing its market capitalization by US $10 billion. Wall Street slashed the share Price of Coca-Cola, Tambrands and many other branded manufacturers.

But 'Marlboro Friday' was not the death of either the Marlboro brand or premium branding. Marlboro's action stopped a Price war that had begun in the early 1990s recession, leading to significant erosion in Marlboro's US market share. Marlboro brand managers had wrongly believed that the brand's absolute Price was sacrosanct. As its competitors increasingly lowered Prices, Marlboro's relative Price premium grew, giving hard-pressed consumers too much of a reason to switch brands. By cutting its Price Marlboro simply restored the relative premium over generic brands. The Wall Street investment analysts, if they had been doing their job properly, would have lowered Philip Morris's share Price well before this and then raised it when Marlboro brand managers reconsidered their mistake. Marlboro rapidly recovered its lost market share and Philip Morris its share Price within two years. By 2007 the Marlboro brand commanded a global market share of 33 per cent by volume (*The Times*, August 2007).

The Gillette razor business model

King Gillette invented the safety razor. But his equally important invention was a new business model. He saw that the value in his business would be the ongoing sale of razors, a continuous need for all men from about the age of 16 who decide to shave every day. He sold them the system comparatively cheaply, but they were then tied in as loyal consumers – because only his blades fitted the system.

Today, Gillette marketing is based on the same principle. It is now a subsidiary of Procter & Gamble, but good though P&G's marketing is it has never come up with such a Powerful scheme. This built-in loyalty has been applied to many other markets and indeed Gillette has applied it successfully to other markets: for example, electric toothbrushes with its Oral B and Braun brands. The consumer is obliged to buy the detachable brushes at huge Prices. An electric toothbrush might cost from £15 to £30 but the individual brushes are sold at about £5 each and may only last a month. Let's say that a system lasts five years: the initial purchase may be only £15 but the five-year value will be more like £300.

Returning to razor blades, Baron Bich applied the same approach that he had first applied to the disposable ballpoint pen market. He took on the system brands, which used the same model as Gillette. Brands such as Parker Pen would sell a pen and then make their money from sales of nibs and ink for fountain pens and, later, refills for ballpoint pens. Bic stripped out all the cost it possibly could to come up with a very low Price. It applied the same philosophy to razor blades, with great success. This is particularly interesting given that one might suppose that the shaver would take extra care about such a personal and, indeed, risky item – but Bic is actually a very good Product, only marginally inferior to Gillette's Product. Years ago I sold Bic razor blades to the UK grocery trade while in possession of secret market research, which showed that in tests the Gillette Product was assessed as only 4 per cent better than the Bic Product, although we were not allowed to divulge this. Admittedly that was before the days of Mach 3 and its successors, which at the last count had got five blades in one – but it was an interesting statistic nonetheless. Thus, in the razor blade market the totally opposite pricing models of system sales with premium-Priced tied blades and low-cost disposable blades coexisted and brought success to both practitioners. But in such a market there is very little middle ground.

Air travel

Another market that appears to have room for both premium Prices and rock bottom Prices is air travel. At one end the premium-Priced carriers emphasize loyalty, building for their pampered business-class passengers with flat beds, luxury lounges and a whole host of loyalty award schemes based mainly on ascribing value to unsold seats with air miles, etc. At the other end the low-cost airlines strip out all non-essential services either completely, or from the base Price, and then sell the services separately.

From the beginning of passenger air travel the airline industry has been singularly unProfitable. Indeed the cumulative combined Profits of the airlines since the beginning of commercial flight have been close to zero. Of course, there have been and still are some very Profitable operators but the majority have lost money. If they have been private companies they have gone bust, although increasingly they are propped up by provisions made for going into administration (such as Chapter 11 provision in the United States) – at the cost of the Profitability of the whole industry. Alternatively they have been flag-carrying national airlines that have been protected by the cartels organized by their government owners.

Yet from that distinctly unpromising primeval swamp have taken off some remarkably Profitable low-cost airlines such as Southwest in the United States, which has posted a Profit for 40 consecutive years; and Ryanair and EasyJet in Europe. Their secret has been to concentrate, with a Passion, on removing unnecessary cost from their model, and sweating their assets – the planes – as much as safety standards will allow. They have also avoided the excessive charges of the monopolist airports of the big cities and cut clever deals with the municipal authorities of nearby airports. These airports might be a few kilometres further away but are much less crowded and little is lost in time by the traveller.

As in all the best low-cost Pricing models this has not only undercut the premium-Priced brands but also created new usage. New routes have opened up and a new type of travel has emerged. Not all of this is desirable from an ecological viewpoint. But I will address the ethical questions later, in the Conclusion. For now let us pay tribute to the cleverness of the people carrying on this kind of trade.

These companies have developed algorithms to vary Price acutely to demand. An airline seat is like a hotel bed for the night, the ultimate perishable Product. Even less-than-fresh foods have some value until it is finally deemed unsafe to eat them. But an airline seat must be sold today for today's flight, as tomorrow it is a statistic of lost opportunity.

When I watch a football match with half the stadium empty I weep for the lost opportunity of variable Pricing. By all means keep your Prices high but if, finally, the seats are unsold, then you have missed an opportunity. Indeed it would be better to give them away as a trial for children, tomorrow's season ticket holders, than to leave them empty.

EasyJet has calculated this to a nicety. They can advertise Prices that are extremely low, although they have now been forced to include all the taxes and charges in the advertised Price, and then vary the Prices right up to the point of travel. You might assume that the Prices would come down nearer the flight time. In fact, as Sir Stelios Haji-Iannou once explained to me when I met him on one of his EasyJet flights, the Prices will probably go up as the available supply reduces. But they are in a very competitive space and average margins are just £2.50 per passenger. Hence there is enormous pressure on cabin staff to potentially double this by selling a drink and a sandwich.

Market segmentation

I have covered the coexistence of apparently conflicting Pricing models in the same market, but some companies seek to control a market through segmentation, with a series of brands Priced according to the spread of the market as a whole. When I was at Pedigree Petfoods we managed a range of canned dog foods from cheap and cheerful brands such as Chappie to more sophisticated brands like Pedigree Chum. Chappie was actually the original brand of the company when it was Chappell Brothers, and subsequently Petfoods Limited had added brands Lassie, then Bounce, then Pal and finally Chum, each of which represented an improvement in quality and so was Priced at a premium to its predecessors. This simple segmentation covered most of the available customers and gave the company the potential to control the market. Whichever way a consumer wished to move, whether up or down in Price, there was a Petfoods brand waiting for them.

Retailers first competed in such FMCG markets with their own label brand competing at or near the bottom of the Price table. Actually, Pedigree Petfoods supplied the Bounce Product, a mid-table candidate, as its own-label competitor for a number of years, until wiser counsels prevailed and it withdrew completely from the own-label market. Later, retailers learnt to segment all of the available market for themselves. Thus Tesco offers Tesco

When I first joined Sony I soon met Ken Iwaki, then one of the top three executives in the company. I asked him why we allowed Aiwa, a company owned 50 per cent by Sony, to compete directly against us in the audio market. Why did we not use it instead to protect Sony from competition from the retail brands and other cheap brands, but keep the best technology for the Sony brand? Iwaki–san was intrigued by my ideas, obvious to me as an experienced FMCG marketer, but perhaps less obvious to a consumer durables company. However, this particular recommendation did not travel very far and over the years Aiwa gradually gained share from Sony as Sony technology ported to Aiwa at lower Prices. This was effectively cannibalization of Sony business and certainly produced a less Profitable position when you consolidated the performance of the two companies.

Value at the bottom of the range, standard own-label in the middle and Tesco's Finest at the top.

Of course, many companies in consumer durables, not least in the car industry, seek to offer a full range from top to bottom and thus control the market. Sometimes they realize that a single brand cannot do this. So my concern was that the Sony brand, with its supreme reputation for quality, should not be compromised by having to devalue to appeal to a broader audience. In the same way Toyota has stretched its brand to cover a large part of the available market but has developed the completely separate Lexus brand offering to compete directly with the more established luxury marques of Mercedes, BMW and Jaguar.

Price points

Pricing often settles around a Price point. Retailers talk of a 'magic Price', a Price where customers' appreciation of value for money comes into balance with the margin requirements of the supply chain. One of the most extreme examples of this in my experience was in Chile where M&M's distributor imported M&M's, the famous candies, mainly in their snack size. The exchange rate was then fixed by the Pinochet régime at 39 pesos to the US dollar, a policy that allowed the regime to successfully squeeze out inflation and force local manufacturers to compete more directly with international manufacturers such as ourselves. This exchange rate allowed the importer to distribute the sachets to be sold in the street at 10 pesos each. Huge quantities were sold at this magic Price. However, when the exchange rate started to move after being fixed for three years, eventually reaching 90 pesos to the US dollar in just three months, the magic Price point was gone and the wholesalers who ran the army of street sales personnel replaced the Product with cheaper locally supplied alternatives. The huge volumes disappeared like snow in summer.

This is an extreme example of elasticity, the concept that demand is elastic to variations in Price. This can be measured quite precisely and in some large industries is a key mechanism of demand management. Some goods are held to be mainly inelastic, eg petrol, where demand tends to change only slightly even when Prices are increased sharply. Here the calculations are probably a little distorted as the customers vary between those whose costs are passed on to employers and whose demand will not change, and those who pay out of their own money and may have to make some adjustment.

The classic 'magic Price' involves the use of '99', ie 99p instead of £1, £9.99 instead of £10, £14,999 instead of £15,000. This is so ubiquitous in the UK that Screaming Lord Sutch, leader of the Monster Raving Loony Party and perennial fighter of elections, actually proposed the introduction of a 99p coin to avoid all the exchange of 1p coins, one of his more imaginative if still loony suggestions. Folk wisdom has it that this practice was initiated by canny retailers who wanted to ensure that shop assistants would be forced to open the till and thus register the transaction rather than just pocketing a bank note, but I find this difficult to believe, as the equally canny but dishonest shop assistant would only have to keep a stock of penny coins in order to frustrate the trap. The real reason is that despite the smallness of the difference mathematically the Price point really does seem much lower in psychological terms. As a practice it is effective and will stay with us for a lot longer yet.

Traditionally Prices were set by manufacturers and suppliers and then followed by retailers. This tradition came under pressure in the UK in the 1960s and some retailers such as Tesco came to national prominence by testing the practice of Resale Price Maintenance. Edward Heath was the minister responsible for taking through Parliament the abolition of Resale Price Maintenance, although some Product categories such as books and newspapers remained exempt. Ironically Mr Heath later was nicknamed Grocer Heath by *Private Eye*, even though this single action was eventually to cause the demise of many thousands of grocers as larger retailers could now compete directly on Price and use their buying Power to exact discounts from suppliers and force smaller retailers out of business.

This action has mixed economic effects. On the one hand it is obviously in the interests of consumers to see Price competition. However, these same consumers have lost a lot of amenity at the community level and Profits are no longer retained in the community but are rather sucked out and centralized at national level by a few players.

That Pricing has a political context is undeniable. This became extreme in the 1970s when inflation took off, largely stimulated by massive increases in oil Prices set by OPEC. In both the UK and the United States, now seen as two of the countries most committed to free markets, legislation was introduced to control Prices. In the UK the ministers responsible to manage this process were Shirley Williams succeeded by Roy Hattersley and, perhaps incredibly, in the United States it was Donald Rumsfeld.

But after this disastrous aberration, which caused massive distortions in markets, a new regime emerged where Price points became a matter for intense negotiation between manufacturers and retailers. As retailers increased their Power (a subject we will return to in Chapter 14), so every change in Price became an opportunity for them to increase their share of the available margin. In the early 1980s I learnt to play this game at Green's of Brighton, a leading player in a relatively small market. As our input Prices changed from time to time for key commodities such as flour and sugar, Packaging and labour, we needed to seek a Price increase. Whereas in the past this would have simply involved the calculation and publication of a new Price list it now involved extensive negotiation with each of the major supermarkets. We had to justify the increase by first demonstrating the changes in our input Prices and showing that we had done everything we could to control them. The retailers were helped by having their own brand Products in the same category and therefore having separate information that would support, or not, our arguments. Once it was agreed that a Price had to change it was then a negotiation over establishing the new Price point and dividing the margin.

In Products selling at Prices below £1 there are several recognizable Price points and some that will simply not work. We have already discussed 99p, but before we get there we will consider 49p rather not 50p, and so on. Thus on a Product previously sold at 47p for which we sought an increase of 5 per cent, we would have to settle for 49p, an increase of just 4.2 per cent, or alternatively go all the way up to 52p, the next recognizable Price point, and thus see the Product go up by 10.6 per cent and risk a serious loss of volume.

In addition the retailers would have a clear sense of which Products were those that were bought so frequently by customers that they knew the Price. As always there is a mnemonic and this one is Known Value Item, or KVI. While politicians, when challenged, usually cannot answer the question 'how much is a loaf of bread', the average shopper can (as they often can for other food items they buy regularly) but will be much less certain over the general range of Products sold in the store. This applies particularly to fresh goods, which although bought frequently are known to vary in Price according to the seasons. Consequently, the supermarket buyers responsible for setting Prices have much more leeway on those items, the great majority not deemed as KVIs.

If the Product is subject to Value Added Tax (VAT) there is a major distortion because of the establishment of Price points. In the United States

Price points are set and sales tax is added afterwards. Thus you may buy a book, for example, with a RSP of $16.99 and then find that 6 per cent sales tax is added at the checkout, thus taking the final Price to $18.01. The rate of sales tax can be varied without affecting the Price point. However, in the UK, VAT is included in the final Price. At the time of writing the rate of VAT is 20 per cent. As I have explained, Price points are supreme, and so if a future chancellor reduces the rate of VAT it may create some artificial situations. However, when the rate of VAT is increased, which has usually been the trend, the effect is a hidden tax on the manufacturer and retailer.

For example, if a television has a RSP of £799 when the tax is 20 per cent, what has actually happened is that the consumer has bought the television for £665.83 and paid £133.17 in VAT to HMRC. If the tax is increased to 22.5 per cent the retailer is faced with two alternatives: either to keep the base Price at £665.83 and the final Price increase to £815.64, thus delivering an extra tax of £16.64, or, more likely, to judge that this is not a viable Price point and so keep the final Price at £799 and reduce the retail base receipt to £652.24. The tax will therefore be £146.76 and the increase in tax will not have been paid by the consumer but by the retailer who will then seek to pass it back to the manufacturer. It is thus a hidden tax on Profits.

'Free' Products

Before leaving the question of Price I want to refer briefly to the idea that some Products are free. This is seen by some as a new area of economics because of the increasing prevalence of online models that purport to offer Products and services at no charge. This is a complex area as this includes a range of business models, from the well-established practice of offering a free additional item to stimulate the sale, to the idea of a 'freemium' where a small subset of users pay for a premium version of something supporting a free version for the majority. The first of these is very long established (see Chapter 4 on Promotion). The idea of a 'freemium' may be new but only a few have succeeded in setting this up as a Profitable model. It does, however, introduce us to the important question of where we buy our Products and services, the subject of the next chapter.

Summary

In this chapter we have:

- considered alternative Pricing models;
- discussed the relationship of premium Prices to lower Prices;
- looked at market segmentation by Price;
- explained the concept of Price elasticity;
- described the role of government in controlling or freeing Pricing and the effect of Value Added Tax;
- introduced the idea of 'free' Products.

Place

Give me but one firm spot on which to stand, and I will move the earth. **ARCHIMEDES 287–212 BC**

Perhaps Archimedes did not have marketing in mind when he made his famous pronouncement about leverage, but *Place* or *Placement* is certainly a vital plank in the marketing edifice. The very word marketing is derived from market, the Place where traditionally People have met to sell and buy, to trade goods and services. To make a market is the act of forming a Place where traders may come together and exchange their Produce. It is interesting to consider what was the first retail outlet. Was it a baker's shop, which began perhaps because one person was more skilled than his or her neighbours in the art of baking bread and so Produced it in quantity and sold it to them, or exchanged it for their Produce? Or, similarly, was one man's wine easier on the palate and so the inn was invented?

History of distribution

We can trace the lineage of such Places of business from the inn to the hotel, the café to the restaurant, the street vendor to the fast-food outlet; from market stalls to shops, department stores, supermarkets and hypermarkets; from the blacksmith to the garage to the showroom. Traditional fairs, or *messe* in Germany, live on in the form of trade shows and exhibitions.

Not all Places are fixed and permanent and there is again a long line of travelling businesses, such as the market trader who takes his or her stall and its speciality goods around the county to trade at different markets on different days of the week. In England such markets were authorized by royal charter and in many cases still are. Such charters were highly restrictive in that not only did they grant the right to a particular town to hold a market or fair on a particular day or days, but by the same token prohibited neighbouring towns from doing the same so that the market would thrive. I live in a town close to St Albans and until recently my own town could not have any kind of street selling because only St Albans had that right in the area. Now we can have one farmers' market per month.

This concept of travelling to get the sale is taken further by selling direct, door to door. When I was growing up in the 1950s in a suburb of Manchester we had delivered to our door not only the milk and newspapers (still widely delivered though in decline) but also meat from the butcher, bread from the baker, a weekly order from the grocer, a soft drinks supplier who collected the empties, and every day in the summer an ice cream van whose jingle announced his presence to us children who then nagged our mothers for a cornet.

Whole business models have been successfully developed based on door-to-door selling, including Avon cosmetics, encyclopaedias, insurance, double glazing and vacuum cleaners. In many cases this was seen as a low-cost method of distribution because it eliminated the middle man and because most of the cost of employing the sales personnel was variable commission. It was also a highly effective method of selling, convenient to the customer and allowing the sellers to make their full pitch.

Developing from this concept has been telephone selling and its modern equivalent of e-mail. Direct mail is also a form of door-to-door marketing, substituting a brochure or other printed enticement for the physical sales person. Every year some 4.5 billion pieces of 'direct mail' are posted through letter boxes in the UK, much of which ends up in landfill.

A further development of marketing direct to home is mail order, a practice that grew in the latter part of the 19th century when the postal service improved enormously with the development of the rail network. In this case, the *Place* of sale is not strictly the home but rather the mail order catalogue. People in that business talk about 'selling off the page' and so the page is the *Place*. There is again a direct line of succession from that to today's online retailing.

So the Place where goods are bought and sold can be everywhere from the home to the supermarket shelf; from selling in the street to huge exhibitions attended by hundreds of thousands of people. The key point for the marketing individual is that he or she must decide how to distribute their Product. They must have a strategy for selling and ensuring that this strategy will work through the whole territory in which they are targeting to sell the Product. This is true for all Products and services whether bought by consumers or businesses. For example, if your business is the theatre then your *Place* is the theatre in which you put on your play – and you will have a strategy to attract people to that theatre. But with the invention of film it became possible to record a film of a 'play' and then distribute copies of the film to thousands of theatres or cinemas to which audiences could come to see the same entertainment.

But wait a minute. Did not Ralph Waldo Emerson say 'Build a better mousetrap and the world will beat a path to your door'? Well actually, no, he did not say exactly that. I will deal with what he did say in the next chapter, because it has relevance to the issue of Promotion. But it is also relevant here. If it is true then all this stuff about Place would not be necessary. The world will beat a path to your door. You don't have to go and find the Place for people to buy your Product: they will find you. A few moments of reflection show that Emerson was wrong. The customer is always right and one thing they are right about is that they decide where they want to buy something. If it's not there, they are more likely to buy something else or not buy at all than to come back and buy it when it is there. Supermarket companies complain to their suppliers about many things but the thing they complain about most is not supplying 100 per cent of the order. They measure themselves and their suppliers on being in stock.

A good example of how this works is the free newspaper *Metro* distributed throughout the London Underground. Rushed commuters only have to break stride, bend down and pick up a free copy of this daily newspaper at thousands of conveniently Placed self-service boxes at each of the London underground and overground railway stations. The newspaper is an adequate daily, easy to read, financed by the advertising inside, which is no more intrusive than that in any other newspaper. Rather than queue at a kiosk for a newspaper that you have to pay for and probably wait for change, the *Metro* is easy to obtain both because it is free and because it is easy to find. It is a highly effective example of using Place to build a business model. There is most probably a cost incurred in that Transport for London most likely charges a rent for the Placing of the newspaper on their stations, just as they charge a rent to the shop owners and kiosks located on their premises.

Importance of location

When your Place of marketing is your own Place different rules apply. Every shopkeeper is in this position. First the shopkeeper will want to be in the right location. There are three priorities: location, location, location. High-street stores have fought over the best location for centuries. The same fight goes on between the big supermarket groups, and the property portfolio of any one of them will be one of the key metrics by which stockbrokers' analysts value the total enterprise. When property developers build large out-of-town shopping malls they will first want to sign up an anchor tenant, preferably one of the big department-store chains such as John Lewis or Marks and Spencer. Retailing is a property game in which the retailer effectively rents out the space. Department stores have for many years operated their stores like a landlord renting out space to brands that need a Place to set out their stall. Cosmetics and fashion brands are mainly distributed in this way.

> When I was at Sony, Harrods reached the conclusion that it would no longer run its consumer electronics section itself. Instead it sought bids from retailers and indeed manufacturers to sell a defined range of TV and audio Products and other related items from the same space. Our Products were sold through a Sony Centre operated by an independent retailer, and reached significantly higher sales than before. Harrods benefited by achieving a guaranteed return on the space and we benefited from the high profile of a dedicated space in the most prestigious store in the country as well as a good rate of sale.

The marketer who does not directly control his or her outlets will need a strategy to manage the distribution through them. And this is where sales management comes in. In an organization where sales are achieved directly to end users, then sales and marketing can comfortably sit with one individual in charge. But if the end user is different from the outlet where the goods are finally sold, as in the case of most consumer businesses, then in my experience it is better to separate the responsibilities of sales and marketing. Marketing will bring the voice of the consumer or end user to the boardroom table. Sales will bring the important and separate voice of the various channels of distribution.

Sales management

Sales management is of great importance in the distribution of Products through Places that are not directly controlled by the owner of the business.

I have never encountered a business that could not benefit by radical improvement of the sales management processes. I was fortunate in beginning my career in sales at Procter & Gamble who invested heavily in sales management. When the company finally decided to launch nationally its toiletry Products, Head & Shoulders shampoo and Crest toothpaste, after several years in test market, the charismatic sales director, Roy Franchi, decided to set up a specialist Commando sales team to achieve wide levels of distribution through outlets that would not normally receive a direct sales call from the company. I was involved in setting up and then managing that team and we set out to achieve coverage of thousands of outlets with a team of 10 salespersons taken from the main sales divisions on a six-month assignment. We targeted ourselves with 30 calls per day, so might have reasonably achieved well in excess of 30,000 calls. We carried stock of each of the Products and sold a small quantity either for cash or for billing through a local wholesaler. It was a wonderful lesson for me of the importance of achieving wide distribution at the beginning of a Product's life, when maximum awareness is likely to be made through advertising and other Promotion.

Today such an exercise might be seen as old-fashioned and expensive, while much of the distribution has been concentrated in the hands of a few players both in the grocery and the chemist trade. This has led to the increasing importance of account management.

Account management

A distinguished Professor of Marketing, Malcolm McDonald of Cranfield University, writes and lectures extensively on the importance of account management in the marketing mix. He emphasizes the need to develop close working relationships between seller and buyer, which he characterizes as 'giving love bites to the buyer'!

Account management is much more than selling, though I do not belittle the art of salesmanship and will return to it in Chapter 7 (Persuasion). Account management requires a thorough understanding of the customer's business, their needs and aspirations, their organization and how the two companies transact their business together. Account managers need to have a good understanding of the overall market in which he or she operates, as this is one of the benefits they can bring to the customer.

> At Sony we used to encourage our account management to know their customers' business better than the customers did themselves. Once a year we would invite our customers' buyers to meet with our account management team at a conference where we shared our Plans for the year ahead, gave our forecast of the markets in which we majored and then demonstrated the new Products that we would be bringing to the market. We then invited our customers' buying representatives to respond with their Plans and their forecast orders for the year ahead. The two sides then worked together to deliver this in the marketplace, and while I cannot pretend that there were not some hurdles along the way the fact that we had started out with a joint endeavour to achieve a mutually agreed set of targets was of great help in overcoming those hurdles. We invested significant time and money in this process but we regarded it as of fundamental importance in delivering our overall business Plan.

Category management

A refinement of account management is category management. Here the seller seeks to establish such confidence in its services by the buyer that the seller takes over some of the responsibility for managing a whole category, not just the Products that its own company supplies. At Procter & Gamble we pioneered this kind of work by seeking to sell a fixture relay to individual store managers. The fixture for a particular class of goods had become outdated and untidy. We would sell the benefits of relaying it, which would undoubtedly lead to better sales. Our carrot was to offer our own labour in actually laying out the fixture and merchandising it. Those days have long gone and the relaying of a fixture is one of the tools of the trade that retailers will reserve for themselves, but if a manufacturer establishes a strong position of trust as Category Manager then the project will be managed jointly. Of course, you cannot establish such trust by only favouring your own Products, but at least you can assure that they get a fair hearing.

Sadly, the relationship between buyer and seller is often characterized by aggressive tactics on both sides with one trying to get an advantage over the other. This is not good business for either party. Good business depends on building mutual advantages that are shared by both. The cake is not fixed in size but can grow and so both parties can benefit. The seller should bring not only its company's Product but a range of marketing support for the Product both in the general market such as advertising to the general consumer and instore support such as training and demonstration. The retailer of course offers the Place – the central point of this chapter – but also can offer its more detailed knowledge of its own customers. In addition the retailer can offer its staff's support and skill in selling on the Product.

Selective distribution

An aspect of the management of distribution that can give rise to difficulty is that of selectivity. Many manufacturers will seek to restrict the distribution of their Products in order to maintain an image of exclusivity. Thus, in simple terms, they will not want their highly priced Product to be sold alongside inferior Products with a much lower image. It is therefore normal to see perfumes, for example, sold in high-class stores but rarely on market stalls. This is a justifiable policy from the manufacturer's point of view. They have invested considerable sums in Product development, Packaging and advertising and want to maintain an exclusive image. The manufacturer also wants to protect the retailer who invests in display, training of staff etc and does not want to see its Product undercut in a lower-cost establishment down the road. However, such desires, while understandable, are fraught with difficulty and are severely curtailed in law.

The Treaty of the Functioning of the European Union

Most of this law in the European Union is covered in or derived from the original Treaty of Rome of 1957 as amended and incorporated in the Treaty of the Functioning of the European Union (TFEU), known as the Lisbon Treaty. The foundations of EU competition law are Articles 81 and 82 of the Treaty of Rome (the EU Treaty). Article 81(1) of the EU Treaty prohibited agreements that may affect trade between EU member states and have the object or effect of preventing, restricting or distorting competition within the EU. Article 81(2) declared that any such agreements are automatically void. The European Commission has the power to impose heavy fines for infringements of Article 81(1). Article 81(3), however, allowed particular agreements or categories of agreements to be declared exempt from Article 81(1). These have been subsumed in Article 101 of the TFEU. Exemptions of categories of agreements are known as 'block exemptions'. Block exemptions have been made for exclusive distribution agreements, exclusive purchase agreements and franchise agreements. The most notable block exemption is for the car industry, which has used its immense political and lobbying influence to protect a system of closed or tied distribution, meaning that you can only buy a particular model of car from an authorized dealer. There are no doubt many good arguments for such a system of distribution but it also usually has the effect of keeping Prices higher than they might otherwise be.

Selectivity

In the most general form of selective distribution system, a supplier appoints retailers who may resell its Products to end users without restraint. The supplier normally supplies only its approved retailers and may undertake not to sell to non-approved retailers or to the general public. Thus, selective distribution almost invariably Produces a closed network of trading outlets. Before the supplier appoints a retailer, it usually requires to be convinced that the potential retailer can satisfy its standards in such areas as management skills, technical expertise, financial resources and quality of premises (depending on the nature of the Product). If the selective system is not also exclusive, the supplier is generally free to appoint any number of additional retailers, even where these are close to its existing retailers, and the retailers are free to retail other Products, including competing brands.

Since 2004 companies have been required to make their own judgements as to how their distribution arrangements comply with European law, but there is also a body of case law decided in the European Court of Justice (ECJ). The ECJ has accepted that selective distribution systems are not necessarily restrictive of competition and that such a system can be compatible with Article 101(1) if certain conditions are met. These can be broadly summarized as follows:

- the Product merits a form of selective distribution;
- resellers are chosen on the basis of objective criteria of a qualitative nature, which are laid down uniformly for all potential resellers and are not applied in a discriminatory fashion;
- the system in question seeks to achieve a result that enhances competition and thus counterbalances the restriction of competition inherent in selective distribution systems, in particular as regards Price;
- the criteria laid down do not go further than necessary.

However, the ECJ has held that with selective distribution systems that meet these requirements there may nevertheless be a restriction of competition where the existence of a number of such systems leaves no room for other forms of distribution.

In my time at Sony I was deeply involved in drawing up a new Pan-European distribution policy to more closely bring the organization's policies in line with European requirements. Sony, like many such companies, had built its distribution country by country without really thinking about Pan-European requirements. Its first European company was a finance organization set up in Switzerland with a view to financing local business initially transacted through third-party distributors. The second company, Sony UK Limited, which I later managed, was set up in 1968. Sony France followed and so on. Each of these companies developed its own policies for trading within a single country. The UK was not even a signatory to the Treaty of Rome when Sony UK was founded. Eventually, after considerable internal negotiation, a single agreement for managing distribution was adopted throughout the countries of the European Union. This agreement operated on selective principles for a group of Products, while another group of Products requiring less servicing and sales know-how were deemed 'open' and could be sold freely.

Exclusivity

Two types of exclusivity may commonly be involved in distribution systems: territorial exclusivity and Product exclusivity. In the most general form of territorially exclusive distribution system, a supplier agrees to supply specified Products to only one retailer in a designated area. This is usually referred to as a 'territory' although some distribution systems use other terminology with the same effect. The retailer is then intended to concentrate on Promoting sales in the territory. Usually, the supplier has no direct sales force of its own in the territory and relies entirely on the retailer to achieve sales penetration there. The retailer is free to choose its customers, who may (in the most general case) include end users and resellers. The supplier may seek to prevent or control the retailer's sales to resellers or to customers who do not reside in its territory.

In exchange for being granted rights in its territory, the retailer may accept some types of Product exclusivity. It may, for example, undertake not to sell competing Products at all, not to sell them within its territory, or not to sell them from the outlet concerned.

Franchising arrangements

Franchising agreements normally create a licence to use a predefined business model for the distribution of goods or services. An important part of this is a licence to use Intellectual Property Rights (IPRs) relating to trademarks, signs and know-how. The franchiser that provides the licence is paid a franchise fee or royalty by the franchisee for the use of the IPRs, the particular business concept and often a model business Plan. Such franchise agreements provide the franchiser with a low-cost method of establishing a uniform network of outlets for distributing its Products or services. Franchisees of a reputable, well-established franchiser have the advantage of access to a comparatively low-risk and well-tested method of starting a new business.

In the case of Burger King, a company that was owned by Pillsbury for a period, while I was on the Pillsbury UK Board we used to meet our opposite numbers from Burger King, although they reported separately through a different management line-up to the corporation's main board. Burger King is now very well established in the UK, but in the early days I think it is safe to say they had one or two teething problems. Their management were drawn from US-based managers with experience of managing groups of restaurants in the Midwest but no previous overseas experience. So when they came to the UK their first restaurant was opened in a high-profile location in London. A second one was opened close by. So far, so good. But then their ambitions got ahead of themselves and their third was opened in Birmingham, a fourth in Manchester, a fifth in Southampton and a sixth in Reading. To them, the distances between all these cities would have appeared small, but in fact they had now covered half the country's TV regions and would have had to spend about 60 per cent of the national weight in order to achieve an advertising campaign with only six restaurants.

Franchise agreements are frequently combined with vertical restraints that may include non-compete clauses and combinations of elements of selective distribution and exclusive distribution.

Franchising is frequently applied in retail distribution systems and in fast-food catering. Companies such as McDonald's and Burger King have built their huge chains of outlets on the back of franchisees' capital. In return they have given the franchisee instant access to a proven business model with a strong brand image and marketing support.

I have also had to deal with issues of cultural understanding in my career as I have done business in over 50 countries and much of that was to do with the management of *Place*. I studied Foreign Market Entry Strategies at the Wharton School in the United States, and on the course met a man who was Planning to bring Anheuser-Busch's range of Products to the UK. Budweiser is now a very successful brand of beer in the UK but that is because its current management has learnt to sell it to the British in a British way, with humour and the occasional quirky approach. Beer drinkers in Britain like to joke about their favourite tipple. However, this man was convinced that the American Way, with strong links to sports, would be the answer. I was not able to convince him of his mistake and Anheuser-Busch lost a lot of money in that first round.

When I was managing Mars's business in Chile I wanted to see the distribution of the Products throughout the country. Chile is a long thin country with duty-free zones at both ends and towns strung along its length. If Chile was Placed in the northern hemisphere it would stretch from Edinburgh to Nigeria. I made it my business to visit every town with over 30,000 inhabitants. On one visit to the south with our Concepçion-based distributor, Emilio, we flew in his private plane to each of the towns in his territory, staying overnight at the farthest based one. On the way back to Concepçion Emilio got the plane airbound, showed me how to keep the plane level and heading north, and then went to canoodle in the back with his girlfriend. I was now flying a plane for the first time in my life.

Pillsbury had a very successful export business in the Middle East, largely based on huge sales of dessert Products during Ramadan. While the faithful fast during the hours of daylight in Ramadan, come nightfall the head of the family lays on a considerable spread for his dependants and, fortunately for us, this was quite likely to include significant quantities of dessert prepared from our crème caramel mix. As the General Manager responsible for this business I was keen to see the distribution of the Products and made a number of visits to all the relevant territories. While in Dubai I was changing my flight arrangements at a travel agency. The owner heard my name and introduced himself. He was also the owner of the distribution company that represented Pillsbury as well as many other businesses. He kindly invited Pillsbury's Export Manager and myself to dine at his home, an unusual offer of hospitality at a first meeting, and we became friends. In his palatial home a large rosewood table was covered with food, even though there were only four of us. After several courses he asked me why I had not had any of the chicken. I apologized and took a piece of chicken. I then noticed that my host had not eaten any chicken either so I asked him why not. He said, 'I don't like chicken.'

I have always wanted to see the Products at the point of sale, the *Place*. To me it is an essential part of understanding a business. Every well-run retailer understands this point and the senior management of most retailers will spend a considerable part of their time in visiting the stores and seeing how their strategies honed carefully in head offices are actually enacted on the ground. Suppliers need to take on the same attitude to the degree that they are allowed to do so. At Sony I always encouraged the management to spend as much of their time in the field as they could. Indeed I laid down a standard that I called 20:20. I expected that they spend a minimum of 20 per cent of their time in the field and 20 per cent coaching and training staff. This still left three days per week for paperwork, sitting in meetings and staring at screens!

Trade shows

In this chapter I have discussed a wide variety of Places where goods are sold but have concentrated on consumer examples, as not only is that the majority of my experience but also the type of business with which everyone can identify. I also think it formed the basis of most of the original thinking behind the four Ps. However, considerable business is transacted on a business-to-business (B2B) basis and much of this takes Place at trade fairs and exhibitions. Even this point is mixed up with the consumer as many of these shows are designed for both consumers and businesses and thus end up serving neither particularly well. The consumer may have an interest in a category such as consumer electronics or video games, wants a day out and goes to an exhibition to see the latest Products. If the same show is open to the trade then the chances are they will already have seen these Products in previous shows and conferences. However, they can benefit from seeing how the public interact with the Products.

The main benefit of any trade show is to enjoy meeting other people in the industry. This is a simple fact. An industry agrees a time and Place to come together somewhere in the world. As a result, great gains in Productivity can be made in the sense of seeing a large number of suppliers and/or customers over a short period of time. Important papers can be delivered of an opinion-leading or technical nature. However, to achieve these ends enormous costs are involved, as huge displays usually of a disposable kind are built and destroyed in short order. I myself have attended over 100 trade shows around the world covering a range of different industries. I have tried to pioneer different kinds of shows to excite the public about a category. For example, in 1993 I was the first signatory on a new show run by a division of News International to promote the consumer electronics industry in Britain. We called the show *Live!* and with Sony's support News International was able to sign up a good range of other exhibitors and put on an exciting show for the benefit of the public.

At Sony we also ran trade shows exclusively for our customers. The industry, through its trade association BREMA, agreed to exhibit in London over a fixed period every spring. However, we refused to hold this under one roof as we reserved the right to invite our customers and didn't want our competitors listening to our conversations. Most of our competitors held their shows in the same hotels every year, but at Sony, where our motto was 'We do what others don't', we always tried to find something different. I did not invent this tradition but was happy to adopt it and develop it further. In the year before my appointment the trade show was held in an underground car park in Hyde Park. During my time we held it in a huge marquee in Battersea Park, on the disused third floor of Whiteley's department store, on the top two storeys of an unlet empty skyscraper in Marylebone Road and, my personal favourite, in the Albert Hall at a gig between a boxing championship and Eric Clapton.

But we continued to come under pressure to participate in an under-one-roof show. Finally I met secretly with a leading independent retailer. He wrote amusing and influential columns in two leading trade papers, one under his own name and the other under a pseudonym. He Persuaded me that there was an overarching responsibility to the industry that mandated the leading manufacturer, Sony, to support such a show. The retailers needed it in order to come together and draw strength from each other and their suppliers. I agreed and from then on we participated in such a show. It did not really fit within our sales Plans and we still held private meetings with our authorized dealers, but we had made a concession to that wider good and it significantly improved our standing with the independent dealers, a position on which my successors have built.

With the development of the internet a lot of business is now transacted online. It is tempting to think, therefore, that your website has become your Place of doing business. This may be true, in which case it will be no different in principle than 'selling off the page' as in the case of mail order, which has been established for over 100 years. It may also be that your website is designed primarily to Promote your business and it is important to distinguish these two different purposes. We will consider the whole question of Promotion in the next chapter.

The managing of *Place*, or *Placement*, is a vital part of the marketing mix. It will be the responsibility of both the sales and the marketing parts of an organization and there needs to be care in how the responsibilities are shared. Perhaps this was in the mind of the printers of the Geneva Bible in the 16th century when they made a classic printing error, which can be seen in the British Library. One of the historically most important translations of the Bible into English is the Geneva Bible, which was translated by a group of English Protestant scholars who fled to Geneva during the reign of Queen Mary of England (1553–58). In the second edition of this Bible, the Gospel of Matthew 5:9 reads: 'Blessed are the Placemakers: for they shall be called the children of God.'

Summary

In this chapter we have:

- shown the development of the marketPlace in marketing;
- described the importance of distribution strategy;

- discussed the role of distribution strategy in developing business models;
- underlined the importance of account management as evidenced by Professor Malcolm McDonald;
- outlined selective and exclusive distribution as governed by the Treaty of the Functioning of the European Union;
- considered the concept of franchising;
- looked at the role of *Place* in B2B marketing.

Promotion

04

Without Promotion something terrible happens: nothing.

PT BARNUM

If a man can write a better book, preach a better sermon, or make a better mousetrap, than his neighbour, though he build his house in the woods, the world will make a beaten path to his door.

USUALLY PARAPHRASED AS 'BUILD A BETTER MOUSETRAP AND THE WORLD WILL BEAT A PATH TO YOUR DOOR', THIS IS GENERALLY ATTRIBUTED TO RALPH WALDO EMERSON

There are many problems with this statement, one of which we dealt with in the last chapter, but the biggest is that there must be market awareness. If no one knows you exist and have built a mousetrap, no one will know that there is a path worth beating. Marketing addresses this with the fourth and final P of the original four Ps – that is, *Promotion*. For most people, Promotion is the activity that is known as 'below the line', ie dealing with the consumer indirectly via other channels. 'Above the line' covers direct communication. For the sake of convenience we will follow this split in this chapter and address advertising or 'above the line' first. We will also exclude public relations (PR) from this definition of Promotion, although it would be captured in traditional texts. The reason is quite simple. Public Relations certainly has an element of Promotion in that a good PR campaign can be part of an effective Promotional campaign. However, Public Relations is not only about the one-way proactive part of communication, but importantly is also about the reactive element of maintaining a dialogue with the public. Companies have to know how to respond to public concerns. This is a long way from Promotion but is an important element of marketing and so we will deal with this in Chapter 8 (Publicity). In the same chapter we will take the special subject of sponsorship. Some aspects of sponsorship are very much connected with an overall Promotional strategy; however, there are other aspects that are far removed from that and are more concerned with corporate reputation than with Product Promotion.

Even with these exclusions, what is left – the traditional subject of advertising and Promotion – is for many synonymous with marketing. I am firmly opposed to that view. For me, advertising and Promotion make up an important element in the marketing mix but not its whole. In the British marketing community there is a level of pride in our creative capacity that seems to say this is an industry on its own, even a branch of the creative arts. It would of course not exist without its clients, and its only success can be measured in terms of its clients' success. If its clients are happy in the knowledge that their objectives have been met then the advertising and/or the Promotion can be said to have been successful. It is simply extraordinary to me that clients have allowed a side show to develop in making awards for creativity etc without always considering effectiveness at the same time.

But we are getting ahead of ourselves. Let us return to the thesis. Having made a better mousetrap how do we communicate that to the potential customer?

History of advertising

In a small community with a passing trade it may be enough for us to put a sign in our shop window inviting passers-by to come in and see for themselves. But if we are ambitious to grow the business to a wider market we will need media with which to communicate the message to that wider market. And so, over time, advertising has found more and more media with which to spread the commercial word. From shop signs to billboards, from newspapers to radio and television, from direct mail to the internet, there have been myriad ways in which advertising messages have been brought to the attention of potential customers. Even back in 1780 Samuel Johnson stated: 'Advertisements are so numerous that they are very negligently perused and it is therefore necessary to gain attention by magnificence of promise and by eloquence, sometimes sublime and sometimes pathetic – promise, large promise, is the soul of an advertisement.'

The Industrial Revolution led to the means of mass manufacture and this in turn led to the need to stimulate mass consumption. The answer was to advertise and new media sprung up – magazines and newspapers with space to carry such advertising. In the Victorian era this continued apace and arguably the first great Promotion, 'The Great Exhibition' of 1851, conceived by Prince Albert, was staged in Hyde Park in the fabulous Crystal Palace that was temporarily erected to house the exhibition. In an early demonstration of globalization the world's manufacturers were invited to take part in the glory of invention and commerce. Over 6 million visitors marvelled at the 15,000 exhibits – and the age of consumerism was launched.

In 1865, a young man joined the House of Pears (soap-makers) as a junior partner. He would later become one of the most remarkable figures in the history of advertising. Thomas J. Barrett created the Pears advertisements, which became famous in their own right and made the brand equally famous. He wrote slogans such as 'Good morning – have you used Pears' soap?' It became so ubiquitous that people refrained from the usual morning greeting because of the predictable response. He also adopted fine art to the same commercial purpose. He bought John Everett Millais's painting *Bubbles* and cleverly had a tablet of soap painted into the picture. Millais was furious until he learnt that thousands of reproduction posters were sold; the painting became the most popular of its day. Barrett also invented the annual 'Miss Pears' contest to find the most beauteous young girl. The contest was to run for a century.

From such pioneers many followed and advertising became more and more influential in media, in consumer buying habits, in street furniture and in the financing of entertainment. The term 'soap opera' comes from the sponsorship by the soap giants of radio and later television serial dramas. Some of the brightest minds have made their careers and in some cases their fortunes in the advertising industry. Roy Thomson, an astute Canadian, started a TV enterprise in the UK after most people's retirement age. He famously said that a TV franchise was a licence to print money. That money came exclusively from advertisers who saw this as the most efficient way to reach the largest possible audience. Today the biggest advertiser in the UK is Her Majesty's Government.

There are two important questions to address when it comes to advertising. First, does it work? And second, if yes, then how does it work?

Does advertising work?

For many people this question is loaded. They don't believe that advertising works on them, even if it works on other people. But this is disingenuous. All of these people will have bought something in their lives as a result of advertising. It may have been a classified advert in the newspapers to which they responded. Or they looked in an estate agent's window, saw a property they liked the look of and, after inspection and due diligence, they made an offer for it. Or they may have been in the market for a new car or television and read the appropriate magazines, then test drove or looked at some samples before making their selection. All of these are examples of effective advertising in action, of help to the customer in making their decision to buy.

Advertising is a highly effective means of providing useful information, and at its best enables effective markets to operate by providing information, encouraging competition, announcing innovation and stimulating demand. But still there is suspicion that it is manipulative and misleading. Many people also see advertising – particularly, though not exclusively, filmed advertising – as a source of entertainment and thus independent of the reason it exists. For a long time in the 1960s and 1970s it used to be said that advertising was the best thing on television. The public loved adverts about Martians who laughed at old-fashioned humans for being behind the times in the way they prepared mashed potatoes, but ironically Smash is no longer with us as a Product while the folk memory of its advertising remains strong. People love the Guinness horses, they chortle at Hamlet cigars and a host of other long-running campaigns, when the fact is that they were never in the market to buy such Products.

Vance Packard wrote *The Hidden Persuaders* in the 1950s and ever since there has been healthy scepticism about advertising. Advertising does work but in a variety of ways and not all the time on all the people. If we approach this only from the economic point of view I think it would be possible to draw a direct correlation between advertising and prosperity. In other words, societies are prosperous in direct proportion to the levels of advertising they are exposed to. This is not necessarily directly causative as a relationship but is still of interest.

It has been famously said, 'Half the money I spend on advertising is wasted; the problem is I don't know which half.' This has been attributed to everyone from Henry Procter of Procter & Gamble to William Lever of Unilever but was actually coined by John Wanamaker, a department-store magnate in the later part of the 19th century who also became US Postmaster General. I will return to this question in Chapter 12 (Productivity), as it is a key metric in that context. But it is also a question of effectiveness. As someone who has spent a career in marketing I am often asked what I think of a particular campaign. I rarely give an answer, as it is technically impossible to judge unless one knows the detail of the brief. What was the target audience? What was the objective of the campaign? Unless one knows the answer to these and other questions it is not possible to judge accurately the strength of an advertisement. Having said that, I must admit that there are many adverts I see that are simply mystifying. Perhaps if I were to see the brief I would find it was a poor brief, badly written, not adequately thought through. In such a case bad advertising is inevitable. It is the same as the principle of computer software – garbage in, garbage out.

As further evidence that advertising works we only have to examine the reaction of whole industries when their freedom to advertise is at risk of restriction by regulators. In the past the tobacco industry was the forerunner and its lobbyists always argued that advertising did not increase the size of the market but was a zero-sum game in which advertisers competed for market share. This ingenuous argument was rightly never accepted and is blown up by the evidence. One particularly disturbing story was in Japan where there had long been an unwritten convention among domestic Producers that advertisers would not appeal to women. Thus penetration of cigarette smoking among women was very low by international comparisons. Then, as a result of political pressure, an American firm gained access to the market. It was not party to this convention and did not recognize it. It launched a number of brands specifically aimed at women. Within a short time a large number of young women had acquired this pernicious habit and we can assume that many of them will have died prematurely.

I find this subject particularly difficult. As a founder member of the CBI Market Strategy Group the then Director General Sir John Banham sought my views on tobacco advertising. I said that while I personally detested the habit – I have the zeal of the reformed addict having smoked for 10 years from the age of 15 – nevertheless I felt that if it is legal to sell a Product then it should be legal to advertise it. I'm not sure that I would say the same today having learnt even more about the dangers of smoking, and at the very least there must be strong limitations on what is allowed. One policy that might work would be for tobacco manufacturers to be forced to spend an equivalent amount of money to their total marketing budget on the counter-campaign.

There are now several other industries that come under pressure to restrict their advertising, from the drinks industry to Producers of children's food. The drinks industry tries to regulate itself and recites the same mantra, that advertising simply moves the pieces around the board. However, a former colleague of mine who has enjoyed a successful career in the drinks industry privately admitted to me what in any case must be obvious, that so-called alcopops have been specially developed to appeal to the young and are then advertised to that community. We will return to the subject of ethics in the Conclusion, but suffice to say that advertisers have a very considerable responsibility.

How does advertising work?

There is a great deal of academic study on this subject. As I said before, for many of us the inclination is to resist the idea that advertising works; that we can be Persuaded to do something by a commercial message. But why not? Life is about Persuasion. Men and women court each other and in the process show themselves in the best possible light. This is mirrored throughout the animal kingdom. An applicant for a job will present themselves in the best possible way both through their initial application and CV and then in the interview. Before I put my house up for sale I will clean it, maybe give it a fresh coat of paint and, when a potential buyer comes to view it, perhaps have a pot of coffee on the go in the kitchen to give it an attractive aroma. The list goes on and on and is quite normal and acceptable. What is not acceptable is for the process to be dishonest – and that is also true of advertising. Advertising must be legal, decent, honest and truthful. When it is not there is machinery by which complaints can be made – and advertising can be, and sometimes is, withdrawn.

Advertising works on two levels as with all human understanding – the rational and the emotional; the left and the right brain. Perhaps people who say it does not work on them are rational people; they are more left-brain and able to resist the emotional appeal of a particular advert. However, great advertising usually does both. One campaign that has always stuck in my mind was run by Abbott Mead Vickers for Sainsbury. It simply said, 'Good food costs less at Sainsbury'. However, this simple statement has both emotional and rational elements. 'Good food' is an emotional idea. It is difficult to prove in the rational sense but we all know what it means. 'Costs less' is entirely rational and is capable of explicit demonstration. The really clever part was that they ran the campaign in two halves. 'Good food' was demonstrated in magazine advertising with beautiful food, lovingly photographed in colour and rapturously described with some of David Abbott's best copy. 'Costs less' was more prosaically explained in black and white in the daily newspapers with details of each week's special offers. But the strapline 'Good food costs less at Sainsbury' was the sign off on both.

This question of emotional and rational aspects to advertising is also a question of timing, as one may need to precede the other. An example from my own experience (or lack of, in this case) was Bounty, the chocolate-enrobed coconut bar from Mars. Readers will no doubt recall the long-running campaign 'Bounty, a taste of Paradise' in which the Product was associated with images of South Sea islands and dusky maidens. When I was in Chile considering which Products from the Mars range should be launched there I thought of Bounty. Back in London over lunch with a leading executive from Ted Bates, the agency involved, I explained my theory: 'The Chileans love the South Seas. Tahiti is one of the Places they aspire to visit; I'm sure they'd love Bounty!' My lunch companion asked dryly: 'Do they know what it is? Long before we showed tropical beaches we spent 10 years describing the coconut and the chocolate enrobing' – the point is that the rational explanation came first and the emotional values were added later. The rational gives you reasons to buy. The emotional makes you feel good that you bought. As Scott Bedbury, the branding expert and former top marketing guru at Nike and at Starbucks, says: 'It's not enough to have a great Product or service any more. The world is full of Products and services that work. You have to take stock of how your brand makes consumers feel.'

When I first made the transition from sales to marketing one of the things I most looked forward to was the opportunity to shoot my own commercials for the brands I would manage. Unfortunately, as previously described, most of these were me-too Products in the armoury, strategically designed to weaken some of our principal competitors' portfolios rather than have a life of their own. Nevertheless, I made an early pitch to my first marketing boss, Chris Bradshaw. Chris was an unusually bright marketer who had (inevitably) gained his training at Procter & Gamble where he had launched Ariel detergent, still a major force in the market. After recruitment by Pedigree Petfoods he had written the strategy that led to the phenomenally successful and Profitable development of the Whiskas cat food franchise. In the mid-1970s the energy crisis precipitated some panic thinking about viability of tin plate in the future and the need to diversify into other forms of packaging that were more compact by relying on semi-moist or dry food technology rather than canning. By the same token these Products were at the time less palatable and cans were to dominate the market for many years yet, although eventually the prediction that dry and semi-moist would take over proved true. A dedicated factory was built and Chris was asked to provide the marketing to sell the factory's output.

In joining his team it was a fabulous opportunity for me to learn from a master as well as my talented colleagues: Paul Jackson, who'd had a long and distinguished career with Mars, and Drummond Hall, who was to go on to become Chief Executive of Dairy Crest.

In an early discussion with Chris I made my pitch to advertise one of my me-too brands. Chris pointed out that advertising was merely a method of communicating with the consumer. The trick was to know what to communicate and then find other ways to do it if advertising was unaffordable. This was a valuable lesson and one I have never forgotten. Robert Louis Stevenson best expressed it when he said 'The difficulty of literature is not to write, but to write what you mean.' In advertising, or indeed in marketing, this is the challenge. To sum up what your brand stands for in a simple message that can be communicated with your end user by advertising, a message on the package or by whatever means. We will return to this subject in Chapter 10 (Positioning).

But later, with a different director in charge, I relaunched the same brand in a new format, merging it with a previously advertised brand. There was a clear need to explain all this to the consumer, and the agency came up with a Powerful idea. We would say that this Product, which was highly nutritious, was good enough to be used by the mountain rescue dogs in the Lake District and so was good enough to be fed to your pooch. This idea is known in the jargon as the torture test. It was an exciting idea and, of course, we backed it up by working with a real mountain rescue team. I remember presenting this idea to the board and the finance director's question was whether the advertising was too good for the Product – an insightful analysis. Nevertheless, I went up the mountain with the agency Production team and, of course, the mountain rescue leader and his dogs. The mountaineer was a natural, with rugged good looks and a willingness to build a long-term relationship. His dogs were a mother and daughter who would double for each other in the film. We also shot the Product comparison at the same time and there was a comparison with fillet steak. The only times that the make-up artist was used was to paint over some grey hair on the mother dog so that she more closely resembled her daughter, and to make the fillet steak look better because, in the director's eye, it did not really look like fillet steak. I think this was still within the meaning of legal, honest, decent and truthful except that the finance director was, of course, right. The story was too strong. The Product did not live up to it. It was not maliciously misleading but simply an over-claim born out of excess enthusiasm and insufficient rigorous testing. I'm sure every experienced marketer has a long list of such war stories, because how else do we finish up with so much banal advertising?

Below the line

Below the line covers the rest of *Promotion*, mainly to support the sales process. Much of this is a legitimate aspect of Promotion, for example in trial-gaining activity, loyalty building or additional incentives to make the sale. But there is some confusion over the role of discounting and where to account for that. Discounts may be deducted legitimately from the top-line revenue or charged to the Promotion account depending on how they are applied, and the custom and practice of the business. There is a great deal of so-called Promotional activity that is little more than discounting by another name.

Throughout time, bargaining has been the normal way of doing business and it still is in large parts of the world. In the so-called sophisticated and developed West we have lost the art of negotiation or haggling. We are embarrassed to ask for a discount and are more comfortable with the non-confrontational nature of self-service. We can go through the supermarket and collect all our weekly needs without once opening our mouths. In the process we may respond to many 'Promotional' messages but the vast majority of these today are variations on a Price theme.

If you walk through your local supermarket you will meet the following variations on a theme: *Two for the Price of One!* or *Buy One Get One Free!*, known in the trade as BOGOF; *Half Price!*; *50% off!*. Is there a difference between these offers? Well, the last two are clearly the same – *Half Price* and *50% off* are identical in meaning and impact. But *Buy One Get One Free* may cost the same to implement but has a different impact. It encourages a higher level of purchase and so takes the consumer out of the market and away from a competitor for a longer period. It also protects the original Price point because although a considerable offer has been made, a whole free extra purchase, the selling point is maintained. The cost of implementing such offers can be considerable. If a manufacturer wants to achieve a reduction in selling Price of say 5p per unit they will have to reduce their own wholesale selling Price by such an amount. This will be a much greater percentage of their own listed selling Price to the retailer than the 5p represents of the final retail Prices, as the following example shows.

Take a Product that normally retails at 50p and is shipped in cases of 12. The manufacturer lists this at £3.60 and so the retailer will make £2.40 cash Profit at recommended selling Price (RSP) or 40 per cent gross margin. Now if the manufacturer stipulates a '5p off' offer the selling Price has to be reduced by 60p per case to £3.00. The retailer sells at 45p, clearing the same cash Profit of £2.40, which is now 44.4 per cent gross margin, while the manufacturer has reduced its Profit by 60p. The manufacturer has simply handed over 60p of margin to the retailer.

To get round this I invented a new form of special offer in the 1970s, while as a young brand manager at Pedigree Petfoods. It was clear that special Packs were effective and the most effective were clear 'money off' offers. However, as just explained, it was necessary to fund the entire offer and so there was a limit to how much we could afford to put into the market. I came up with the idea of the 'Special Low Price' offer Pack. Each Pack was marked with the words 'Special Low Price!' Consequently the customer could expect a discount from the usual Price. However, the level of the discount was not fixed and so as the manufacturer I could vary that according to what I could afford. I then asked my sales force to try to negotiate an additional contribution to the offer from the retailer and thus achieve close to the original offer we were trying to replicate. This was very successful and we ran such offers for a number of years.

Most trade Promotion is little more than supporting the listing. As retailers have gained Power at the expense of all but the most Powerful global manufacturers a great body of trade merchandising has built up. The retailer has become more and more skilled in squeezing its suppliers. When I was a young sales manager at Pedigree Petfoods we had developed quite sophisticated arguments denying requests for overriding discounts that retailers sought on their overall level of turnover. Most of these arguments revolved around our investment in the market, in Product development, in educating the consumer and so on. In my own case, these arguments were invariably successful.

However, since that day the retailer has learnt countervailing arguments, which are mainly about its Power over the supplier. Grant the retailer their requests or they will delist you. This threat of delisting is all pervasive and even the listing itself, the agreement to stock a particular line, will carry a fee. The retailer will charge the manufacturer for agreeing to stock their Product, then for stocking it and at the end of the year for having stocked it. I remember in the 1980s one particularly bloodthirsty buying director of a major supermarket chain, after another bout of removing the toenails from a supplier, would go into his staff canteen, ring a bell for attention and then announce, 'another manufacturer bites the dust'. I'm glad to report that the world is round and he got his comeuppance when the retailer was acquired by an even more aggressive predator who decided it did not need the services of that particular buying director.

Such abuse of Power has regularly been investigated but seldom proven. This is because no supplier will provide the evidence that will prove the case, because they are afraid at the corporate level of losing their business and at the individual level of losing their job. Everyone knows it goes on. Very few can do anything about it except those very large companies that have a global business and so can hold individual retailers at arm's length and not give in to all their demands. Even here there is an increasing trend for retailers to travel around the world. I used to think that retailing was largely a local business relying on local knowledge and that it did not easily transfer across cultures. There were many examples of retailers that enjoyed dominant positions in their own countries but failed to establish an international business unless the business was 'retailing in a box', ie a formula that could be exported without much variation. Thus we saw the immensely successful

Marks and Spencer fail to establish itself in the United States, and J Sainsbury had a similarly disappointing experience there.

Fast-food retailers such as McDonald's and Burger King took a while to iron out the local cultural variations but have now established very successful global businesses. Of the grocery companies, Walmart with its acquisition of Asda in the UK, and Tesco with clever forages into Eastern Europe and Southeast Asia, are showing that after all it can be done, although Tesco has had to bite the bullet on its US experiment, Fresh & Easy.

As I have said, most of so-called Promotion is simply reductions in Price or is designed to support the listing. Marketers often talk of building loyalty through such schemes when all they are doing is devaluing their brand or offering bribes to their end user. This form of Promotion has its role to play, providing we do not exaggerate its effect.

Above the line versus below the line

A brand owner will want to run a campaign with both 'above' and 'below' the line elements. They will want to maintain direct communication with their consumer while giving an appropriate level of trade support. However, what will be their decision if their overall funds are limited and they are unable to achieve both tasks adequately? In all probability they will withdraw the advertising because they will not want to upset their trade buyers by withdrawing their support. The effect of withdrawing advertising may not be immediate but they will think that if they do not support the trade buyer then the buyer will be delisted and they will have no business.

I was faced with a similar dilemma when I was in charge of Green's of Brighton in the early 1980s. As General Manager it was my decision to allocate the advertising and Promotion budgets. I had been trained in the hard school of Mars, where we had developed strict rules as to the minimum levels of spend necessary to support an advertising campaign. We believed that unless those minimum levels of reach and frequency were achieved then the advertising was in a sense a waste of money as it was effectively invisible. Insufficient consumers would see it and levels of recall would be too low.

I therefore decided to allocate all of my spend to below the line activity. I gave the budget to a leading sales Promotion house, which was of course understandably delighted. They came back with an imaginative Plan for a programme of activities throughout the year. On one brand they proposed a free gift of a calendar, which we would Produce especially to encourage year-round use of that brand; on another there was to be a tie-up with

Barnardo's charity, and so on. My CEO, Bruce Noble, an excellent manager trained at Colgate Palmolive and with previous stints at McKinsey and a leading London advertising agency, expressed his doubts on the Plan and tried to dissuade me from it, but I was convinced it was better value for money than anything we could achieve above the line.

I was wrong. The campaign was very unsuccessful and few of the Promotions met their objectives. Spreading Promotional money around in that way was even less effective than it might have been with advertising. The particular error was to send a message that the brand was no longer an advertised brand. This message not only went to consumers, although I doubt whether they ever really acknowledge such things, but more importantly went to direct stakeholders, especially our employees and particularly among them our sales force. They no longer had the Power of advertising behind them, and their customers also saw that this was a brand that had lost its confidence.

The following year I moved the available money back above the line and this time briefed Abbott Mead Vickers, our residual agency. As we had been a founder client of theirs, despite our small budget they retained considerable loyalty to the brand, Placed some of their best talent at our disposal and delivered some high-quality magazine advertising that restored some of the fortunes of the brand. Bruce Noble graciously acknowledged that I had learnt my lesson and underlined it by pointing out to me that in his opinion a brand should maintain some advertising support even if it was reduced to tiny ads in the corner of a weekly such as the *Radio Times*. It was a statement of its position in the world.

I remembered the lesson when I was at Sony. Here I had substantially greater budgets to disburse. However, when a recession hit in the early 1990s many of my competitors reduced their advertising support in some cases to naught. They of course did not reduce their trade support but had moved over that line that Bruce had defined for me. I, by contrast, increased the level of advertising support so that Sony appeared to be almost the only brand in serious communication with its audience. Our share of voice rose to over 75 per cent, which may seem excessive but the result was a substantial increase in our overall market share and significant increases in sales even at a time of falling market demand. We were able to hang on to these share gains in subsequent years and during this period actually reduced our percentage of turnover allocated to advertising and Promotion.

So when we ask ourselves the question 'How does advertising work?' as well as considering the emotional and rational appeal to the end user we must also take into account the attitudes of all the other stakeholders, especially the sales force and the trade.

In the first four chapters of this book I have dealt with the traditional four Ps of marketing. In the next chapter I will start the journey of expanding coverage and consider one more core P, that of packaging.

Summary

In this chapter we have:

- described the development of advertising in the marketing mix;
- explained how advertising works;
- considered the importance of maintaining an advertised stance;
- looked at various methods of 'below the line' Promotion;
- discussed the risks of excessive Price Promotion.

Packaging

05

An egg is a work of art, a masterpiece of design, construction, and brilliant Packaging. **DELIA SMITH**

In this chapter I will explain why the four traditional Ps of marketing require at least a fifth P, *Packaging*. Packaging might be felt to be either part of the Product or the Promotion, depending on whether we are talking about the function of the Packaging or the design on the Packaging. But that is exactly the point. Packaging serves two entirely separate purposes and is therefore both an art form and a science. The question of form and function has to be addressed.

Consider the Product Coca-Cola. This is a well-known beverage. Whether we drink it from a bottle, a can or a soda fountain matters little as they are each delivery systems, but in the context of marketing these delivery systems convey a whole business model. Coca-Cola is manufactured in syrup form with its secret formula only known to a handful of individuals. The syrup is then distributed throughout the world to bottlers (which these days are also canners, etc); they add carbonated water and then sell bottles and cans and other forms of the final Product. In this context the Packaging has taken on a whole new meaning.

When I managed Green's of Brighton, a dry mix food business, my raw material costs and Packaging costs were roughly equal. The Product proposition was that a customer could make a cake or dessert by buying a mix of the critical ingredients, except for one final fresh ingredient such as an egg or some milk. The received wisdom had it that by adding this ingredient the customer felt as if they were adding something of their own and so felt less guilty than if they had bought a ready-to-eat cake. They then baked the cake in the oven and produced something they could serve as their own. In this scenario the Packaging was all important. It had to deliver all the ingredients in good condition and in the right quantities so that the purchaser could achieve their finished Product.

And what appeared *on* the Packaging was also all-important. There had to be a photograph of what the end Product should look like. This was both to attract the customer to want to buy it and also to reassure them after they had made the cake. Then there had to be a list of instructions, the equivalent of the 'recipe' from the cook book. There were lots of other regulatory and legislative requirements. And finally, overarching all these, there had to be evidence that this was a reliable Product from a reputable brand name; there had to be the trademark or logo.

The words brand and trademark are not synonymous but have become almost interchangeable. Originally a brand was the mark that the farmer made with a hot iron on his cattle or sheep. It marked out his property both for his own and his neighbours' reference. The word then became used to stand for a trademark, signifying the manufacturer of a Product. It is a promise that goods from this source can all be held to be of similar quality to others with the same mark. The first registered trademark in the United Kingdom was the Red Triangle used by Bass, the brewers, as long ago as New Year's Day 1876, when the Trade Mark Registration Act 1875 came into force.

Function

Packaging must first act as a protective barrier and a delivery mechanism. It is the same principle as architecture. Before we judge the cosmetic appearance of the building we must know if the building is fit for purpose. Will it stand up? Will it withstand wind and rain? Does the plumbing work? Designers of Packaging can draw lessons from some of the wonderful examples in nature. I quoted Delia Smith at the beginning of this chapter, who paid tribute to the qualities of the egg as a Packaging design. It protects the precious contents until it comes to life, or in the kitchen is needed to add a unique blend of proteins and minerals to the cuisine. A banana gives another outstanding example of Packaging. Protective but easy to peel it does not even require any energy in order to enjoy a nutritious and delicious snack.

History of Packaging

Early forms of manmade Packaging used the natural materials available at the time: baskets of reeds, wineskins, stone jars, wooden boxes and barrels, pottery vases, ceramic amphorae, woven bags etc. Processed materials were used to form Packages as they were developed: for example, early glass and bronze vessels. The study of old Packages is an important aspect of archaeology.

In 1800, Napoleon Bonaparte offered an award of 12,000 francs to anyone who could devise a practical method for food preservation for armies on the march; he is widely reported as saying 'An army marches on its stomach'. After some 15 years of experiment, Nicolas Appert submitted his invention and won the prize in 1810. The following year, Appert published *L'Art de conserver les substances animales et végétales* (or *The Art of Preserving Animal and Vegetable Substances*). This was the first cook book of its kind on modern food preservation methods.

The tin can was patented in 1810 by the English inventor Peter Durand. Durand's patent was dedicated to the preservation technique rather than to the vessel. The technique was successful (despite insufficiently clean Production conditions) because of the high temperature of the treatment: 100 °C instead of about 70 °C used in modern pasteurization (though higher temperatures did also destroy some of the food flavour). However, Appert used exclusively glass vessels whereas Durand was the first to mention in a patent the use of tin cans.

Durand seems to have been somewhat suspicious of the invention and did not produce any food cans himself, but sold his patent to two other Englishmen, Bryan Donkin and John Hall, who set up a commercial canning factory and by 1813 were producing their first canned goods for the British Army. In 1818 Durand introduced tin cans in the United States by re-patenting his British patent there. By 1820, canned food was a recognized article in Britain and France and by 1822 in the United States.

Early cans were sealed with lead soldering, which led in some cases to lead poisoning. Notoriously, in the Arctic expedition of Sir John Franklin in 1845, crew members suffered from severe lead poisoning after three years of eating canned food.

In 1817, the first paperboard carton was produced in England. Folding cartons first emerged in the 1860s and were shipped flat to save space, ready to be set up by customers when they were required. The year 1879 saw the development of mechanical die cutting and the creasing to give the cartons the corrugated effect. In 1911 the first kraft sulphate mill was built in Florida; in 1915 the gable top milk carton was patented and in 1935 the first dairy plant was observed using them. Ovenable paperboard was introduced in 1974.

> About 10 years after that, when I was General Manager of Green's of Brighton, I introduced a very successful mix to make brownies. The mix came with an ovenable tray that fitted exactly inside the standard Green's carton. All the consumer had to do was add a little water to the mix, bake it in the tray in a hot oven and 30 minutes later there was a very appetizing tray of brownies ready to eat. It did away with the necessity for the customer to have all the right baking equipment at home. The Product went straight to number four in the dry mix market charts!

Packaging advancements in the early 20th century included bakelite closures on bottles, transparent cellophane overwraps and panels on cartons, increased processing efficiency and improved food safety. As additional materials such as aluminium and several types of plastic were developed, they were incorporated into Packages to improve performance and functionality.

Many Arctic communities would preserve food in holes or larders dug into the ice. There is a tradition in Scandinavia of preserving fish, especially herrings, in this way. Freezing food is a common method of food preservation, which slows both food decay and, by turning water to ice, makes it unavailable for most bacterial growth and slows down most chemical reactions. American inventor Clarence Birdseye, who developed the quick-freezing process of food preservation in 1932, is considered the father of the frozen-food industry. The famous brand name Birdseye is derived from him, despite the more emotive aspects of the logo.

Chilled food is prepared food that is stored at refrigeration temperatures, which are at or below 8 °C (46 °F). The key requirements for chilled food Products are good quality and microbiological safety at the point of consumption. They have been available in the UK, United States and many other industrialized countries since the 1960s. While tinned foods could be stored for decades in a larder, frozen and chilled foods required the presence of a freezer and/or a refrigerator in the household. Thus when introducing a new type of Packaging the marketer needs to research the household ownership of such appliances.

This section has concentrated on food Packaging as this is probably, along with drugs and medicines, the most challenging use of Packaging. In any new development process, Package design and development are an integral part. Package design starts with the identification of all the requirements: structural design, marketing, shelf life, quality assurance, security, logistics, legal, regulatory, end use, environmental, etc. The design criteria, time targets, resources and cost constraints need to be established and agreed upon.

Before leaving the functional aspects of Packaging we should consider two cautionary issues: first, although increasingly there is pressure for theft-proof and tamper-evident Packaging, nevertheless we must remember that it must be capable of being opened by its intended user. As the American comedian, Dave Barry, puts it: 'more and more Products are coming out in fiercely protective Packaging designed to prevent consumers from consuming them. These days you have to open almost every consumer item by gnawing on the Packaging.' Second, we need to use less. Many Products are over-Packaged, sometimes for the dubious reason of suggesting that the contents are more substantial than is the case. As well as needing to recycle and reuse, the best way to achieve a sustainable position is to use less in the first place. Thus, as Dave Wann puts it, 'the Packaging for a microwavable "microwave" dinner is programmed for a shelf life of maybe six months, a cook time of two minutes and a landfill dead-time of centuries.'

Packaging of identity

An individual person is identified by their name and appearance. Some individuals, in order to market themselves in particular markets such as film acting or popular music, will invent a new identity complete with new name and stylized appearance. It is the same in Product marketing. We need to create a complete identity that has a hierarchy of design elements to assist easy recognition by the target consumer.

The first of these is obviously the name itself. If our Product is baked beans we need to distinguish it from any other mark of baked beans by a name. Even the cheapest value offering from a supermarket will carry that supermarket's own brand. There is a great deal of mystique in the selection of names and it seems to have taken on much of an art form. However, as Shakespeare's Juliet said:

> 'What's in a name? That which we call a rose
> By any other name would smell as sweet.'

To unpick some of this mystique I examined a group of 50 famous names in order to understand their derivation and classification. In 2009 the Marketing Society, of which I am a Fellow, celebrated its 50th anniversary. As a mark of this it selected 50 Golden Brands. Like all such lists, this one is somewhat subjective. The criteria for being assessed as 'golden' are not obvious to this author and seem to be based more on a distinctive advertising campaign than anything else. As I hope this book is making clear, there is very much more to marketing and brand management than that. At least the list does not fail the usual test of excessive recency, as one brand is selected from each year. But this in turn has led to the focus on short-term activity rather than sustained brand building. The list contains Ariel but not Persil; Barclaycard but not American Express; Channel 4 but not the BBC; Dove but not Gillette, and so on. Perhaps one of the strangest omissions is Vodafone, while BT, O_2 and Orange are all included – Vodafone went from a standing start to become Britain's most valuable company in a few years, one of the greatest developments of shareholder value in modern history.

However, for my purpose the list is as good as any other list. Table 5.1 is a brief summary of the derivation of each of these names together with a simple classification. A health warning: my research has been based on desk research supported by some personal knowledge. Mythology can build up about the development of names over time, and different interpretations are possible in some cases.

This analysis shows that we can classify the derivation of brand names into just six categories with various combinations of the categories as well. In this group of 50 leading brands, 13 are family names while another seven use an element of family name derivation. Eight are symbolic, with six more using symbolic elements in combination. Six are simply descriptive, with another four having a descriptive element in combination. Four are invented, with another four using an invented element in combination. Three are portmanteau, or composite, words with eight more having a portmanteau element in combination. Just one, Tango, is simply emotive.

But how important is the selection of any of these names? Would John Cadbury have been any less successful if he had been called John Sainsbury? Or John Sainsbury if he'd had the family name of Cadbury? What if Louis Perrier had artificially carbonated water rather than finding a naturally carbonated source and Jacob Schweppe had discovered the mineral water spa in the south of France (or in his native Switzerland)? Sony was visionary in inventing a name that could be used easily all over the world but its Japanese competitors Toshiba and Hitachi managed perfectly well behind them.

What distinguishes a name is tried and trusted experience over time. There have been occasional overnight stars but the majority of respected brands built their reputation over decades. They take on meaning rather than starting with that meaning. Thus Smith & Wesson is known for its guns while Brown & Poulson is known for its cornflour. As names both are

TABLE 5.1 Marketing Society 50 golden brands 1959–2009

No.	Brand	Type of Name	Derivation of Name
1	*Andrex*	Invented	The name *Andrex* comes from St Andrew's Mill in Walthamstow, north London, where the toilet tissue was first made in 1942.
2	*Apple Computer*	Symbolic	Established in California in 1976 the company was called Apple Computer, Inc. for its first 30 years, but dropped the word 'Computer' in 2007 to reflect the company's expansion into the consumer electronics market in addition to its traditional focus on personal computers.
3	*Ariel*	Symbolic	*Ariel* is a marketing line of home laundry detergents made by Procter & Gamble. *Ariel* is a name from the Hebrew 'Lion of God' and also a character in Shakespeare's *The Tempest*.
4	*Audi*	Family/Symbolic	The name *Audi* is based on a Latin translation of the surname of the founder August Horch, itself the German word for 'listen'!
5	*Barclaycard*	Family/ Portmanteau	Barclays Bank traces its origins back to 1690 when John Freame and Thomas Gould started trading as Goldsmith bankers in Lombard Street London. The name '*Barclays*' became associated with the business in 1736, when James Barclay, son-in-law of John Freame, became a partner in the business. *Barclaycard* is a global credit provider owned by Barclays plc in the UK. The *Barclaycard* was the first credit card introduced in the UK, coming into service in 1966.
6	*Benetton*	Family	Benetton Group S.p.A. is a global fashion brand, based in Treviso, Italy. The name comes from the Benetton family who founded the company in 1965.

(*Continued*)

TABLE 5.1 *(Continued)*

No.	Brand	Type of Name	Derivation of Name
7	*Benson & Hedges*	Family	*Benson & Hedges* was founded in 1873 by Richard Benson and William Hedges as Benson and Hedges Ltd. The company was formed to make cigarettes for the then Prince of Wales, Albert Edward.
8	*Birds Eye*	Family	Founded by General Foods, which in 1929 bought the rights to use a fast-freezing process patented by Clarence Birdseye. The brand was owned in Europe by Unilever until it sold it in 2006.
9	*British Gas*	Descriptive	British Gas plc, the former gas monopoly in the UK and its successor company Centrica, which has the rights to the *British Gas* name in the UK.
10	*BSkyB*	Portmanteau/ Symbolic	By 1990 both Rupert Murdoch's Sky Television and the BSB alliance were beginning to struggle with massive losses, which led to a 50:50 financial merger in November 1990. The new company was called British Sky Broadcasting (*BSkyB*) but marketed as *Sky*.
11	*BT*	Initials/ Descriptive	Formerly *British Telecom* (from BT Group, formerly British Telecommunications plc).
12	*Cadbury*	Family	In 1824, John Cadbury began producing and selling drinking chocolate in Birmingham. He later moved into the production of a variety of cocoas and drinking chocolates. A partnership was struck between John Cadbury and his brother Benjamin. At this time the company was known as 'Cadbury Brothers of Birmingham'.

13	*Channel 4*	Descriptive	The channel was established to provide a fourth television service to the UK that would break the duopoly of the licence fee funded BBC's two established services and the single commercial broadcasting network, ITV.
14	*Coca-Cola*	Portmanteau	Derived from the coca leaves and kola nuts used as flavouring. *Coca-Cola* creator John S. Pemberton changed the 'K' of kola to 'C' to make the name look better.
15	*Direct Line*	Descriptive	It was the first telephone insurer in the UK when launched in 1985 by founder Peter Wood, and soon became the UK's largest provider of motor vehicle insurance.
16	*Dove*	Symbolic	Unilever acquired soap factory *De Duif* (Dutch: *The Dove*) in the Netherlands, from which the English brand name *Dove* is derived.
17	*Dulux*	Invented/ Portmanteau (?)	*Dulux* is a brand of paint produced by Imperial Chemical Industries. The brand name *Dulux* was also used by DuPont since 1931 and is probably a portmanteau of DuPont Luxury.
18	*Duracell*	Portmanteau/ Descriptive	*Duracell* originated via the partnership of scientist Samuel Ruben and businessman Philip Rogers Mallory, who met during the 1920s. The P.R. Mallory Company produced mercury cells for military equipment use, superior to the battery technology used then in most applications. In 1964, the term '*Duracell*' was formally introduced as a brand. The name is a portmanteau for 'durable cell'.
19	*easyJet*	Portmanteau	EasyJet Airline Company Limited (styled as *easyJet*) is a British airline.

(*Continued*)

TABLE 5.1 *(Continued)*

No.	Brand	Type of Name	Derivation of Name
20	*EBay*	Portmanteau	Pierre Omidyar, who created the auction web trading website, had formed a web consulting concern called Echo Bay Technology Group. '*Echo Bay*' didn't refer to the town in Nevada; 'It just sounded cool', Omidyar reportedly said. Echo Bay Mines Limited, a gold mining company, had already taken EchoBay.com, so Omidyar registered what (at the time) he thought was the second best name: *eBay.com*. (There are alternative stories behind this.)
21	*Fairy Liquid*	Symbolic	In 1837, Thomas Hedley & Co. was established in Newcastle-upon-Tyne making soap and candles. The company bought the rights to the word '*Fairy*' and launched the first all-purpose soap in 1898. To this day, *Fairy* remains one of the best-known household product names. In 1930, Procter & Gamble established its first overseas subsidiary with the acquisition of Thomas Hedley & Co. Ltd.
22	*Google*	Invented/ Symbolic	Originated from a misspelling of the word 'googol', which refers to 10^{100}, the number represented by a 10 followed by 100 zeros. Some say it was inspired by '*Googleplex*' in *The Hitchhiker's Guide to the Galaxy* by Douglas Adams.
23	*Guinness*	Family	Arthur Guinness started brewing ales from 1759 in Leixlip, later in Dublin.
24	*Habitat*	Descriptive	Terence Conran opened his first furniture shop in Kings Road in Chelsea, west London, at the height of the swinging sixties. A habitat is defined by characteristic physical conditions and the presence of other organisms.

25	*Heinz*	Family	Henry John Heinz (1844–1919) was a German-American businessman. In 1869, Heinz founded Heinz Noble & Company with a friend, L.C. Noble, and began marketing horseradish. The company went bankrupt in 1875, but the following year Heinz founded another company, F & J Heinz, with his brother and a cousin. One of this company's first products was tomato ketchup. The company continued to grow, and in 1888 Heinz bought out his other two partners and reorganized the company as the H.J. Heinz Company, the name it carries to the present day.
26	*Hovis*	Portmanteau/ symbolic	The name was coined by London student Herbert Grime in a national competition set by S. Fitton & Sons Ltd to find a trading name for its patent flour, which was rich in wheat germ. Grime won £25 when he coined the word from the Latin phrase ***ho**minis* ***vis*** – 'the strength of man'.
27	*Lego*	Invented	Ole Kirk Christiansen, founder of the company, came up with the name *Lego* from the Danish ***le**g* ***go**dt* ('play well') and the company grew to become the Lego Group.
28	*Levi's*	Family	Levi Strauss, born Löb Strauss, was a German-Jewish immigrant to the United States who founded the first company to manufacture blue jeans from denim, or De Nimes cloth. His firm, Levi Strauss & Co., began in 1853 in San Francisco.
29	*M&S*	Family/ Initials	The company was founded by Michael Marks, a Polish Jewish immigrant. He first opened a penny bazaar (Marks' Penny Bazaar) in Hartlepool, the port of his entry into England, selling imported goods from his native Poland. Marks then ventured to Stockton-on-Tees and eventually on to Leeds in 1884 as a single market stall. After Thomas Spencer joined the company in 1894 it was known as '*Marks and Spencer*', later known colloquially as '*Marks and Sparks*', '*Marks's*', or '*M&S*'.

(*Continued*)

TABLE 5.1 *(Continued)*

No.	Brand	Type of Name	Derivation of Name
30	*McDonald's*	Family	The business began in 1940, with a restaurant opened by brothers Dick and Mac McDonald in San Bernardino, California.
31	*Microsoft*	Portmanteau	Coined by founder Bill Gates to represent the company that was devoted to microcomputer software. Originally christened *Micro-Soft*, the '-' disappeared in 1987 with the introduction of a new corporate identity and logo.
32	*Mini*	Descriptive	The *Morris Mini Minor* was shown to the press in August 1959. It was commercialized as *Austin Seven* and *Morris Mini Minor* and later changed to *Austin Mini* and *Morris Mini*.
33	*Nescafe*	Family/ Portmanteau	*Nestlé* – named after its founder, Henri Nestlé, who was born in Germany under the name 'Nestle', which is German (actually, Swabian diminutive) for 'bird's nest'. The company logo is a bird's nest with a mother bird and two chicks.
34	*Nike*	Symbolic	Named for the Greek goddess of victory.
35	*O^2*	Symbolic	The *BT Cellnet* consumer brand was renamed *O^2* – the chemical symbol for unbound oxygen – as were all the group's other businesses (other than Manx Telecom). The rebranding was engineered by the Lambie-Nairn design agency, which developed the idea of the company supplying services that were essential, much the same as oxygen is essential for life.

36	*Orange*	Symbolic	The *Orange* brand was created by an internal team at Microtel. The brand consultancy Wolff Olins was charged with designing the brand values and logo and advertising agency WCRS created the *Orange* slogan '*The Future's Bright, the Future's Orange*' along with the now famous advertising.
37	*Oxo*	Invented	Concentrated meat extract was invented by Justus Liebig around 1840 and commercialized by the Liebig Extract of Meat Company starting in 1866. The original product was a viscous liquid containing only meat extract and 4% salt. In 1899, the company introduced the trademark *Oxo* for a cheaper version; the origin of the name is not known, but presumably comes from the word ox.
38	*Perrier*	Family	The spring in southern France from which *Perrier* is drawn. It has been used as a spa since Roman times. Local doctor Louis Perrier bought the spring in 1898 and operated a commercial spa there; he also bottled the water for sale.
39	*PG tips*	Descriptive/ Invented	In the 1930s Arthur Brooke launched *PG Tips* in the UK tea market under the name of *Pre-Gest-Tee*, as it was thought that tea aided digestion. This was soon abbreviated to *PG* by grocers and van salesmen. The company adopted this as the official name and added '*tips*', referring to the fact that only the tips (the top two leaves and bud) of the tea plants are used in the blend. By 1951 the name *PG tips* was officially adopted.
40	*Sainsbury's*	Family	*Sainsbury's* was established as a partnership in 1869 when John James Sainsbury and his wife Mary Ann opened a store in Drury Lane in Holborn, London. He started as a retailer of fresh foods and later expanded into packaged groceries such as tea and sugar.

(*Continued*)

TABLE 5.1 *(Continued)*

No.	Brand	Type of Name	Derivation of Name
41	*Schweppes*	Family	Johann Jacob Schweppe, a German-born naturalized Swiss watchmaker and amateur scientist, developed a process to manufacture carbonated mineral water, founding the Schweppes Company in Geneva in 1783.
42	*Shell*	Symbolic	Royal Dutch/Shell was established in 1907, when the Royal Dutch Petrol Society plc and the Shell Transport and Trading Company Ltd merged their operations. The latter had been established at the end of the 19th century by commercial firm Samuel & Co (founded in 1830). Samuel & Co was already importing Japanese shells when it set up an oil company, so the oil company was named after the shells.
43	*Smirnoff*	Family	The *Smirnoff* brand began with a vodka distillery founded in Moscow by Pyotr Arsenievich Smirnov (1831–98), the son of illiterate Russian peasants.
44	*Sony*	Invented	From the Latin word '*sonus*' meaning sound, and '*sonny*', a slang word used by Americans to refer to a bright youngster, 'since we were sonny boys working in sound and vision', said Akio Morita. The company was founded as Tokyo Tsushin Kogyo KK (Tokyo Telecommunications Engineering Corporation) in 1946, and changed its name to *Sony* in 1958. *Sony* was chosen as it could be pronounced easily in many languages.
45	*Stella Artois*	Family/Symbolic	In 1708, Sebastian Artois became the master brewer at Den Horen, and gave his name to the brewery in 1717. In 1926, *Stella Artois* was launched, initially as a seasonal beer for the Christmas holiday market.

46	*Tango*	Emotive	*Tango* is a carbonated soft drink that was launched by Corona in 1950. Corona was bought by the Beecham Group in 1958, and Beecham Soft Drinks was bought by Britvic in 1987. Originally, *Tango* was the name of the orange flavour in a range of different flavoured drinks that each had its own name.
47	*Tesco*	Family/Initials/ Portmanteau	Founder Jack **Co**hen – who sold groceries in the markets of London's East End from 1919 – acquired a large shipment of tea from **T.E. S**tockwell. He made new labels by using the first three letters of the supplier's name and the first two letters of his surname.
48	*The Body Shop*	Descriptive	It has been suggested that Anita Roddick and her husband, Gordon Roddick, got the idea while on a visit to San Francisco, where they encountered stores on Union Street and on Telegraph Avenue in nearby Berkeley named *The Body Shop*, which sold shampoos, lotions and body creams in small plastic containers. In 1976 Anita and Gordon opened a new store in Brighton, also calling it '*The Body Shop*', which of course is also a pun on a car repair garage. The Roddicks deny that they copied the name but did pay the US company for naming rights in the United States.
49	*Toyota*	Family/ Invented	From the name of the founder, Sakichi Toyoda. Initially called *Toyoda*, it was changed after a contest for a better-sounding name. The new name was written in katakana with eight strokes, a number that is considered lucky in Japan.
50	*Virgin Atlantic*	Symbolic/ Descriptive	Founder Richard Branson started a magazine called *Student* while still at school. In his autobiography, *Losing My Virginity*, Branson says that when they were starting a business to sell records by mail order, 'one of the girls suggested: "What about *Virgin*? We're complete virgins at business."'

interchangeable, but after over a century of specialization the identity has been clearly established. Charles Rolls met Henry Royce in Manchester in 1904. Mr Rolls provided the salesmanship and the financial backing and Mr Royce the engineering. It sounds like the ideal partnership except that Rolls's real passion was in flying; ironically he tried and failed to persuade Royce to manufacture an aerial engine. By 1909 Rolls had withdrawn to a non-executive position and in 1910 was the first Briton to be killed in a flying accident. Yet the combination of the two men's names is immortal and one of the greatest examples of an unqualified luxury brand that has entered the language.

Generics

Entering the language is not without danger as if it is fully achieved the brand owner may be said to have lost control of his or her brand as it becomes a generic name for the category. Brands that began as commercial trademarks and have been lost to their owners include Linoleum floor covering, which was ruled as generic in 1878 following a lawsuit for trademark infringement and may have been the first Product name to become generic. Aspirin was patented by Bayer, which still controls the trademark in some countries but it has been declared generic in the United States and elsewhere. Bayer also trademarked Heroin! Other names that have become generic include Cellophane, originally a trademark of DuPont; Escalator – originally a trademark of the Otis Elevator Company; the Thermos was declared generic in 1963 and the Yo-Yo in 1965.

Changing a brand name

Changing a name is fraught with danger and should usually only be tried if there is some overwhelming reason. The nuclear power reactor at Windscale suffered an embarrassing accident and was renamed Sellafield to try to reassure the public that under the new name the management would be more careful. However, when the Post Office decided to spend lots of money on a new name for the Royal Mail, arguably one of the longest established, most trusted and even best-loved brands in the UK, they must have lost their marbles in the post. They came up with Consignia, an utterly meaningless name, but fortunately within a short time it had been *consigned* to the history books of case studies.

Top management at Mars wanted to rationalize their brand names throughout the world and lost a lot of fans in the process. In the UK, Opal Fruits was subsumed in Starburst, and Snickers replaced Marathon, despite the fact that Marathon had built up valuable equity as the first sponsor of the London Marathon (I remember the late Chris Brasher, founder of the London Marathon and chairman of Brasher Boot where I was a director, telling me of the wrangling they had had over that decision). There are still consumers in the UK who resent Unilever's decision to standardize its names throughout Europe so that Jif, which resonates with 'in a jiffy', was ousted by Cif, which to British ears sounds like a disease.

Clearly mistakes can be made in trying to spread names across linguistic borders. There are many stories about this, such as calling a car Nova in Spain when *no va* in Spanish means *does not go*.

I have collected my own examples of international Product names that sound unusual to native English speakers and use them in lectures, but this does not mean that any of these are badly chosen for their domestic markets. I have samples of *Pschitt* soft drink from France and *Mucki* milk from Italy. I have *Creap* coffee powder and *Sour Balls* candies from Japan. I actually like the Japanese drink, *Pocari Sweat*, a health drink that replenishes water and electrolytes in the body that are lost through perspiration. Whenever I get to Narita airport after a long overnight flight I get a can from the vending machine and it's the first step in getting back to normal.

Logo

For many People it would seem that the logo is the most important part of brand management. Except in a few cases (which I will consider), for me it is one of the least, but it is a step in the hierarchy of creating an identity. It is difficult to conceive of any logo being of itself inspiring, and many of the press releases that are written about the launch of new logos are nothing but candidates for *Private Eye*'s 'Pseuds Corner'. Logos or symbols have been with us for millennia. Throughout most of human history most People have been largely illiterate so two-dimensional symbols of simple graphical design

FIGURE 5.1 Mercedes and CND logos

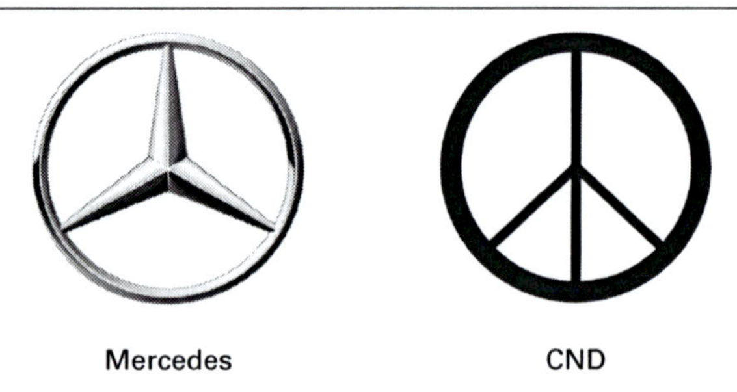

were important rallying posts for humans to flock to. Religious leaders adopted naive but powerful symbols, with the Christian Cross and the Mohammedan Crescent being long-lived examples. Military campaigners had their emblems, which evolved into coats of arms and then national flags. There is archaeological evidence for the swastika in Neolithic times and in the East it was used in the Hindu, Jain and Buddhist traditions. Notoriously it was adopted by the Nazis and is now banned in Germany and is taboo in the rest of the Western world.

All such symbols are simple enough to enable easy recognition but with sufficient distinctiveness that they can be identified separately from their rivals and in the modern context legally protected. Analysis of a range of logos will reveal that many are quite unsophisticated but nevertheless serve their purpose perfectly well. To a car enthusiast, the Mercedes logo is instantly recognizable and brings to mind all the qualities of Mercedes cars: engineering excellence, reliability, efficiency and so on. However, if you add one extra stroke the logo looks remarkably like the universal symbol for the campaign for nuclear disarmament, as shown in Figure 5.1.

Logos are of particular importance in the sportswear market. During the 20th century a number of brands of athletic wear were introduced, which over time were skilfully managed so that the clothing and footwear became used much more widely than in its strict sporting context. However, to legitimize its adoption as a fashion brand there were two universal rules. The brand would attach itself to leading sportsmen and women or to national or club teams. Second, a stylish logo would be an ever-present feature of the design of the apparel. This last was quite a trick because prior to that labels were always worn *inside* the clothing to mark the designer's branding. The owner would know the brand – the admirers would have to guess.

Adolph Dassler was one of the first to follow this strategy. He shortened his own name to coin *adidas*. He then set out to persuade leading athletes to wear his shoes so that ordinary people would want to emulate their heroes. In the 1936 Olympics held in Germany the great Jesse Owen wore adidas spikes while winning four gold medals and soon the German national football team was wearing Dassler's football boots. However, the famous three stripes logo was acquired from a Finnish company, Karhu Sports, in 1949 for (the equivalent of) €1,600 and two bottles of whisky. In the 1980s I visited the headquarters of adidas in the town of Herzogenaurach near Nuremburg, and saw the museum with the long consistent history of building a brand based on close partnership with sports stars and the easy recognition of the three stripes. Adidas has been fastidious in its defence of the logo and has been involved in numerous disputes, some over logos that are clearly different but, it can be argued, are derived from the adidas motif, such as logos with two or four stripes.

Nike was founded in 1964 by Phil Knight with the vision to 'Beat adidas'. It has achieved this aim in terms of annual revenue, as Nike has overtaken adidas as the largest sportswear manufacturer in the world. It has followed a similar strategy, though tracing a slightly different path through the various sports. It first entered athletics as adidas had done – after all, the simple running shoe is the most widely used article of sportswear. But it then famously entered basketball with the sponsorship of the extraordinary Michael Jordan. Jordan was one of those sportsmen who transcend their sport, and the sight of Jordan sinking basket after basket wearing the Nike logo that resembles a stylized tick, or sign of endorsement, embodied its slogan, '*Just Do It*'. The complete Packaging of name, logo (as worn by all conquering sports stars) and slogan is well-exampled by Nike, which has followed up its relationship with Michael Jordan with long-term deals with similarly iconic stars such as golfer Tiger Woods and tennis ace Roger Federer. But we will return to this subject of sponsorship in Chapter 8 (Publicity).

A brand that does not try to achieve the volume position of a Nike or an adidas but is highly successful in its own right is Lacoste. This brand follows a similar model but was founded by the eponymous tennis star of that name. René Lacoste was one of the so-called 'Four Musketeers', French tennis stars who dominated the game in the 1920s and early 1930s. He won seven grand slam singles titles in the French, US and Wimbledon championships without ever making the long voyage to compete in Australia. He was world number one in 1926 and 1927 and was nicknamed 'the Crocodile' by his fans because of his ferocious style of play.

In 1933, Lacoste founded La Société Chemise Lacoste, with André Gillier. The company produced the tennis shirt that Lacoste often wore when he was playing, which had an alligator (generally thought to be a crocodile) embroidered on the chest. The company had many firsts. It was probably the first to introduce coloured tennis shirts and, later, non-wooden tennis racquets. It gradually diversified into golf and sailing but kept careful control of its brand. In 1963 René passed the management of the company to his son Bernard, who did an outstanding job in building both the brand and the volume without sacrificing quality in Product or reputation.

> I had the honour to work closely with Bernard Lacoste when I was responsible for the footwear license granted by Lacoste to Pentland. Bernard taught me many lessons in the strict control that he and his small team exercised from their tiny headquarters in Paris over a global sports brand. Sadly, Bernard died in 2006, but I still have the restaurant guide to Paris that he gave me. He called it *Crocodile Gourmet* and published it on the occasion of the 65th anniversary of the foundation of Chemise Lacoste – in an inevitable green cover with the famous logo.

Livery

Next in the hierarchy of design elements is the livery. In some cases this is a simple colour scheme; in others it has more complex components. Some whole markets have segmented by colour, as in the case of petrol stations: BP (green), Shell (yellow), Esso (red, white and blue), and so on. This is mirrored almost exactly in the supermarkets: Tesco (red, white and blue), Asda (green), Morrisons (yellow). Sainsbury's skews the pitch with orange!

This is all part of the need to Package a total identity and thus facilitate identification. A market where that need might be thought to be paramount is air travel, where most airlines are flying the same aeroplanes along the same routes and so they distinguish themselves through the service proposition, the livery and so on. I recall one of British Airways' more distinguished marketing directors, Liam Strong, explaining to me the trouble they went to in designing and buying the many thousands of items his department was responsible for procuring. These ranged from uniforms to cutlery to toiletries to serviettes and they all followed strict rules of corporate identity. How, then, could his successors have reached the conclusion that the most visible part of the design Package, the tail fin, should be given over to a random selection of international modern art with no cohesive theme at all? Their most keen British competitor, Sir Richard Branson, immediately saw the opportunity and adopted some patriotic design motif on his Virgin Atlantic aircraft. Eventually the BA management saw reason and returned to being a flag carrier, but it is impossible to calculate the damage done to its brand image over this episode.

Packages as business model

A variation on the theme of Packaging is to *Package* all the elements of a series of connected purchases in order to make the purchase a single easy-to-complete contract. A familiar and successful example of this is the 'Package holiday'. Most of us will have bought at some time a Package holiday from a travel agent. We have then travelled abroad, usually by air, been met at the airport, decanted in our hotel, and have all or most of our meals paid for – all via one transaction made back home. For many people unable to speak the local language and afraid to take the risk of buying such travel in individual components this has been a boon and a highly successful piece of marketing. There are hidden benefits too, in that the individual traveller who does buy these components separately may not have adequate cover if any of the providers goes bust before the contract is completed. Usually the Package provider is bonded and, if a company goes down, the bond kicks in and the travellers are shipped home with another carrier.

A further example of the importance of Packaging is the software market, where software programs are bundled up in a computer. Microsoft has established a dominant position in this market – despite a common view that there are better offerings available – largely because of its success in getting acceptance of such Packages by a wide variety of PC manufacturers. We will return to this theme in Chapter 13 (Partnership).

In summary, Packaging is a fundamental plank in the fabric of marketing. It brings together all the design elements that contribute to the identity of the Product. When you see a Rolls-Royce, for example, it is immediately recognizable from the name, from the 'Spirit of ecstasy' mascot, its own three-dimensional logo and from the very design of the vehicle itself.

From time to time in this book I will recommend another business book that has been of particular value to me out of the scores that I have read. In the case of Packaging, however, I would not recommend a book but a museum, the Museum of Brands, Packaging and Advertising in Notting Hill, west London. The museum was founded by Roger Opie who has put together the largest collection of individual examples of Packaging and supporting material to illustrate over 250 years of social and marketing history. I strongly recommend a visit in order to understand some of the above themes in more detail.

That completes Part 1, based on the original four Ps of marketing and with the addition of *Packaging*. In the next section we will address the actions necessary to successfully manage the Ps. The first of these is planning, because as John Lennon sang in 'Beautiful Boy': 'Life is what happens to you when you're busy making other plans.'

Summary

In this chapter we have:

- identified Packaging as the fifth of the core Ps of marketing;
- described the history of Packaging in its functional form;
- looked at the Packaging of identity;
- considered the use of logos and livery in Packaging;
- examined the use of Packaging as a business model.

PART TWO
Actions

Planning

06

If a man does not know what port he is steering for, then no wind is favourable to him. **SENECA**

Everybody has got a plan until they get punched in the mouth. **MIKE TYSON**

In this second section of the book I explore five Ps that all relate to the actions of marketing. This begins with *Planning*, for as Plato said, 'The beginning is the most important part of the work.' I began my career as a fresh-faced law graduate of Oxford University and did the only sensible thing you can do with a law degree, I became a soap salesman. Procter & Gamble is rightly famous for its training and I was first taught the so-called 7 × 6 call, ie the seven steps of the sales call together with the six sales tools. I won't go through all this here except to say that the first step of the call was Planning and preparation. Sometimes these words seem to become conflated but they are quite distinct in meaning. As a Boy Scout I knew the meaning of our motto, *Be Prepared!* When I go for a country walk I Plan the walk by looking at a map or a guide book and selecting a suitable circular route. I then prepare for the walk by collecting my outdoor gear and my rucksack, containing all manner of items that I hardly ever use but might in an emergency. I don't *Plan* on getting lost but *prepare* for that eventuality by taking a map, a compass and my mobile phone. I don't Plan on cutting myself on barbed wire but prepare for that eventuality by taking my first aid kit. You get the picture.

In marketing, Planning is an essential process. To dispense with it is like building a house without a Plan or sailing the ocean without a chart. As the famous Norwegian explorer Roald Amundsen said, 'Adventure is just bad Planning.' If you plan, you do not guarantee success, but if you fail to Plan then effectively you are Planning to fail. I was trained in a company where Planning was an essential part of any process, whether it was engineering or sales. I came to realize that marketing was no different. But I fear I have come across many businesses where such practice is not known. Just as one cannot imagine building a car or any other Product without engineering drawings so we should not be able to imagine taking Products to market without a plan.

A good plan is like a good story: it will have a beginning, a middle and an end. The beginning should state the goals of the Plan. What are we trying to achieve? The middle will state the method in the Plan. How are we going to achieve our goals? And the end will state how we are going to measure that we have achieved our goals. I have read or received a great many business or marketing plans that usually have a beginning and an end, but are very light or even non-existent in the middle – the 'how?'. But for me this is the most important part. I want to know what the business is going to do to achieve its goals. It is easy (though actually harder than it seems) to set goals but the really hard part is execution. What are we going to do? As Alan Kay says: 'The best way to predict the future is to invent it.' And the best way to invent it is to Plan the actions by which it (the prediction) will be achieved.

Managing by objectives

At Procter & Gamble I was taught a more formal method of this process, which we called BOMMB. This was simply a restatement of Peter Drucker's 'management by objectives' (as set out in his 1954 book *The Practice of Management*). First you establish where you are. This is your 'Base'. Then you set the 'Objective'. Then you decide the 'Method' by which you will achieve the objective. Then you work out the 'Measurement' criteria by which you will know that you have achieved your objective. And this will bring you to a new 'Base' where you can start the process again:

Base
Objective
Method
Measurement
Base

In the process of 'managing by objectives' we must concentrate on outputs not inputs. Thus we assess the cleaner's work by observing that the house is clean, not by watching her/him swish the duster and wield the broom. It is the absence of dirt that is our evidence.

New Labour, obsessed with target-setting, failed to understand this, no doubt because the People implementing the changes were not themselves experienced in the process. Thus Sir Christopher Meyer, former ambassador to Washington, writes in his book *Getting Our Way – 500 Years of Adventure and Intrigue: The inside story of British diplomacy* (2009):

> In Washington as ambassador, I had to engage in an annual objectives setting exercise. I was instructed by London to put into my personal objectives a set number of public speeches for the year. There was no interest in their subject or audience. I plucked the number 35 out of the air. Fine, was the response. At the end of the year I duly reported that I had met my quota. Well done, was the response.

At least the objective was measurable.

Setting objectives is easy in the sense that we are talking about the future and so anything is imaginable. But it is difficult in that an objective must follow certain criteria to be of any use. I was first taught the acronym SMAC, which stood for Specific, Measurable, Achievable and Compatible (with other objectives). Later I learnt a more helpful acronym, SMART, and this is what I now recommend. An objective should be Specific, Measurable, Achievable, Relevant and Time-based:

Specific
Measurable
Achievable
Relevant
Time-based

We can combine our two acronyms as follows:

S
BOMMB
A
R
T

If, for example, we are setting an objective in volume sales we might say: *Objective: increase volume sales of widget X*. This would be 'measurable' only after the event. It is not 'specific'. And we can only know if it is 'achievable' by reference to other factors. Is it 'relevant'? Probably, but only after a study of the status of this Product. And is it 'time-based'? Not so far. Then if we say: *Increase volume sales of widget X by 20 per cent over next calendar year*, this is 'specific' (though a specific quantity would be even clearer). It is 'measurable'. It is 'time-based'. The other criteria again can only be answered in context.

I have followed this process at various times in my career and have usually found it rewarding. When it wasn't it was either because I did not follow it closely enough or I forgot to consider the other criterion in Planning, which is to follow your Plan B when Plan A (for whatever reason) does not work.

In 1980 I visited Chile for the first time with a colleague from Mars. I was very impressed with the openness of the economy and after my next visit we made a recommendation to Mars that it should form a marketing company to manage the business on the ground. After a further fact-finding visit I was asked to head up the new company. That had not been my intention in making the recommendation but it fitted in with my personal goals. So in 1981 I became Gerente General of Effem Chile Ltda based in Santiago de Chile, and wrote the business Plan. I still have a copy of the document, which was issued in numbered copies to the owners and senior management of the corporation and to our advisers in Chile. It was described as the Medium Term Plan 1982–85. It was divided in four sections as follows:

1. General Market Analysis of Chile.
2. Development of Effem (Chile) Ltda 1981–85.
3. Marketing Strategy 1982–85.
4. Financial Date 1981–82.

The total Plan was about 60 pages and I wrote all of it myself, though of course with help from colleagues and advisers. Most importantly I worked through all the financial schedules myself and this was in the days before personal computers. I worked through the details of how the company would evolve over the period of the Plan and what our marketing developments would be; the whole Plan rested on a number of assumptions.

In the first year on the basis of the Plan considerable success was achieved. The Plan was exceeded, most of the Planned actions were implemented and overall volumes doubled versus the previous year. However, in the second year Chile went into a catastrophic economic crisis leading to a deep recession that was listed in *The Economist* in an article in 2009 as the seventh deepest depression in modern global history. Our business rested on one key assumption: that the exchange rate that had been fixed at 39 pesos to the US dollar in 1979 would continue. It remained fixed until June 1982 when it was devalued. It was further devalued over the next few months, declining to 90 pesos to the

US dollar – and our importing business was blown away. There were no forward hedging mechanisms, and so by the time we had collected peso debt it was not enough to buy the dollars to pay our dollar debt to our US-based suppliers. I recommended closure and, after a day of negotiation in Brazil with Forrest Mars, one of the owners of the corporation, this was accepted.

In Mike Tyson's words I'd had a Plan but I had then been punched in the mouth. There were many mistakes but the key one was not to Plan for the possible eventuality of a devalued exchange rate. I'm not sure it would have made a lot of difference to the outcome but we might have restricted our exposure. The lesson is that a detailed Plan is required, but so is consideration of the alternative scenarios that might develop and a proper assessment of the risks run by the business. This should focus on the probability of risk and the impact of the event if it happens.

In 1988 I joined the Sony Corporation, initially as Managing Director of Sony Consumer Products Company UK. The company was emerging from the VHS debacle; at its nadir the UK subsidiary for which I now became responsible had lost £30 million in one year. I was now charged with increasing sales from £150 million the previous year to £250 million over three years. In addition I was set objectives in Profitability, market share, brand image and service performance. Again I set out to write the Plan by which these would be achieved. This was detailed for each area of the business and each of the objectives in six-monthly intervals. I then set out to engage my management team in accepting these objectives and agreeing the methods by which they would be achieved. These actions meant that the objectives became firmly embedded in everyone's targets, reviews and appraisals. In the three-year period we achieved £300 million in sales, thus doubling the business, and met all the other targets as well. We continued to work in this way and eventually, when I left to go to Pentland in 1998, the company had grown to £523 million turnover. We never had to face a recession as bad as that I had faced in Chile, but the recession of the early 1990s still bit hard and our markets for consumer durables went into decline. Our sales did not decline, as we invested more in advertising, Promotion and in our distribution – and continued to grow. We had a Plan B.

Features of a good marketing Plan

So what should we look for in a good marketing Plan? A marketing plan is a written document approved by the senior management of a company that summarizes the actions required to achieve one or more marketing objectives. Typically it will cover between one and five years. A traditional process is the development of a five-year Plan of which the first year is the next year's budget. A marketing Plan may be part of an overall business plan for the company or business unit. Well-conceived marketing strategy must be the foundation of a good marketing Plan.

The corporate vision

The most important factor in successful marketing is the 'corporate vision'. While the popular business book *In Search of Excellence*, by Tom Peters and Robert Waterman, has been to some extent discredited because of the subsequent decline and even failure of many of the so-called excellent companies in its pages, its main message was '*Nothing drives progress like the imagination. The idea precedes the deed.*'

If the company in general, and its chief executive in particular, has a strong vision of where the company's future lies, then there is a good chance that it will achieve a Powerful position in its markets (and attain that future). This will be not least because its strategies will be consistent, and will be supported by its staff at all levels.

Jim Collins and Jerry Porras covered this in their highly successful book *Built to Last: Successful habits of visionary companies* (1994). The book outlines the results of a six-year research project into what makes enduring great companies. A primary objective for the authors' research was: 'to identify underlying characteristics that are common to highly visionary companies'. They identified 18 companies that met all their criteria and contrasted them with good companies that fell short of greatness, with the companies all founded before 1950 in order to qualify for the test of lastingness. A common theme in the great companies was that they had adopted a 'Big Hairy Audacious Goal'. For example, Henry Ford's vision for his automobile company was 'To democratize the automobile', in other words make it available to every man, not just the rich. Ford was still following this in the 1980s with cars like the Mondeo in Europe, but perhaps part of their more recent problems comes from the fact that the original vision had been achieved. Once that is the case a new vision is required.

Strategic management

The discipline of strategic management began in the United States in the 1950s and 1960s. In 1957, Philip Selznick introduced the idea of matching the organization's internal factors with external environmental circumstances.

This core idea was developed by the Harvard Business School General Management Group into what we now call SWOT analysis. Strengths and weaknesses of the firm are assessed in light of the opportunities and threats from the business environment. A PEST analysis is often used within a strategic SWOT analysis. It is a business measurement tool, looking at factors external to the organization. PEST is an acronym for Political, Economic, Social and Technological factors, which are used to assess the market for a business or organizational unit. The PEST analysis headings are a framework for reviewing a situation, and can also be used to review a strategy or position, direction of a company, a marketing proposition, or idea. There are many variants on this model, including PESTLE analysis, which adds Legal and Environmental factors; STEEPLE analysis, which adds Education; and even STEEPLED, which adds Demographic.

Alfred Chandler recognized the importance of coordinating the various aspects of management under one all-encompassing strategy. Chandler also stressed the importance of taking a long-term perspective when looking to the future. In his 1962 groundbreaking work *Strategy and Structure,* Chandler showed that a long-term coordinated strategy was necessary to give a company structure, direction and focus. In Igor Ansoff's 1965 classic *Corporate Strategy* he developed the gap analysis still used today, in which we must understand the gap between where we are currently and where we would like to be, then develop what he called 'gap reducing actions'.

In the 1970s much of strategic management dealt with size, growth and portfolio theory. The PIMS Study was a study over nearly 20 years, started in the 1960s, that attempted to understand the Profit Impact of Marketing Strategies (PIMS), particularly the effect of market share. Started at General Electric, moved to Harvard in the early 1970s, and then to the Strategic Planning Institute in the late 1970s, it contains decades of information on the relationship between Profitability and strategy. Its initial conclusion was unambiguous: *The greater a company's market share, the greater will be its rate of Profit.* The high market share provides volume and economies of scale. It also provides experience and learning curve advantages. The combined effect is increased Profits.

Portfolio management

Out of the financial industry came the idea of portfolio management, which was developed into a business theory. Harry Markowitz and others had concluded that a broad portfolio of financial assets could reduce specific

FIGURE 6.1 Boston Consulting Group matrix

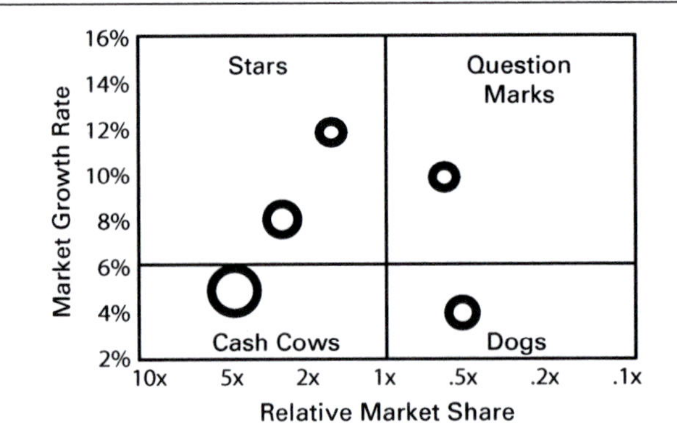

risk. In the 1970s marketers extended the theory to product portfolio decisions, and managerial strategists extended it to operating division portfolios. The Boston Consulting Group (BCG) took this further and in 1970 produced the famous BCG matrix to help corporations allocate resources, as shown in Figure 6.1.

To use the chart, analysts plot a scatter graph to rank the business units (or products) on the basis of their relative market shares and growth rates:

- *Cash Cows* are units with high market share in a slow-growing industry. These units typically generate cash in excess of the amount of cash needed to maintain the business. They are regarded as staid and boring in a 'mature' market, and yet every corporation would be delighted to own as many as possible. They are to be 'milked' continuously with minimum investment, since such investment would be wasted in an industry with low growth.
- *Dogs* are units with low market share in a mature, slow-growing industry. These units typically 'break even', generating barely enough cash to maintain the business's market share. Though owning a break-even unit provides the social benefit of providing jobs and possible synergies that assist other business units, from an accounting point of view such a unit is worthless, not generating cash for the company. They depress a Profitable company's return on assets ratio, used by many investors to judge how well a company is being managed. *Dogs*, it is thought, should be sold off or closed.
- *Question marks* (also known as problem children) are growing rapidly and thus consume large amounts of cash, but because they have low market shares they do not generate much cash. The result is

a large net cash consumption. A *question mark* has the potential to gain market share and become a *star*, and eventually a *cash cow* when the market growth slows. If the *question mark* does not succeed in becoming the market leader, then after perhaps years of cash consumption it will degenerate into a *dog* when the market growth declines. *Question marks* must be analysed carefully in order to determine whether they are worth the investment required to grow market share.

- *Stars* are units with a high market share in a fast-growing industry. The hope is that *stars* become *cash cows* over time. Sustaining the business unit's market leadership may require extra cash, but this is worthwhile if that's what it takes for the unit to remain a leader. When growth slows, *stars* become *cash cows* if they have been able to maintain their category leadership, or they move from brief *stardom* to *dogdom*.

As a particular industry matures and its growth slows, all business units become either *cash cows* or *dogs*. The natural cycle for most business units is that they start as *question marks*, and then turn into *stars*. Eventually the market stops growing, thus the business unit becomes a *cash cow*. At the end of the cycle the *cash cow* turns into a *dog*. As the BCG stated in 1970:

> Only a diversified company with a balanced portfolio can use its strengths to truly capitalise on its growth opportunities. The balanced portfolio has:
>
> - stars whose high share and high growth assure the future;
> - cash cows that supply funds for that future growth; and
> - question marks to be converted into stars with the added funds.

The General Electric (GE) Business Screen was originally developed to help marketing managers overcome the problems that are commonly associated with the BCG matrix, such as the lack of credible business information, the fact that BCG deals primarily with commodities not brands or Strategic Business Units (SBUs), and that cash flow is often a more reliable indicator of position as opposed to market growth and share.

The GE Business Screen introduces a 3 × 3 matrix, which includes a medium category. It utilizes industry attractiveness as a more inclusive measure than BCG's market growth and substitutes competitive position for the original's market share.

A large corporation may have many Strategic Business Units (SBUs), which essentially operate under the same strategic umbrella, but are distinctive and individual. The point is that successful SBUs will do well in attractive markets because they add value that customers will pay for. Weak companies do badly for the opposite reasons. To help break down decision making further, you then consider a number of sub-criteria:

For market attractiveness:

- size of market;
- market rate of growth;
- the nature of competition and its diversity;
- Profit margin;
- impact of technology;
- environmental impact.

For competitive position:

- market share;
- management profile;
- research and development;
- quality of Products and services;
- branding and Promotions success;
- Place (or distribution);
- efficiency;
- cost reduction.

You then adapt the list above to the needs of your strategy. The GE matrix has five steps:

1. Identify your Products, brands, experiences, solutions, or SBUs.
2. Answer the question: what makes this market so attractive?
3. Decide on the factors that Position the business on the GE matrix.
4. Determine the best ways to measure attractiveness and business Position.
5. Finally, rank each SBU as either low, medium or high for business strength; and low, medium or high in relation to market attractiveness.

Now follow the usual words of caution that go with all boxes, models and matrices. Yes, the GE matrix is superior to the Boston matrix since it uses several dimensions, as opposed to BCG's two. However, problems or limitations include:

- There is no research to prove that there is a relationship between market attractiveness and business Position.
- The interrelationships between SBUs, Products, brands, experiences or solutions are not taken into account.
- This approach requires extensive data-gathering.
- Scoring is personal and subjective.
- There is no hard and fast rule on how to weight elements.
- The GE matrix offers a broad strategy and does not indicate how best to implement it.

Michael Porter made significant contributions to the canon. Porter was originally an engineer, then an economist before he specialized in strategy. He described a category scheme consisting of three general types of strategies that are commonly used by businesses to achieve and maintain competitive advantage. These three generic strategies are defined along two dimensions: strategic scope and strategic strength. *Strategic scope* is a demand-side dimension and looks at the size and composition of the market you intend to target. *Strategic strength* is a supply-side dimension and looks at the strength or core competency of the firm. In particular he identified two competencies that he felt were most important: Product differentiation and Product cost (efficiency).

He originally ranked each of the three dimensions (level of differentiation, relative Product cost, and scope of target market) as either low, medium or high, and juxtaposed them in a three-dimensional matrix. That is, the category scheme was displayed as a 3 × 3 × 3 cube. But most of the 27 combinations were not viable (see Figure 6.2).

FIGURE 6.2 Porter's generic strategies

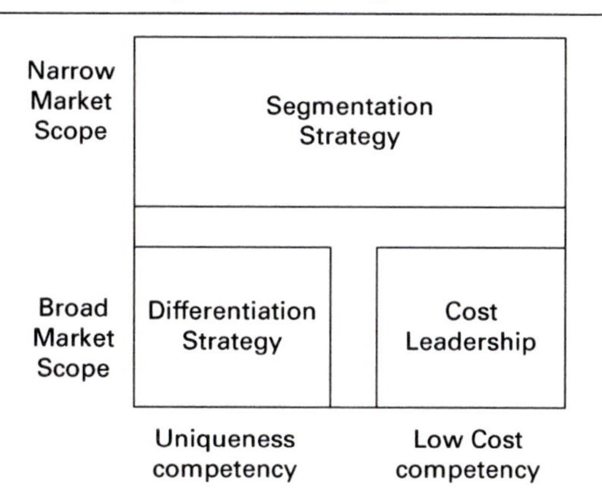

In Porter's 1980 classic *Competitive Strategy: Techniques for analyzing industries and competitors*, he simplified the scheme by reducing it down to the three best strategies. They are cost leadership, differentiation, and market segmentation (or focus). Market segmentation is narrow in scope while both cost leadership and differentiation are relatively broad in market scope.

This process while popular can tend to narrow around the norm. Others have taken a view that success is better found in niche strategies or – as in a more recent book by W. Chan Kim and Renée Mauborgne *Blue Ocean Strategy* (2005) – the challenge is to create uncontested market space and make the competition irrelevant.

I joined NXT as CEO in 2000 at the height of the technology boom. The company's share price had been fuelled by great excitement and a business that was loss-making, and turning over a few million was valued at £1.6 billion. However, the company lacked focus as it was chasing every possible lead for its ground-breaking flat loudspeaker technology. With the support of the senior management team and the help of a few MBA students from London Business School I put together a business Plan focusing on seven key sectors. Over the next few years products were launched by major original equipment manufacturers (OEMs) in each of these sectors. Sales never reached the heights that had been hoped for but this focus on a few key sectors gave the company much needed direction.

Once we have agreed our strategic objectives we can turn this into detailed Planning. Here we will want to consider the 'how', the specific methods by which the objectives will be achieved. We will consider many of the Ps that are described in this book and develop our thinking as to what actions to take in each area to achieve the agreed objectives. Here, timing is of the essence. Getting your timing right in business is as important as it is in sport.

Project management

To help this process there have been several techniques developed, again largely by US-based organizations. The critical path analysis is a mathematically-based algorithm for scheduling a set of project activities. It is an important tool for effective project management. It was developed in the 1950s by the DuPont Corporation at about the same time that General Dynamics and the US Navy were developing the Program Evaluation and Review Technique (PERT). Today, it is commonly used with all forms of projects, including construction, software development, research projects, Product development, engineering, and plant maintenance, among others. Any project with interdependent activities can apply this method of scheduling. There is no reason that these excellent techniques developed primarily with engineering projects in mind cannot be applied to marketing programmes. Indeed, good marketers will always use one or other of these techniques.

The essential technique for using the Critical Path Method (CPM) is to construct a model of the project that includes the following:

1 a list of all activities required to complete the project;
2 the time (duration) that each activity will take to completion;
3 the dependencies between the activities.

Using these values, CPM calculates the longest path of planned activities to the end of the project, and the earliest and latest that each activity can start and finish without making the project longer. This process determines which activities are 'critical' (ie on the longest path) and which have 'total float' (ie can be delayed without making the project longer.) These results allow managers to prioritize activities for the effective management of project completion, and to shorten the Planned critical path of a project by pruning critical path activities, by 'fast tracking' (ie performing more activities in parallel), and/or by 'crashing the critical path' (ie shortening the durations of critical path activities by adding resources).

A Gantt chart is a type of bar chart that illustrates a project schedule. Gantt charts illustrate the start and finish dates of the terminal and summary elements of a project. These elements comprise the work breakdown structure of the project. Some Gantt charts also show the dependency relationships between activities. Although now regarded as a common charting technique, Gantt charts were considered revolutionary when they were introduced. The first known Gantt chart was developed in 1896 by Karol Adamiecki, who called it a *harmonogram*. Adamiecki did not publish his chart until 1931, however, and then only in Polish. The chart is commonly known after Henry Gantt, who designed his chart around the years 1910–15. Although a Gantt chart is useful and valuable for small projects that fit on a single sheet or screen, they can become quite unwieldy for projects with more than about 30 activities.

Forecasts

An inevitable feature of any Plan is that it will contain a forecast. Another feature is that it is almost inevitable that this forecast will be wrong. None of us can tell the future with any accuracy. As Winston Churchill said: 'I always avoid prophesying beforehand, because it is much better policy to prophesy after the event has already taken place.' The great baseball player, Yogi Berra, put it even more succinctly when he said: 'It's tough to make predictions, especially about the future.'

Here are a few examples of mankind's ability to tell the future, particularly as it relates to innovation:

> '*Everything that can be invented has been invented*' (Charles Duell, an official at the US patent office, 1899).
>
> '*The telephone has too many shortcomings to be seriously considered as a means of communication*' (a memo at Western Union, 1878).
>
> '*The cinema is little more than a fad. It's just canned drama*' (Charlie Chaplin, actor, producer, director and co-founder United Artists, 1916).
>
> '*Flight by machines heavier than air is unpractical and insignificant, if not utterly impossible*' (Simon Newcomb, mathematician,1902).
>
> '*The horse is here to stay, but the automobile is only a novelty, a fad*' (the president of the Michigan Savings Bank advising Henry Ford's lawyer not to invest in the Ford Motor Company, 1903).
>
> '*Television won't last*' (Mary Somerville, pioneer of radio, 1948).
>
> '*Nuclear powered vacuum cleaners will probably be a reality in 10 years*' (Alex Lewt, president of vacuum cleaner firm Lewt Corporation, in the *New York Times*, 1955).

We can develop statistical models that can improve our rate of accuracy but it is important to start off with the knowledge that we will be wrong – and then we can Plan to manage that process. Having said that, I do believe that greater accuracy in forecasting is a source of competitive advantage. At Sony we had a very talented market research manager who used all available commercial sources and then added his own interpretation to put together a remarkably accurate set of forecasts about the market development. We then used these as the basis of our Plans, which we shared with our major customers. We invited them to give us their forward orders based on these Plans. However, their orders would of course be very inaccurate. It was one thing to forecast the size of the market; it was quite another to forecast how many of a particular model would sell. Competitors might put more of their resources behind a particular model or indeed simply drop the price in order to make one of our lines uncompetitive.

Contingency Plans

Here again is the importance of Plan B. We need a contingency Plan, a fund to bring into Play when one of our products is in trouble. Retailers work on much shorter Planning horizons.

> Mark Souhami, former deputy chairman of Dixons Store Group, the largest retailer in the UK of consumer electronics, once told me that the strategic Planning horizon of a retailer was about 10 minutes. Our factories liked to operate on long-range plans with long lead times. Our customers wanted to react to the weekend's sales figures. John Clare, the then chief executive of Dixons, had the sales figures for the week sent to his home on a Saturday night (I know because I've been a guest at a dinner party in his home on a Saturday evening when he would excuse himself for a while and go and study the figures). On Monday mornings he would review these with his buying and marketing teams and calls would go out to suppliers for help with slow-selling lines. I imagine all this process, short term as it was then, will have speeded up with faster computers and better electronic communications.

In a fast-changing environment with little certainty about the future the best approach is to constantly review your objectives and progress towards them. If the vision is clear there may be many ways to get there. A sports coach sets a game Plan but will not stick rigidly to it if his or her side goes behind. When I joined Pillsbury UK in 1984 to run its Green's of Brighton division as General Manager, the Pillsbury Corporation was then quoted on Wall Street and had delivered 13 consecutive years of quarterly growth in earnings per share. It was financially driven with strong controls and demands made on its business units. Green's was regarded as a cash cow and I was tasked with delivering a specific contribution figure. These targets were set by US management and the UK managers' job was to achieve them.

Green's factory was in a mining town in South Yorkshire. We were the second largest employer after the National Coal Board, whose employees went on a national strike that year. Those terrible industrial relations spilled over into our factory. Our budget was carefully calculated and allowed no room in negotiation with the trade union over the annual pay rise. My boss, the UK managing director and I delivered that message to the shop stewards who promptly recommended strike action to the workforce. They returned after nine days of negotiation, which obviously cost more than some concession in the original round. Thus the inflexibility imposed on us by US management, which we in turn attempted to impose on our workforce, led to a worse result. (I'm glad to say that before I left the company four years later relations had improved significantly.) In business I advocate rolling Plans and forecasts updated for every major change in outlook. This has to be carefully managed and may impact on the kind of remuneration scheme that an organization adopts. But just as it is better to evaluate historic performance on a moving annual total (MAT) basis to appreciate trends, so it is preferable to roll forward the forecast by updating it with every piece of major news. It is also better to Plan for a range of scenarios. Three obvious positions might be:

- Target: the position the company is aiming for.
- Budget: the position the management is committing to.
- Fallback: the minimum position to be achieved before cuts in cost and/or investment will have to be made.

Summary

Planning is an essential part of the marketing mix. But the Planning needs to be of a practical nature concentrating on setting SMART objectives with detailed Planning and good contingency Planning to back it up in the event of serious deviation from the original Plan. In the next chapter we will look at the importance of Persuasion in the marketing mix.

Further reading

As well as the books referenced in the text I recommend *Marketing Plans: How to prepare them: how to use them* by Professor Malcolm McDonald. I had the great pleasure to work with Malcolm when I was at Pentland. I had been asked by the CEO to introduce Professionalism into the marketing across the company. I introduced Malcolm and his colleagues at Cranfield University to help me with this and we started by introducing a proper Planning process into each business unit.

Persuasion

07

Would you Persuade, speak of interest, not of reason.

BENJAMIN FRANKLIN (1706–90), AMERICAN STATESMAN, SCIENTIST AND PHILOSOPHER

In this chapter I intend to show the importance of *Persuasion* in the world of marketing. In my view marketing should take the lead because it represents the market in the decision-making process. To do this it needs to champion its cause. It will be an advocate for the brand, Persuading colleagues in other functions to follow that lead and ultimately Persuading customers and end users to buy the company's Products and services. To do this it will need the skills of Presentation and in most cases of public speaking.

In the previous chapter I recalled learning the 7 × 6 sales call in the Procter & Gamble business school of sales training. One of the most important steps of the call, and the one that most People think of as salesmanship, was the Presentation. It was in the Presentation that one used the six sales tools. However, I think what was taught was basic in outline. It would serve, and it did serve, but it was not particularly Persuasive. It lacked structure other than in use of the sales tools and, of course, the step that is actually the most important, 'the close'.

After a little time with the company I was identified as someone who might progress and so attended a head office course in sales skills. There was a very senior and experienced US sales manager there. He was frankly horrified with the lack of sales skills that this group of would-be stars demonstrated and, soon after, perhaps as a result of that experience, everyone in the sales force went through a course of training in a more advanced type of salesmanship. We were taught a new five-step Presentation, *Persuasive selling*. We were given an aide memoire with the steps enumerated in a little plastic wallet to carry around with us, so that we would never forget them. I still carry mine around today some 40 years later. They are as follows.

Persuasive selling steps:

- Summarize the situation:
  - conditions;
  - buyer's needs;

  - limitations;
  - opportunities for benefit.
- State the idea:
  - simple, clear, concise;
  - meet buyer's needs;
  - suggest action.
- Explain how it works:
  - what... when... where;
  - how is it practical?
  - anticipate questions and objections;
  - ensure understanding.
- Describe and reinforce key benefits:
  - how does the buyer benefit?
  - are the benefits related to the situation?
  - are the benefits specific?
- Make the next step easy – ask a closing question:
  - direct;
  - alternative;
  - minor point;
  - easy to do now.

This has served me well throughout the past 40 years and, as far as I know, has never been surpassed. There are always developments in thinking about salesmanship but the key elements are summarized in those five steps of Persuasive selling. For many People, Presentations are limited to internal meetings, but the rules are similar. You might not think of colleagues as buyers but you are trying to get them to buy your idea. They are unlikely to do that if they cannot see the benefits to them, either personally, through their department or for the good of the company as they perceive it. So the skills of Persuading a colleague or group of colleagues are no different from the skills of Persuading a customer. It is necessary to establish a mutuality of interest.

Mutuality of interest

I learnt many of my skills at Procter & Gamble but I learnt much of my philosophy at Mars. Forrest Mars Sr developed tremendously powerful ideas about business, which have pervaded many other companies as Mars has exported its talent around the world. One of the most important he called 'mutuality of interest'. He believed that by establishing mutuality of interest between his company and its suppliers, its customers and its employees, superior performance would be achieved. As his family-owned business is now one of the very largest privately held businesses in the world we can presume he was right. I will explore this further in Chapter 13 (Partnership).

Abraham Lincoln, former president of the United States said: 'If you wish to win a man over to your ideas, first make him your friend.' This is a further development of the concept of mutuality of interest. It establishes the idea that we are more likely to buy from People we like. This leads sales personnel to try very hard to get to be friendly with the customers – and it can lead buyers to put up lots of barriers to this. Some companies might try to abuse the position of trust that should exist between seller and buyer, and I have certainly heard of stories where the practice of entertaining or giving gifts to customers went too far. Many companies now exert strong controls over the situation, and rightly so, even if only to protect the buyer from accusations of being influenced in his decisions by the generous hospitality of the supplier.

But surely friendship is not based on such things. Friendship comes from mutual respect, liking and a common interest. Friendship in business is perfectly possible without the potentially corrupting influence of hospitality or gifts. However, I have made numerous friends in business where hospitality was involved – but was not directly because of that hospitality.

Perhaps more important than friendship is trust. As a trainee manager at Procter & Gamble I worked with all the sales representatives in a certain region of the country. I was supposed to observe their performance and offer constructive assessment, perhaps recommending a new skill or approach where appropriate. One of the more experienced sales People I worked with, Derek, had been covering the same patch for many years. Everyone knew him and he knew everyone. He tended to skip out of that part of the call I have been talking about, the *Presentation* and the *close*. He would walk into the store, wave at the manager, carry out his stock check, calculate the order requirement, and say to the manager on the way out, 'I've taken care of you. I'll see you in two weeks' time.' And then he posted off the order. The store managers all trusted him that when he said he'd taken care of them, he would not abuse their trust. We used to classify our calls as A, B or C. In A calls we had control. In B calls there was a dialogue. And in C calls we had no control and just collected an order. An ongoing objective might be to increase the level of control from C to B, or from B to A. All of Derek's calls were A. There was nothing I could teach him.

But the best sales representatives are the ones who listen the most. As Dean Rusk, former US Secretary of State under President John F. Kennedy, said 'One of the best ways to Persuade others is with your ears – by listening to them.' You should use your ears in ratio to your mouth, ie two to one.

I am not a religious person but I believe that the central message of Christianity and indeed of other major religions is a good one. 'Do unto others as you would have them do unto you.' Or, as it has come down in the vernacular, 'do as you would be done by': the golden rule. If everyone followed it the world would be a better place. Selling is no different. It is not about getting one over the other person. At Procter & Gamble we did not believe that selling ice to the Eskimos was clever, because there would be no repeat purchase.

Persuasion of colleagues

Persuasion of colleagues is an important task for any marketer. Too much of this is attempted via one-way PowerPoint Presentations. PowerPoint is one of those technical improvements that has made life worse because it is so easy to use and so pervasive. It becomes a crutch for People who lack the skills of Persuasion. Before PowerPoint and its ilk we used to produce acetate charts that were magnified by overhead projectors onto a blank screen. Older readers will remember this. Younger ones will wonder in what museum they can find such objects. Perhaps the same one that has slide rules, and fax and telex machines etc, all of which I also used to use. When I worked in marketing for Pedigree Petfoods I was assigned to what was referred to as 'non-canned Products' to distinguish them from canned. Our canned pet food business was immensely successful with brand leaders such as Pedigree Chum for dogs and Whiskas for cats each returning in excess of 30 per cent return on total assets. Overall, our canned business returned 27 per cent. But when the oil crisis hit in 1974 there was a knock-on effect for many other commodities, including tin plate. As mentioned earlier, the management decided that they needed to offset the risk of rocketing tin-can cost by investing in other non-canned technology, ie dry and semi-moist products in which other competitors such as Quaker Oats and Carnation had carved out a lead. A new factory was built at Peterborough. By 1978 when I joined the marketing team there, despite a lot of effort the non-canned business was very far from successful. It was unProfitable and although a number of new Products had been launched none of these had made much of an impact. The man in charge of marketing, Chris Bradshaw, was often called into the weekly board meeting to review performance and discuss strategy. The three of us who supported him in marketing were frequently required to produce charts to back up his arguments. A significant part of our time went into this endeavour and we came to see ourselves as the chart factory. We researched our ideas, checked our facts, wrote out the chart in longhand, got it typed up, then turned it into an acetate chart on a special machine and handed it to Chris for his Monday morning appointment with the board. It was a requirement that all of these charts should show the source of any fact quoted. This was often research purchased from Nielsen, AGB or our own in-house agency, Mars Group Services (MGS). However, on one occasion I developed my own forecast for which I had no source. I wrote at the bottom of the chart F.I.T.A., which might seem like another agency or trade association but in fact stood for 'finger in the air'.

In Sony the sales companies met formally with the *Jigyobu* or Business Group twice a year in Tokyo. These meetings were very intense all-day affairs customarily followed by dinners with senior management. As the man in charge of consumer Products I would go to all of these meetings over a two-week timetable. Persuasion was the order of the day. We were very well prepared with a good understanding of our markets but often found the product planners and engineers on the other side difficult to convince. After all, they had these meetings with all the sales companies over several weeks and needed to maintain a coherent Plan for the whole world.

On one occasion we were Presented with a new CD player. This was intended to replace a phenomenally successful player that had five-star reviews in all the hi-fi press and was permanently on back order. We asked what was new about the new Product. We were told it was better. But in what way was it better? Well, the Planner explained, it had a better chip. But in what way? This went on for some time and we were quite unable to elicit any more information. I then asked if we could continue with the existing machine as it was so successful. No, that was quite impossible, we were told. They were already committed to the new machine. When the new machine arrived on the market it turned out to be a dog. It was badly reviewed. We had to sell off the stock at a huge loss.

Overall our hi-fi business was very successful. It had been built up by Steve Dowdle who was later to succeed me as UK Managing Director. He had come from a retail background and understood what the buyers wanted in their ranges. He Persuaded the factory to set up a line of rack systems. These became known as midi systems based on the width of a turntable. They were one- or two-piece systems with a combination of components: turntable, CD player, cassette mechanism, amplifier, tuner and matching loudspeakers. They were Priced competitively at all the magic Price points from £199 to £599. This strategy worked well for several years but gradually we lost share to Aiwa who were selling a similar range based on Sony technology at lower Prices. What made this particularly galling was that Sony owned 50 per cent of Aiwa. It seemed to us that we were giving our technology to a sister company who then undercut us in the market and stole market share. We complained about this for years and got nowhere. Then after a major reorganization that set up a powerful business group in Tokyo – combining all the consumer AV Product groups in one – two of the top management of the new group, Mr Tamiya and Mr Nakamura, came to visit us. I knew them both well. Tamiya-san was one of the corporation's top salespeople. He had spent many years in the United States building up the company. He had hosted visits that I had made to Tokyo with Dixons' senior management after Dixons had bought Silo in the United States and so tried to position themselves as a global retailer. Suehiro Nakamura, known to us as Tiger, had been a spectacularly successful manager of the Bridgend TV factory in Wales and a fellow director of Sony UK. I presented our overall business to them. Most of it was going well but there was the continued decline in hi-fi. I explained the story as we saw it and the fact that we had been making this complaint for a long time. Tamiya-san looked at me and said, 'Maybe you lack convincing Power!' It was a tough lesson in the importance of Persuasion.

I had more success with a different Mr Nakamura. Hideo Nakamura had been one of the engineers who developed the compact disc format. As a reward for this contribution he was given the opportunity to build a new business in in-car entertainment, which he called mobile electronics (ME). My predecessor as managing director of Sony Consumer Products UK had not seen much of an opportunity here and had assigned a salesperson to the product group who was aggressive but lacked sophistication. Our strategy seemed no better than to follow all the other Japanese brands, Pioneer, Kenwood, Panasonic etc, who were already established in the in-car aftermarket. I used to go and see Mr Nakamura and tell him how well we were doing in the UK in every other Product group. He would get angry and say he didn't care. 'Why were we doing so badly in ME?', he wanted to know. Finally, I Persuaded him to send one of his best engineers, Joe Usui, to head marketing in the UK. Joe's English was a little weak so we assigned to him a British marketing manager, John Anderson, (later to take charge of all audio marketing in Europe), and the two of them developed a new strategy: to supply Sony in-car Products to car dealers as an option upgrade. This was extremely successful and sales grew fast. Mr Nakamura came to visit us. We took him to Aston Martin to see the cars made with Sony Products fitted as standard. Our annual mobile electronics sales went from £1 million to £53 million and we became the leading market for Sony ME outside Japan.

Public speaking

I stated earlier that public speaking is a key skill in Persuasion. The great Roman orator Marcus Tullius Cicero (106–43 BC) said: 'He who wants to Persuade should put his trust not in the right argument, but in the right word. The Power of sound has always been greater than the power of sense.'

One of my favourite examples of this was not even a speech but a signal – and the right word was found by accident. The Treaty of Amiens in 1802 ended the Revolutionary War during which Admiral Horatio Nelson had distinguished himself at the Battles of Cape St Vincent, the Nile and Copenhagen but it was an uneasy peace and it was known that Napoleon Bonaparte was preparing for renewal of war. Immediately before the resumption of war in May 1803 Nelson had been appointed Commander-in-Chief in the Mediterranean and hoisted his flag on HMS *Victory*. Then followed a persistent blockade of Toulon with the object of preventing a union between the French fleet in Brest and, after Spain declared war on Britain, the Spanish ships at Cartagena and Cadiz.

In early 1805, as a part of a grand design, Napoleon ordered the combined fleets to rendezvous in the West Indies and then to sail to take command of the English Channel so as to permit an invasion. Nelson chased the fleet to the West Indies but missed them and returned to Gibraltar, where he made dispositions for the blockade of Cadiz by Admiral Collingwood and proceeded home.

On receipt of confirmation that the combined fleets had fallen back on Cadiz, Nelson sailed on 18 September 1805 in HMS *Victory* to join the blockading fleets. On 20 October the French Commander, Admiral Villeneuve, sailed out of Cadiz. At dawn the next day, the Franco-Spanish fleet was silhouetted against the sunrise off Cape Trafalgar and Nelson formed the two divisions in which they were to fight, one to be led by Nelson and the other by Collingwood. As the opposing fleets closed, Nelson sought to inspire the fleet with a signal. Admiral Nelson summoned the *Victory*'s signals officer, John Pasco, and said to him: 'Mr Pasco. I wish to say to the fleet "*England confides that every man will do his duty.*"' Pasco, noting that the word '*confides*' was not in the signal book, suggested the word '*expects*' instead. Nelson agreed, adding 'You must be quick, for I have one more signal to make which is for close action.' The message '*England expects that every man will do his duty*' was greeted with three cheers in every ship. Nelson died in the ensuing battle but it was an overwhelming victory for the British fleet and indeed it was not to lose another battle at sea for more than a century. Nelson's famous message became a familiar and well-used patriotic exhortation. Even the abbreviated form, '*England expects!*' came to have resonance.

As a young salesman at Procter & Gamble I used to look forward to sales conferences sometimes called to announce the launch of an exciting new Product. The brand managers would make their case with great skill and humour and I always came away properly motivated to do my best in selling the new Product target. When I became a brand manager myself I set out to emulate the performance of these other managers and would try to make it both motivational and entertaining. We used to hire an actor to polish our performances. He had been one of the early stars on *Doctor Who* and gave several great tips in public speaking. Later at Sony I was surprised with the relatively poor performance of the public speakers. Embarrassingly at one sales conference the event went on so long – partly due to the fact that none of the speakers had bothered to rehearse – that the senior Japanese delegation present had to leave early to catch their plane. The exit of four very senior Japanese from the front row did not contribute to the desired effect on morale. After that, I made it a rule that we would always rehearse and put on as slick a show as we could. Rehearsals often took place at weekends but everyone came to understand the importance of them. After that our sales conferences were of a high standard, both for internal meetings with our sales force and for big production numbers with the dealers.

At Sony one of our biggest events was (and still is) the annual Sony Radio Awards. Those in the industry used to say they were the Oscars of the radio industry. As UK Managing Director I introduced them on a number of occasions. One year Chris Evans was moved to say on his radio show the following day:

> And the guy from Sony got up at the beginning and he gave this speech and he was very good, this guy. He looked like Bill Gates, didn't he? He was very good, a very assured speaker in front of 1,200 People. I really admire People who can do that. I can talk on the radio when no one can see me, and on the TV when no one's really there but to get up in front of that many People… I have a problem and I said to John, 'he was very good, this guy wasn't he? He was a good speaker', and John said… 'Well, Sony do have good speakers!'

Persuasion of end users

Persuasion is, of course, a key requirement in our relationship with the consumer or end user. At Sony we put a great deal of effort into training the staff of the dealers who sold our products. Our Products were technically advanced and often required demonstration and explanation. This needed to be of a high quality if the customer was to be Persuaded to buy. The brand name and the advertising counted for a lot but still the end user might need a lot of convincing. Ticket Prices were high and the risk of getting the purchase wrong considerable. All of this contrasts with other, usually cheaper Products, such as a new soft drink, for example. I don't think I can remember anyone personally Persuading me to buy a new type of cola or lemonade. But when a consumer buys a new television it is on average seven years since he or she was last in the market and so there is likely to have been substantial developments in technology in that time. This makes the consumer uncertain and keen for reassurance.

The best example of this I came across was the strategy that Sir James Dyson adopted to establish his famous bag-less vacuum cleaner in the UK. I met Sir James at the opening of a huge new-format Curry's store near Spaghetti Junction in the Midlands. He explained that he had given a sample cleaner to each of the sales representatives in Curry's. They had taken it home and seen for themselves its effectiveness in cleaning while not requiring replacement bags, which invariably ran out just when you needed them. Thus the sales People at Curry's had great confidence in Persuading their customers to buy this new type of cleaner. It sounds an expensive strategy but it was probably a relatively small cost compared with other more remote forms of Promotion. As a piece of Persuasion it was highly effective. As Blaise Pascal, the 17th-century French scientist and religious philosopher said, 'People are usually more convinced by reasons they discovered themselves than by those found out by others.'

Psychology in marketing

Persuasion is a central aspect to advertising, which we partially covered in Chapter 4 (Promotion). The subject of psychology in marketing has long been studied with a view to enhancing understanding of consumer motivation and how to influence it. Ernest Dichter was a US-based psychologist and marketing expert who is considered to be the '*father of motivational research*'. He received his doctorate from the University of Vienna in 1934 and emigrated to the United States in 1937. In 1946 he founded the Institute for Motivational Research in New York State and later founded similar institutes in Switzerland and Germany. Dichter pioneered the application of Freudian psychoanalytic concepts and techniques to business – in particular to the study of consumer behaviour in the marketplace. This was a significant influence on the practices of the advertising industry. According to a *New York Times* article in 1998, Dichter 'was the first to coin the term *focus group* and to stress the importance of image and Persuasion in advertising'.

Credited with originating the Esso slogan, 'Put a tiger in your tank', in collaboration with a Chicago advertising copywriter, Dichter's work and that of others in the same field came to the attention of a much wider audience when Vance Packard, a US magazine writer, published his seminal work, *The Hidden Persuaders* in 1957. Packard explored the use of consumer motivational research and other psychological techniques, including depth psychology and subliminal tactics, by advertisers to manipulate expectations and induce desire for products, particularly in the United States post-war era. He also explored the manipulative techniques of Promoting politicians to the electorate. The book questioned the morality of using these techniques. However, subsequent research has demonstrated that techniques like the use of subliminal messaging are unlikely to change long-term behaviour and may even be counterproductive.

It is said that the brain is the last frontier of human science and our understanding is growing. We may one day discover a way to influence others by directing energy to the brain in a certain way. If we are successful in such research it seems to me that the human race is doomed, as politicians and others will not be able to resist the abuse of such technology, just as the inventor of the machine gun believed his invention would stop war as no one would be able to countenance the use of such a horrible weapon.

In the meantime, more modest research into more gentle Persuasion has been quite rewarding. In 2008 Richard H. Thaler and Cass R. Sunstein of the University of Chicago published a book called *Nudge: Improving decisions about health, wealth and happiness*. Their approach to what they call 'choice architecture' is to help People make better decisions on topics ranging from personal investments, to schools for our children, to the meals we eat. Thus, a food supervisor in a school system was able to consider how supermarkets lay out their Products and then apply it to the way different food choices were offered to children – and then get them to eat more healthy alternatives. Another example is the British system of writing on the roadway 'look left' or 'look right' in order for pedestrians to make the safe choice. Politicians of all parties are looking at Thaler and Sunstein's work to see if the lessons can be applied to behaviour on a grand scale.

My own experience tells me that Persuasion is not a complicated science. Rather it is a simple understanding of People's motivation, whether as consumers or otherwise. You should talk in simple terms. David Ogilvy, as one of the foremost experts in 20th-century advertising, when asked what the rules of grammar in advertising are, said: 'I don't know the rules of grammar. If you're trying to Persuade People to do something, or buy something, it seems to me you should use their language.'

In the next chapter we will consider Publicity and, in particular, Public Relations (known universally as PR). This branch of marketing is quite separate from advertising and Promotion, because while they are usually unidirectional proactive activities PR has an inevitable passive form, as when it is necessary to respond to a public reaction to an action, whether Positive or negative.

Summary

In this chapter we have:

- considered the importance of Persuasion in the marketing mix;
- described the steps of Persuasive selling;
- looked at Persuasion in the context of mutuality of interest;
- discussed the problems of using Presentation aids in attempts to Persuade;
- referred to the development of understanding the psychological processes of Persuasion.

Further reading

As well as the books referred to earlier I recommend *The Will To Win*, by Nick Heptonstall. Nick promoted me to be his District Field Assistant when he was a District Manager at Procter & Gamble and, later, when he set up his own strategic sales consultancy, I retained him and his colleagues to help me improve the sales performance of the Sony UK sales force. The book is a handbook on unlocking one's potential and improving one's personal dynamism; it contains useful chapters on Persuasion and related skills.

Publicity (public relations)

08

Some are born great, some achieve greatness and some hire public relations officers.

PROFESSOR DANIEL J BOORSTIN, US SOCIAL HISTORIAN AND EDUCATOR

Publicity is not the same as advertising. The management of public relations (PR) is both an active and a passive function. An enterprise will set out a proactive strategy to develop its PR but will need the capacity to respond to events, both negative and Positive. At its most skilled PR can turn an event that might have generated negative Publicity into one that has a Positive impact on the reputation of the enterprise.

Definition of Public relations

Public relations (PR) is the practice of managing the communication between an organization and its various publics. PR gains an organization or individual exposure to their audiences using topics of public interest and news items that do not direct payment. Common activities include speaking at conferences, working with the press, and employee communication. It is something that is not tangible and this is what sets it apart from advertising.

PR can be used to build rapport with employees, customers, investors, neighbouring communities, or the general public. Almost any organization that has a stake in how it is portrayed in the public arena employs some level of PR. There are a number of related disciplines all falling under the banner of corporate communications, such as media relations, investor relations and internal communications, including employee relations. Corporate communications may and usually will report separately in the organization from other marketing functions but that makes it no less a part of marketing, as it clearly covers the reputation of the company and its brands. Indeed one of the most important aspects of PR is that of Product PR, which deals with gaining Publicity for a particular Product or service through PR tactics rather than using advertising.

In Chapter 4 (Promotion) we quoted Ralph Waldo Emerson who is reputed to have said, 'Build a better mousetrap and the world will beat a path to your door.' The original quote from Emerson, writing in his journal in 1855, was: 'I trust a good deal to common fame, as we all must. If a man has good corn, or wood, or boards, or pigs to sell, or can make better chairs or knives, crucibles or church organs than anybody else, you will find a broad hard-beaten road to his house, though it be in the woods.'

The popular version was born when in 1889 Sarah SB Yule and Mary S Keene, preparing a lecture, tried to recall Emerson's exact words. They could not. But they came close, deciding that he had said: 'If a man can write a better book, preach a better sermon, or make a better mousetrap than his neighbor, though he builds his house in the woods the world will make a beaten path to his door.'

As I said before this is not true. We need to Promote our better mousetrap in order to make the world aware of it and give reasons why it is better. But we also need a PR campaign to help the world understand why it is better. In fact many companies will not have the funds to advertise their new Product but will be able to mount a cost-effective Publicity campaign.

At Mars we used a different name for PR, that of 'external relations', or ER. In this respect we were defining it as any aspect of the company's external relations with all of its publics. That was 35 years ago and the idea is now common, although the name PR has survived. Practitioners are likely to use the plural 'publics' as much as the singular 'public'.

The press release

The most common tool in the PR tool box is the press release. This document is issued to the press to announce something that the organization wishes to Publicize and to be put into the public domain. It is not a trivial task to produce such a document and the skill of writing one is well worth developing. It needs to cover all the important information but be written in such a way that the reader, usually harassed and likely to cut corners, will be attracted to the story by its headline and its opening words and will get to the end wanting to know more. It is customarily signed off by a senior officer of the company and its facts must be very carefully checked because once released there is very little chance of correcting what is now out of the bottle.

It may not be quite fair but I have the suspicion that journalistic standards today are not what they were in previous generations. In times past, journalists were trained on actual stories written for local newspapers before being Promoted to the national press. They were taught to check their sources and that meant always getting corroboration for every fact or assertion they wanted to print. The film *All the President's Men* (1976) describes one of the greatest press scoops in history, the discovery of a conspiracy to cover up the fact that a break-in at the Democratic Party Headquarters in the Watergate Hotel during the 1972 US presidential election had been financed directly by the committee to re-elect the sitting Republican president, Richard M. Nixon. During the film, based on a best-selling book by the reporters involved, Bob Woodward and Carl Bernstein, the efforts of the investigators to get confirmation of every allegation before printing it is an eloquent testimony to the quality of the journalism involved.

Today I am not so sure. I suspect that much of what passes for news in the newspapers is in fact not much more than gossip interlaced with direct quotes from press releases.

It is an unedifying exercise to read a newspaper, even one of the so-called broadsheets (even though few of them are broad-sheeted any more), and ask what the derivation of a story might be. A surprising number of them are likely to have originated on a PR executive's desk.

I have conducted this exercise myself in a class taught at the University of Bedfordshire where I used to be a governor. I helped a class of undergraduate marketing students to interpret an edition of *The Times* and it was extraordinary how with some analysis one might assume that the majority of stories were in some way probably influenced by external agency.

This has led to the rise of the spin doctor, someone who is so practised in the art of PR to be able to spin the story and turn it from black to white. The spin doctor is seen as a political creature and this effect is best observed in politics. For example, New Labour developed the trick of announcing government investments as new when they had previously been announced. However, such skills were frequently learned on the battlefields of marketing and need not have such pejorative connotations.

The father of PR is undoubtedly Edward L Bernays (a nephew of Sigmund Freud, the father of psychoanalysis), who became styled as publicist number one. In his seminal book *Public Relations* (1945) he makes clear that PR is not Publicity, press agentry, Promotion, advertising, or a bag of tricks, but a continuing process of social integration. It is the field of adjusting private and public interest. This book is important because it tells us how to adjust ourselves to our publics by presenting a thorough analysis of PR, its origin and development, its aims and responsibilities, and fixes its place in the modern world.

The Companies Act 2006

I believe this was ahead of its time because the modern attitude to business has changed. For example, in the UK company law was for a long time enacted under the principle that a director's primary duty was to the shareholders of the company, in other words its owners. Then the Companies Act 2006 was passed. It has the distinction of being the longest in British parliamentary history, with 1,300 sections and covering nearly 700 pages, and containing no fewer than 15 schedules (the list of contents alone is 59 pages long.) The act was brought into force in stages, with the final provision being commenced on 1 October 2009. It superseded the Companies Act 1985 and placed a new emphasis on corporate social responsibility. The codified duties are as follows:

1. S171 *to act within their powers* – to abide by the terms of the company's memorandum and articles of association and decisions made by the shareholders.
2. S172 *to promote the success of the company* – directors must continue to act in a way that benefits the shareholders as a whole, but there is now an additional list of non-exhaustive factors to which the directors must have regard. This was one of the most controversial aspects of the new legislation at the drafting stage. These factors are:
   - the long-term consequences of decisions;
   - the interests of employees;
   - the need to foster the company's business relationships with suppliers, customers and others;
   - the impact on the community and the environment;

- the desire to maintain a reputation for high standards of business conduct;
- the need to act fairly as between members.

This fundamental shift in a director's responsibilities may have major implications as the courts interpret the statute and the case law develops. Boards would be best advised to seek to manage the relationships that they have with all these stakeholder groups and thus the importance of PR will be extensively enhanced.

Bad Publicity

It is often said that there is no such thing as bad Publicity but this is palpably untrue. Publicists such as Max Clifford earn a great deal of their fees from prominent celebrities anxious to keep the wrong kind of stories out of the press. In the recent past Tiger Woods, arguably the world most famous sporting celebrity, has been hounded out of the golf circuit for a period after lurid tales of his private life became public. Several of his major sponsors were forced to drop him as spokesperson for their brands.

Products that have suffered badly from adverse Publicity have included Perrier, whose reputation for purity suffered a blow in 1990 when a North Carolina lab found benzene in several bottles. Perrier shifted from explanation to explanation on the issue, finally stating that it was an isolated incident of a worker having made a mistake in the filtering procedure and that the spring itself was unpolluted. The incident ultimately led to the recall of 160 million bottles of Perrier and arguably it has never fully recovered its exclusive cachet since. By contrast, the recall of a drug called Tylenol was much better handled. Tylenol is a North American brand of drugs for relieving pain, reducing fever and relieving the symptoms of allergies, cold, cough and flu. On 29 September 1982 a Tylenol scare began when the first of seven individuals died in Chicago after taking Extra Strength Tylenol that had been deliberately contaminated with cyanide. The crime was never solved and Tylenol sales temporarily collapsed, but the brand was rebuilt and recovered in a few years. The brand was rescued with the invention of the first inherently tamper-proof capsule, recapturing 92 per cent of capsule segment sales lost after the cyanide incident. The scare led to the introduction of tamper-evident Packaging across the over-the-counter drug industry.

> I was involved in a major Product recall at Sony. Soon after I joined the company I became aware of a fault in a German-sourced switch used in some of our TVs. On occasion this switch would ignite and could cause a domestic fire. Obviously the company took this very seriously but had only instituted what it called a 'soft recall', ie as each incident was reported a service engineer would visit the home and talk with the owner and arrange for a replacement set. If the Product was returned for any other service then the part would be replaced. I insisted on a full Public recall with national press advertisements listing the set numbers of the affected models. This was well supported by the trade, who got behind the recall and swapped over the part on all the sets for which they had full records. In this way we were able to limit the sets at risk by a substantial margin. The reaction to the recall was entirely Positive as the public said that was what they expected a company like Sony to do. Arguably the reputation of the brand was enhanced by this experience.

Bad Publicity about Products does not always stem from problems in quality or criminal tampering. Sometimes it can come from the adverse reaction of the public to the make-up of the Product. In the mid-1980s there was a great deal of negative Publicity about the use of E numbers in food Products, particularly those eaten by children. Some ingredients such as flavouring or colourings were associated with bad reactions by some children. Even bad behaviour was attributed to the presence of E numbers such as tartrazine, a synthetic yellow food colouring. This was ironic to us food manufacturers – I was then working for Pillsbury and was responsible for its Green's of Brighton cake mix business – as E numbers were a classification of food additives that were allowed in food preparation by the European Community because they were adjudged to be safe. Some E numbers were allocated to natural ingredients and others to vitamins, eg vitamin C (E300) or lycopene (E160d), the colour in tomatoes. To have a diet without any components that have an E number is basically impossible. A food manufacturer was obliged to list all the ingredients in its Product in order of the presence by weight. The manufacturer could choose between using an E number and using the full technical term. This became a difficult choice as the technical term might be an impenetrable chemical expression while all E numbers were associated by the public with bad and artificial things. Some manufacturers resorted to making claims that their Products were 'Free of E numbers' but this referred mainly to the lack of additives, not to the absence of components with an E number.

> At Pillsbury we tried to reduce the number of E numbers but some of these were fundamental to the safety or acceptance of the Product. All the PR we tried had very little effect on public opinion. I went on television and gave a robust defence of the practice of using E numbers but it had little effect. As today, with misunderstandings of scientific advances such as genetically modified foods, the public's lack of scientific know-how caused long-term damage to the industry. The customer is always right.

On this occasion the government at the European level had tried to help the public make better informed choices, but the practice had been misunderstood. On other occasions governments seek to interfere with established business practice. In the late 1970s the then Labour government sought to introduce some particularly ill-conceived piece of legislation that would have had the effect of putting up manufacturers' costs without any obvious benefit to the public. I was assigned to a working party to represent Mars's interests in the UK. After a full review of the issue, all of us agreed that this was a piece of legislation that would have no positive outcome. One very senior marketer from the confectionery side of the business, Paul Curtis, joked in exasperation, 'Well, can we at least get a change of government?' A few months later the Callaghan government fell and the legislation never hit the books.

Sponsorship

The use of sponsorship is a form of PR. Sponsorship consists of giving financial support to an event, a celebrity, an activity or a charity in return for naming rights and other privileges. Some sponsorships are very well established while others come and go with a great deal of frequency. They range in scale from the butcher who might sponsor a fast bowler with a free steak for every wicket he takes, to the enormous sums committed to sponsorship of world events that attract global audiences such as the Olympic Games.

I first encountered sports sponsorship at Pentland where I had global responsibility for brands such as Speedo, ellesse and Berghaus. We also had the footwear licence for Lacoste, which ran a full programme of sponsorship in its favoured sports of tennis and golf. Speedo was a brand built on performance in the Olympic pool, and at the Atlanta Olympic Games of 1996 swimmers wearing Speedo costumes had won over 70 per cent of the medals available. Ellesse had been built on its sponsored links too. It was first a ski brand developing the first jet pant and then the quilted jacket. In the 1970s it sponsored the Valanga Azzurra, the Italian national ski team, and so marked a milestone as it became one of the most successful and visible ski brands of the 1970s and 1980s. At one point in the 1980s it was the official supplier to 10 national ski teams (West Germany, Italy, Switzerland, Canada, the USSR, Belgium, Luxembourg, the Netherlands, Norway and Bulgaria). In 1975 it decided to move into tennis in order to make its business all year round, and in 1980 it signed sponsorship agreements with Chris Evert and Guillermo Vilas. In 1983 it signed the 15-year-old Boris Becker and at the beginning of the 1980s six of the world's top 10 ranked women players were under contract to ellesse, including British stars Jo Durie and Virginia Wade. This policy of sponsoring top stars in skiing and tennis was continued throughout the 1980s and 1990s and even extended into other sports too. The 1982 World Cup-winning Italian nation soccer team had a contract with ellesse to wear its casual clothing off the pitch; and in the United States it sponsored the famous New York Cosmos and a number of New York and Boston marathon winners.

In sportswear, sponsorship is a critical part of most manufacturers' strategies. Nike and adidas have been playing the game this way for many years. However, the costs have become extraordinary. Only the biggest brands can really justify these sums and agents have become extremely skilled at negotiating contracts that heavily favour the sponsored star or team. Some of the contracts I saw on some of the weaker brands were not sustainable. One leading football club, now in the Premiership, was sponsored to wear a particular brand of shirt and effectively all of the Profit generated through that sponsorship flowed to the club.

Much of the sponsorship I observe seems little more than indulgence of the company chairman's whim. However, at Sony I had very happy experiences of sponsorship as an effective way of generating Publicity in relevant markets and keeping the brand in the Public eye.

The Radio Awards have been sponsored by Sony in the UK since 1983. Working closely with representatives of the radio industry, Sony sponsors awards for excellence made to programme makers and artists. These awards are presented at a well-attended dinner in the spring every year and are then widely reported in both press and, of course, on radio stations particularly by the winners! It is an especially happy association for Sony as it is a major manufacturer of the equipment used by broadcasters to record and then broadcast their programmes and is also a major manufacturer of the radio receivers on which the public receive the programmes. Radio in the UK is a very healthy industry because of the unique mix of publicly financed and commercially financed broadcasters. Sony has established a unique relationship with the industry as a whole.

In 1991 the Rugby World Cup was held in the British Isles for the first time. Various sponsorship opportunities were presented to Sony, including the opportunity to be one of eight named sponsors of the competition itself. However, what I felt was of much more interest was the opportunity to be the unique sponsor of the broadcast rights, which had been won by the independent commercial channel ITV. Broadcast sponsorship was still in its infancy. In the previous year one of the power companies had been the broadcast sponsor of the football World Cup. But key matches in that competition were shown on both BBC and ITV and usually when the public have that choice they favour BBC for both traditional reasons and to avoid the advertising. This time ITV had exclusive rights. I decided to only sponsor the broadcasting and leave the event sponsorship to others. I believed that far more people would watch the matches on television than in the stadia and I did not like the idea of sharing sponsorship with seven other parties. So it proved. The majority of people thought that Sony had actually been the event sponsor, giving rise to allegations by the official event sponsors that Sony had ambushed the competition. But that was false. We had chosen legitimately from the choices put to us by the agency representing the World Cup organizers and the host broadcaster.

With the help of our advertising agency, Bartle Bogle Hegarty, we introduced a brand new concept. Before each advertising break we introduced a message from Sony and asked a trivia-type question about rugby. We then gave the answer at the end of the break. Thus we encouraged viewers to stay with the break and be exposed to all the other messages – and we offered a bit of fun in the process. It was a highly successful innovation that was much imitated afterwards. We of course linked our Promotional campaigns to the event and used it to drive awareness of our Products as we built up to the crucial Christmas peak season. It is a truism of sponsorship that for every £1 you spend on the event itself you must spend another £1 (or five!) on making the sponsorship work. We launched our new TV campaign during the Rugby World Cup Final on 3 November that year. The following week the editor of *ERT*, the leading electricals trade paper, wrote in his editorial:

On the ball

In recent weeks, UK TV audiences of over 14 million have been glued to their sets watching the Rugby World Cup.

Most of those viewers will have been left with the impression that Sony was largely responsible for the entertainment the match provided.

Now Sony was not the only sponsor of the Cup series. But how many in the audience can remember the names of the other sponsors?

By clear use of first and last shots in each commercial break, Sony made sure its brand dominated match coverage.

Sony made inspired use of the opportunity it bought with its several-million-pounds-worth of sponsorship and airtime, by intelligent use of its resources.

Other advertisers take note – you can get a lot of impact out of your spend by dint of creative thinking. And all of us, manufacturer and dealer alike, can benefit.

My only disappointment? England lost the final to Australia 12–6.

Corporate social responsibility

In the past few years a new concept has developed that is closely linked to PR, that of corporate social responsibility (CSR). There is no single definition of this but a serviceable definition might be that CSR is about how companies manage the business processes to produce an overall Positive impact on society. The reason why PR is closely linked to this is that companies that make massive contributions to the overall benefit of society will have achieved nothing for their own reputation if this is not recognized and appreciated by society at large. A truly altruistic firm might not worry about this. It is enough to have done the good deed. However, any board of directors that is accountable to shareholders and has the legal responsibilities I outlined earlier would be foolhardy if it did not make an effort to see its contribution acknowledged. As John D Rockefeller said: 'Next to doing the right thing, the most important thing is to let people know you are doing the right thing.'

Companies need to consider two aspects of their operations: 1) the quality of their management – both in terms of People and processes; 2) the nature and quality of their impact on society in various areas.

Outside stakeholders are taking an increasing interest in the activity of the company. Most look to what the company has actually done, good or bad, in terms of its Products and services, in terms of its impact on the environment and on local communities, or in how it treats and develops its workforce. Out of the various stakeholders, it is financial analysts who are predominantly focused on the quality of management – as well as on past financial performance – as an indicator of likely future performance.

The World Business Council for Sustainable Development, in its publication *Making Good Business Sense*, by Lord Holme and Richard Watts, uses the following definition:

> Corporate Social Responsibility is the continuing commitment by business to behave ethically and contribute to economic development while improving the quality of life of the workforce and their families as well as of the local community and society at large.

Traditionally in the United States, CSR has been defined much more in terms of a philanthropic model. Companies make Profits, unhindered except by fulfilling their duty to pay taxes. Then they donate a certain share of the Profits to charitable causes. It is seen as tainting the act for the company to receive any benefit from the giving.

The European model is much more focused on operating the core business in a socially responsible way, complemented by investment in communities for solid business case reasons. I believe this model is more sustainable because: 1) social responsibility becomes an integral part of the wealth creation process – which if managed properly should enhance the competitiveness of business and maximize the value of wealth creation to society; 2) when times get hard, there is the incentive to practise CSR more and better – if it is a philanthropic exercise that is peripheral to the main business, it will always be the first thing to go when push comes to shove.

Charity

Charitable giving is a complex question for any company that has more than one shareholder. If you own and run your own business then subject to tax law you can do what you want with the Profits. But as soon as you sell some of your shares to another person then you need to agree with that person through a board meeting what is your policy on charitable donations. It is possible to take a very strict view that a Public company should not give anything to charity. It is owned by the shareholders and any Profits belong to them. They can make charitable donations out of their dividends. However, in modern society this is probably not an acceptable view to the majority. It is therefore important to have a policy on charitable donations and to follow it.

At Sony UK we had a policy that worked very well. As a famous company with a brand that in some ways was much bigger than the business, we received countless requests for charity. Our first rule was to delegate the management of this to a committee chaired by a senior manager with representatives from different parts of the company. Accordingly, no director sought to influence the giving with their own views or those of their spouse; equally, directors were protected from the moral pressure that can come to someone in their position. The charity committee was then allocated an annual budget out of earned Profits. Our second rule was to give priority to three groups of charity:

1. The first were those members of society who could not fully enjoy our products because of their own disability or disadvantage, eg a blind person cannot fully enjoy a Sony TV.
2. The second were those local communities in which we worked.
3. The third were charities that were important to our workforce, eg if someone lost a loved one to cancer then there might be a request to support a particular cancer charity.

We also used our Products as gifts where possible, rather than giving cash.

New media

New forms of media are changing the practice of PR as much as any aspect of marketing. In the past, PR departments measured the effectiveness of their campaigns by the number of column inches they achieved in the press. A slightly more sophisticated model, the one we used at Mars, was to deduct the negative column inches from the number of Positive column inches in order to achieve an overall score.

What matters now is to know what is being said about your company and its Products in the blogosphere. You have to be able to track attitudes as expressed through social media such as Facebook. As the public learns that not only can it have an opinion on anything and everything but it can also express it to the world, you have to know which of these are influential and what the general view of the tweeting classes is. You ignore this at your peril.

Reputation management

Another recent trend is the development of the concept of 'reputation management'. For me, those who espouse this are barking up the wrong tree. You own your brand and so can manage it in all its forms. You do not own your reputation; that is the outcome of all the things you do, and so is not directly managed. Rather it is the result.

But reputation is directly linked to PR. Public relations have become 'mission critical' to success. An organization needs the most talented, well-rounded practitioners, experienced in the 'art and science' of PR, to lead it to higher standards of communications and better, more mutually beneficial relationships with key stakeholders.

The world has become increasingly complex for decision makers. This complexity is growing at a disturbing rate because of a number of issues, including:

- the sheer speed of communication on a global scale;
- the enormous increase in channels of communication, especially digital;
- shifting patterns of influence, and the rise of citizen reporting and blogging;
- the elevated expectations of all stakeholders, and the rise of consumer Power;
- new and rapidly changing communities of interest, enabled by digital technologies and a new sense of emPowerment;
- increased regulation and the consequent communications requirements;
- the aggressive pursuit of information by journalists, and the 'tabloidization' of business reporting;
- declining levels of trust.

Good relationships are the engines of success in today's world. These relationships can only be built and maintained through superior communications as well as excellence in performance. The problem is... that which represents superior communications today will be different tomorrow.

Summary

In this chapter we have:

- established the importance of Publicity or PR in the marketing mix;
- looked at examples of dealing with negative Publicity;
- described the role of sponsorship;
- discussed corporate social responsibility;
- considered attitudes to charity;
- referred to the impact of new media;
- questioned the concept of reputation management.

Push-Pull

09

Pull the string, and it will follow wherever you wish. Push it, and it will go nowhere at all.

DWIGHT D EISENHOWER, 34TH PRESIDENT OF THE UNITED STATES

Marketing theory distinguishes between two main kinds of promotional strategy – *Push* and *Pull*. The practice of Push versus Pull derived from supply chain management, or logistics. With a Push-based supply chain, Products are Pushed through the channel, from the Production side up to the retailer. The manufacturer sets Production at a level in accord with historical ordering patterns from retailers. It takes longer for a Push-based supply chain to respond to changes in demand, which can result in overstocking or bottlenecks and delays, unacceptable service levels and Product obsolescence.

In a Pull-based supply chain, procurement, Production and distribution are demand-driven so that they are coordinated with actual customer orders, rather than forecast demand. A supply chain is almost always a combination of both Push and Pull, where the interface between the Push-based stages and the Pull-based stages is known as the Push-Pull boundary. An example of this would be Dell's build-to-order supply chain. Inventory levels of individual components are determined by forecasting general demand, but final assembly is in response to a specific customer request. The Push-Pull boundary would then be at the beginning of the assembly line. Dell's response to the difficulty of managing the Push-Pull dilemma is unusual in the world of technology, which has a particular problem with this aspect of marketing.

A technology Push is mainly driven by internal R&D activities while market Pull is driven by the external market forces. A Push-Pull system in business describes the movement of a Product or information between two subjects. On markets the consumers usually 'Pull' the goods or information they demand for their needs, while the offerers or suppliers 'Push' them towards the consumers. In logistics or supply chains the stages are operating normally both in Push and Pull manner.

You might think that in my early experiences at Procter & Gamble we would have evolved largely Pull strategies based on generating demand for our Products. You would be wrong. We also relied heavily on a Push strategy with enormous emphasis on sales force pressure on the retail trade to stock up in high numbers and Push the Products through. We used to talk about stock-room pressure, ie selling in so much stock that the store manager would be more likely to build extra displays of our Products. We learnt how to sell against what we called the Business Cover Plan, a simple mathematical technique of persuading retailers to stock additional quantities against the possibility of extra demand or a failure to supply, or any other reason we could think of.

Today's retailers are much more sophisticated and have gained control of their ordering process. They are very concerned about 'stock-outs' and are likely to penalize suppliers who fail to complete orders, but they hold the supplier responsible to maintain adequate inventories from which they can call off their requirements at short notice. Over the intervening 40 years or so there has been a massive move in Power down the supply chain and, in the process, a massive destocking of Britain's retailers, with consequent benefits to their balance sheets. They are among the best in the world at running this aspect of their operations and a large retailer such as Tesco may only hold four days' inventory in its total system at any one time. This has even raised eyebrows in Whitehall as the government has learnt that inventories of vital Products are very low – if there is disruption to supply through bad weather or industrial action, or any other external force, supplies can quickly fall to a critically low level.

Shelf life

In food companies, and others with a perishable Product, there is the additional factor of shelf life to consider. I first encountered this when I went to South America to set up Mars's business in Chile. I had only previously been responsible for Petfoods that were in cans with almost infinite shelf life, or dry or semi-moist Products that lasted for a long time. Chocolate, however, has a very short life and must be stocked inside quite tight temperature boundaries. If it melts it is, of course, unsaleable. Thus the Push strategies were really not appropriate. We did not benefit from selling in excessive stock but worked hard to maintain good balances. Later I worked at Pillsbury where our shelf life was typically about nine months. Most of our Products contained flour, which loses its quality over time. If we included a raising agent this would also lose potency. This restricted the stock we would manufacture and seek to sell and so again this circumstance directed us much more to a Pull strategy. Retailers also insisted on a proportion of shelf life being left before they would accept the Product. This might be, say, two-thirds of life and so a Product that claimed a shelf life of nine months had to at least retain six months on shipment.

Shelf life does not only relate to food Products. Yesterday's newspaper has little or no value, although when I lived in Santiago de Chile, keen for news from home I often paid a premium for British newspapers even several days old. On one occasion I bought a copy of *The Times* from a kiosk in the city centre. The crossword had been completed by someone else and it was all too apparent that there was some black-market recycling going on.

Indeed shelf life does not only relate to physical Products. A hotel cannot sell last night's empty bed. An aircraft costs the airline more or less the same to fly empty or full. A theatre wants to put up a 'house full' sign every night. At NXT, where we operated a licensing model and held no physical inventory, nevertheless our inventions were patented and so we were still subject to the shelf life of the patents, which would expire 20 years after grant. As already mentioned, some businesses have become much more sophisticated as to how they manage demand through manipulating their Pricing. As I explained in Chapter 2, for example, the cut-Price airlines will vary Pricing right up to the last minute through complex algorithms.

Service businesses also have an inventory that cannot be sold after time elapses. A consulting business aims to sell a certain proportion of its billable hours. Anything unsold short of this target cannot be sold at a later date. So billable time is simply another form of perishable goods and must be managed along strict lines of Push-Pull marketing. A telephone company has made its investment in fixed-line capacity. In this sense the inventory is fixed. After that it will do everything it can cost-effectively do to maximize usage because this will impact Profitability. The late Stafford Taylor, when he was in charge of BT's consumer business, told me that he had a strategy of 'one more minute'. At that time the average usage by British consumers of their landline telephone was just eight minutes per day. If BT could increase that by 'one more minute' it would deliver an additional £500 million annually to the bottom line. Thus he invested significantly in well-loved advertising campaigns featuring popular actors such as Maureen Lipman and Bob Hoskins who advocated 'It's good to talk'.

Fashion is also a form of perishability. At Pentland where we managed a range of sportswear brands we knew that our styles were likely to go out of fashion each season and so had to manage our procurement with great care. Even publishing is subject to such rules. *Private Eye* magazine in its literary review section likes to taunt celebrity authors whose works were much hyped and are now being sold off at very low Prices or, in the terminology of publishers, 'remaindered'. *Private Eye* calls this feature '*remainders of the day*'.

There is also a fashion element to consumer electronics and at Sony, contrary to the image you might have of the company, I found myself more often in a Push situation rather than a Pull. Undoubtedly Sony had an excellent brand image and sought to create consumer demand for our Products but realistically we could never advertise all the Products we sold. Every year I launched about 250 new Products in the Sony range and very few of our Products stayed in the catalogue for more than four years, the majority being discontinued and replaced after two years; in some categories the rate of new Product introduction was much faster than this. In my time the camcorder market was still new and the rate of Product introductions very fast. New models were introduced every six months or so. This was compounded by the problem of television standards. Colour television was first introduced in North America in the 1950s and standards set by the National Television System Committee (NTSC). This system was used in not only North America but also Japan and some other Asian countries. In Europe, however, a different system was developed. Europeans could see problems with the NTSC system, which some wags designated 'Never Twice the Same Colour'. PAL was developed by Telefunken in Germany. The format was first unveiled in 1963, with the first broadcasts beginning in the United Kingdom in 1964 and Germany in 1967.

Camcorders have to play back in the format on the consumer's television and so Products were first released in the NTSC markets of Japan and North America and then, if successful, launched in PAL format six months later in Europe. Thus we were always a generation behind. The markets knew what improvements were coming and so tended to hold back their orders if particularly significant improvements in size, or resolution, or magnification or battery life were expected. The inertia this threw into the market was very difficult to counteract and our customers tended to get clogged up with several generations of Products. Dixons Stores Group, not only our largest overall customer, but also a retailer with a strong photographic tradition, could not afford to miss out on the latest models but as a consequence might have as many as eight or nine generations of old Products layered in their warehouses like geological seams.

Far worse problems had been encountered by my predecessors in Sony who had to deal with the difficulties created by the video format war, between the Betamax format developed by Sony and the VHS format favoured by JVC and others. Much has been written about this elsewhere, not all of it accurate, but for the purposes of this chapter the point is that Sony was following too much of a Push strategy. The manufacturing company responsible for video Production in Japan considered the Product sold when it was shipped, when in reality the inventory was piling up around the world in the sales companies. Sony UK alone lost around £30 million one year on discounts and write-offs. The process of forecasting and ordering was known by the Japanese word *seihan*, which covers the whole logistics process. After the Betamax debacle, strong controls were introduced and I'm glad to say that such disasters were avoided in my time with the company. I would personally chair a monthly *seihan* meeting to review and monitor, and indeed modify, the forecasting and ordering being placed on the factories. However, we never succeeded in re-engineering the total business process in order to get into a situation where we made what we sold rather than selling what we made. In durable Products such as consumer electronics few companies will destroy the inventory rather than limit supply, but perhaps that is what they should do to maintain Pricing levels and healthy demand. To take an example, following the credit crunch in 2008–09 sales of champagne slumped. In France the producers destroyed some of their excess inventory rather than see Prices fall but in the UK, which is one of the largest markets in the world for champagne, retailers who held excess stocks simply discounted them with the inevitable consequences to Producers' carefully nurtured brand images.

We used to say that nothing sells like a back-order. In other words, creating some kind of shortage often led to even greater demand as the psychology of the market shifted. A few companies make this a business practice. Some of the more prestigious car marques limit Production and generate a waiting list – and then their cars' owners find that far from losing value the minute they drive the vehicle off the forecourt, a prestigious vehicle of this kind will actually gain a premium.

Product life cycle

The key to managing the Push-Pull of marketing is to understand the rhythm of marketing – and the key to this is to understand the Product life cycle.

To say that a Product has a life cycle is to assert four things:

- that Products have a limited life;
- Product sales pass through distinct stages, each posing different challenges and opportunities to the marketer;
- profits rise and fall at different stages of the Product life cycle;
- Products require different marketing, financial, manufacturing and procurement strategies in each stage of the life cycle.

The different stages in a Product life cycle are shown in Table 9.1.

This is a useful model but there are severe limitations on its application. First and foremost and right at the heart of marketing it is vital to define the Product correctly. Thus this cycle may be true of individual models and even of technologies but it is unlikely to be true of whole categories. For example, the television has been with us as a mass consumer Product since the 1950s but has gone through several technology cycles and, within that, manufacturers have managed countless model changes.

Sony made a huge proportion of its Profits out of Trinitron technology in the colour television (CTV) market. Trinitron was introduced in 1968 as a significant improvement over RCA's shadow-mask technology used by most other manufacturers. Sony gradually built a leading position in the market. Each year it would introduce new models with numerous enhancements over several decades. Thus the Product life cycle was a useful model in managing those changes. However, it was less useful in managing technology change as it did not really fall within the normal Planning cycle as a way of predicting when cathode ray tube (CRT) technology, of which both shadow mask and Trinitron were subsets, would be replaced by plasma or liquid crystal display (LCD) technology. It was clear that as the demand for larger television screens grew over time CRT technology would not be appropriate as the sets would become too large for most people's living rooms. This is because the tube would need to be longer and so the depth of the set would increase to unacceptable levels. The demand for a flat screen technology, which would be less obtrusive and allow a greater screen size, had been there for a long time but it took the industry time to develop technologies that gave sufficient picture quality and were capable of achieving Price competitiveness. Sony was tempted to hang on to its Trinitron technology with which it continued to enjoy market leadership, when it would have been wiser to more aggressively replace that with LCD and possibly plasma technology. Finally it lost competitiveness in the race to develop these new technologies and in order to retain a significant market share in the overall CTV market was forced into a joint venture with Samsung, the Korean giant, to source its LCD Products. Such a strategy would have been unthinkable just a few years before.

TABLE 9.1 Stages of a product life cycle

Stage	Characteristics
1. Market introduction stage	1. costs are high 2. slow sales volumes to start 3. little or no competition – competitive manufacturers watch for acceptance/segment growth losses 4. demand has to be created 5. customers have to be prompted to try the Product 6. makes little or no Profit at this stage
2. Growth stage	1. costs reduced due to economies of scale 2. sales volume increases significantly 3. Profitability begins to rise 4. public awareness increases 5. competition begins to increase with new players in establishing market 6. increased competition leads to Price decreases
3. Mature stage	1. costs are lowered as a result of Production volumes increasing and experience curve effects 2. sales volume peaks and market saturation is reached 3. increase in competitors entering the market 4. Prices tend to drop due to the proliferation of competing Products 5. brand differentiation and feature diversification is emphasized to maintain or increase market share 6. industrial Profits go down
4. Saturation and decline stage	1. costs become counter-optimal 2. sales volumes decline or stabilize 3. Prices, Profitability diminish 4. Profit becomes more a challenge of Production/ distribution efficiency than increased sales

Supply and demand

Economics is known by many as 'the dismal science'. This is because it seeks to establish laws of predictability that define norms of behaviour, but fails because the behaviour is not only mathematical but human and is therefore not capable of certain predictability. As George Bernard Shaw said: 'If all economists were laid end to end, they would not reach a conclusion.' However, one law of economics is generally agreed as reliable and that is the law of supply and demand. Supply and demand is an economic model of Price determination in a market. It concludes that, in a competitive market, Price will function to equalize the quantity demanded by consumers, and the quantity supplied by Producers, resulting in an economic equilibrium of Price and quantity.

Most People will relate to that and countless examples can be quoted to prove it. However, even in a competitive market, demand may vary in elasticity. Some markets are highly inelastic. One example is petrol, where Prices are increased substantially by both government action through tax and market action – and demand does not vary hugely. However, if competitive brands of foodstuffs attempt to raise their Prices faster than the general market they will usually see retraction in demand. Mars had a deliberate policy of keeping their Price rises linked to the Retail Price Index and adjusting Product formulae accordingly.

Nevertheless Price is not the only regulator. Supply may be restricted deliberately, as in the example I gave before of prestigious car marques, or because of a genuine shortage. And not all markets are competitive. The British economy is a mixed economy of both private and public ownership of means of Production and delivery of services. In such an economy there are two ways to manage supply and demand. Price is generally favoured by the private sector. Rationing is the default method of the public sector. Another term for rationing is 'the queue'. Thus in the war years, and indeed right up to 1954, a system of rationing was introduced under wartime statute to limit the supply of scarce goods such as petrol, clothing and certain foodstuffs in order to manage supply and seek to ensure fairness in distribution. One inevitable result was the emergence of a parallel or 'black' market of the same goods, where Price was the factor for those willing and able to pay more to get hold of goods probably illegally sourced. I am just old enough to vaguely remember some of the last Products coming off rationing.

We might like to think that such days have gone, but several public services are still rationed. The National Health Service was set up with the philosophy of providing a minimum standard of health provision free at the point of use. Payment was made separately and quite independently by those in work through a system of National Insurance pursuant to the recommendations of the Beveridge Committee. The committee's proposals were quickly accepted by the Conservative and Liberal parties but were rejected, ironically, by the Labour Party. However, over the next few years the Labour Party gradually accepted most of the proposals and implemented them in the creation of the welfare state.

So in the market for health provision there is no Price mechanism at point of use that controls demand. Demand is therefore uncontrolled and since it is impossible to meet uncontrolled demand a system of rationing takes place with queues, ie waiting lists, prioritization and the so-called postcode lottery where different decisions about rationing are made in different areas of the country. It seems to me that this is an inevitable consequence of the design of the system.

For most of us there are three basic needs – food, shelter and health care. After that in a civilized society there is a long and ever-growing list of additional needs such as education, policing and so on. In Britain most of our food is provided in a free – though regulated – market. Supply of foodstuffs is subject to a complex series of regulations at the level of agricultural land. These regulations were introduced at a time of shortage in the post-war era when the feeding of Europe's surviving population was a matter of crisis. They no longer serve well in an era of plentiful supply. But in the final stages of supply where the value has been added and a competitive market exists, while the Products are heavily regulated as to contents, descriptions, weights etc, there is no regulation of supply and demand. Thus Price is the regulator and we find there is abundance in the shops and no need for rationing, except for highly infrequent shortages of some individual foodstuffs.

Shelter in Britain is also largely a matter of private provision. The availability of land is indeed restricted as God is not making any more of it. And politicians rightly restrict its use through measures such as the green belt. Some housing is built by public providers to ensure the availability of affordable housing, but in the large the market is private. There is no actual shortage of housing, which is not to say that there are no homeless people – but the reasons for these are largely social.

Thus of our three basic needs we choose to supply two through a predominantly private market with Price as the denominator. In one of these, food, there is no rationing and abundant supply. In the second, housing, there is plentiful supply and many hold most of their wealth in their property. But with the third basic need, health care, the market is largely a state monopoly with the inevitable result of queues. If we look at the former Soviet communist model where all three needs were provided by the state there were queues for all three needs. Bread queues, overcrowded houses and similar standards of health care to the West, though with much reduced life expectancy.

Privatization should have restored competitiveness to many public monopolies – where it was done well, as in the case of telecommunications. People may have forgotten that you used to have to wait, or queue, to have a line connected by British Telecom when it was a state monopoly. Now it is a fiercely contested commercial market. Even where it was botched as in the case of British Rail, and private monopolies replaced a public monopoly, still their commercial sense and concentration on Promotion has led to a huge increase in passenger journeys.

Another public good that is rationed is the road network. There is a popular misconception that the public has already paid for the roads to be built through the Road Fund Licence and therefore there is a very strong antipathy to the idea of paying tolls to use the roads. In many other countries road tolls are normal and indeed they were in Britain in the past before the age of the car. This means that demand at peak times often exceeds supply and the result is heavy congestion, which costs the economy some £20 billion per year (according to the Eddington Report). There have been a few attempts to deal with this: notably the London congestion charge but this covers less than 4 per cent of the Greater London area and may have done little more than displace some congestion to other areas.

Traffic is largely a function of economic activity. Since we want the economy to grow it follows that we want more traffic. But we feel as individuals that the congestion is someone else – when of course it is us. If we are going to reduce traffic we need to change our behaviour, make fewer journeys, share cars etc. But few people seem to take this message on board.

Incidentally, traffic is also affected by the Push-Pull dilemma. Companies such as Toyota, in seeking to improve the efficiency of their operation, introduced the concept of Just-in-Time (JIT) delivery. Working with their suppliers they encouraged a system whereby key components were delivered just in time for their insertion into the Production line rather than being held in vast quantities all over the factory. Actually, a common practice of suppliers to comply with such demands was simply to load up their trucks and wait in line outside the factory for the decision to call them in. Looking at the operation from the manufacturer's point of view, its inventory had been rationalized. Looking at the supply chain as a whole, the inefficiency had just been moved upstream.

The importance of scarcity

In digital media there have been some dramatic changes in the business model, caused by the disruption of the internet and other forms of digital media. The internet works on an entirely open basis, which was the intention of Sir Tim Berners-Lee, inventor of the world wide web. It is free to all, and once information has been placed there it can be widely distributed. Thus generations of consumers are growing up believing it to be normal and entirely justified to download content free that traditionally was sold in hard format with royalties flowing back to its publisher and ultimately its creators. This was true of the recorded music industry, which is now going through significant year-on-year declines. The ethics are clear. The creators should be rewarded for their efforts. The publishers should be rewarded for their efforts and the risks they take in agreeing to publish unknown writers and artists.

But some models work perfectly well in this new world. They are invariably those where the element of scarcity has been maintained. Thus satellite television operators are able to charge high subscriptions for content, particularly sport, which is shown usually in real time as sport is of the essence with the result unknown. To protect this position the operators encode their broadcast and only make it available to subscribers who also contract and may pay for a set top box that can decode the signal. The future looks bleak for content owners who are unable to control the scarcity of their Product. On the other hand, digital media allows organizations to transform much of their communication to a Pull strategy where empowered consumers seek information online rather than the treadmill of the old Push communication strategies.

Summary

In this chapter we have:

- described the Push-Pull of marketing as it relates particularly to the supply chain;
- considered the difference between types of Product, both physical and perishable, and noted the wide variety of perishability;
- evaluated the advantages and disadvantages of the Product life cycle;

- looked at the law of supply and demand and reviewed its application when Pricing is not a factor, as in public sector monopolies;
- underlined the importance of scarcity as a way of creating Profitable Pull strategies rather than commoditized Push strategies.

In the next chapter we will consider the last action in this section of the book, Positioning.

Positioning

10

Give a man a fish; you have fed him for a day. Teach a man to fish and you can sell him fishing equipment.

AUTHOR UNKNOWN

Great communicators have an appreciation for Positioning. They understand the people they're trying to reach and what they can and can't hear. They send their message in through an open door rather than trying to push it through a wall.

JOHN KOTTER, HARVARD PROFESSOR AND LEADING LEADERSHIP GURU

Marketing should not be a war of attrition. With clever use of *Positioning*, resources can be used most efficiently, brand image can be enhanced and Profitability improved. In marketing, Positioning has come to mean the process by which marketers seek to create an image or identity in the minds of their target market for their Product, brand, or organization. Repositioning involves changing the identity of a Product, relative to the identity of competing Products, in the collective minds of the target market.

Neil McElroy's ground-breaking memo on brand management that I referenced in the Introduction was based on an assessment of the need for Positioning. McElroy wanted to see Procter & Gamble's personal soap brands Positioned so that they did not compete directly with each other but rather versus other companies' Products. Later academic work on Positioning was not as much focused on the question relative to competitive Products as much as it was focused on cutting through the ambient 'noise' and establishing a moment of real contact with the intended recipient. In the classic example of Avis claiming '*We're No.2, We Try Harder*', the point was to say something so shocking (it was by the standards of the day) that it cleared space in your brain and made you forget all about who was number one, and not to make some philosophical point about being 'hungry' for business.

Although there are different definitions of Positioning, probably the most common is: identifying a market segment or niche for a brand, Product or service utilizing traditional marketing strategies (ie Price, Promotion, Placement, Packaging and competition).

The term was first published in 1969 by Jack Trout in the paper '"Positioning" is a game people play in today's me-too market place' in the publication *Industrial Marketing*, in which the case was made that the typical consumer is overwhelmed with unwanted advertising, and has a natural tendency to discard all information that does not immediately find a comfortable (and empty) slot in the consumer's mind. It was then expanded into the ground-breaking book *Positioning: The battle for your mind* (1981), in which Trout and his co-writer Al Ries defined Positioning as 'an organized system for finding a window in the mind. It is based on the concept that communication can only take place at the right time and under the right circumstances.'

Contrary to what some observers say, I distinguish *Positioning* from *Perception*, with which we will deal in Chapter 15. Perception is that which happens in the minds of the target market. It is the aggregate Perception that the market has of a particular company, Product or service in relation to their Perceptions of the competitors in the same category. A company's management should be proactive about the ongoing process of evolving a Position, and Positively influence the Perceptions through enlightened strategic actions.

Noel Peebles, author of *How to Sell Your Business the Easy Way!* (1999), writes:

> Positioning is the marketing tool that helps prospects and customers identify what's unique about your Product, service or company. Use Positioning to give your advertising purpose, to give it a message, and to give it the appropriate tone. Then and only then, are you on your way to developing a good advertising strategy.

Product Positioning process

Generally, the Product Positioning process involves:

1. Define the market in which the Product or brand will compete (ie who are the relevant customers).
2. Identify the attributes that define the Product 'space'.
3. Collect information from a sample of customers about their Perceptions of each Product on the relevant attributes.
4. Determine each Product's share of mind.
5. Determine each Product's current location in the Product space.
6. Determine the target market's preferred combination of attributes.

7 Examine the fit between:
- the Position of your Product;
- the preferred combination of attributes.

8 Position.

The process is similar for Positioning your company's services. Services, however, don't usually have the physical attributes of Products. So you need to ask first your customers and then yourself: what value do customers get from my services? How are they better off from doing business with me? Also ask: is there a characteristic that makes my services different?

Noel Peebles again:

> What's the ONE WORD or phrase that comes to mind when customers think of your business? Is it service, Price, selection, convenience, quality or something else? Do you really 'own' that word or phrase in the customer's mind?

Write out the value that customers derive and the attributes your services offer in order to create the first draft of your Positioning. Test it on people who don't know what you do or what you sell, watch their reactions and listen for their response. When they want to know more because you've aroused their interest and started a conversation, you'll know you're on the right course.

The excellent Professor Mark Ritson wrote in an article in *Marketing Magazine* in October 2009:

> A great marketer can create Perceptual maps and uses them to derive a clear, tight, three-word Positioning for their brand. No wheels or triangles here, just a clear articulation of what the brands stands for. If ever there was a question that sorts the wheat from the chaff, it's: 'What is your Positioning?' Too often this is met with a stream of generic crap about integrity and innovation or a ridiculously over-complex, six-slide presentation that attempts to capture the 'essence' of the brand. A good marketer answers with a confident smile and few words.

Defining the market

Theodore Leavitt joined the staff of Harvard Business School in 1959 and at the age of 34 published an historic article in the *Harvard Business Review* that he was later to edit. Called 'Marketing Myopia' it asked: 'What business are you in?' It is an essential step in market analysis and subsequent segmentation to define the business in which you are in and therefore with whom you compete. Classically the US railroad companies could satisfy themselves that they retained significant shares of the railroad industry vis-à-vis each other. However, that industry so defined was in long-term decline, first to automobiles and then to aeroplanes. The rail industry should have defined its market as transportation and then it would have seen the dangers much earlier. I call this process 'defining away the competition'.

But it would be equally unhelpful to define it too widely. As General Manager of Green's of Brighton I could call our company brand leaders of the cake mix market, which we held by some margin. More correctly we included other forms of shop-bought cakes in our market definition in order to acknowledge the much more powerful and growing business of brands of ready-to-eat cakes such as Mr Kipling. However, it would have been fatuous to define our market as 'food' because then our share would have been miniscule and everything from fishcakes to baked beans would have been our competition. This would not have given us any useful indicators for action.

Once we have defined our market correctly, neither too broadly nor too narrowly, then we can segment the market by behaviour or some other attribute of the customer. We can then go through the rest of the process defined above. Positioning concepts might be divided into three general categories:

1. A Product can adopt a functional Position in that it solves problems or provides measurable benefits to customers. Here the customer is invited to use rational thought to appreciate the Positioning.
2. A Product can adopt a symbolic Position in that it enhances the customer's self-image, or sense of belonging or fulfilment. Here the customer will react emotionally.
3. A Product can adopt an experiential Position in that it provides sensory or cognitive stimulation. Here the customer reacts viscerally or by instinct.

In going through this process we will be also defining the target market for our Product. This may use evidence of demographics but it can also be about attitudes, behaviours, social class, geography and many other subdivisions of society. It is also important to remember the issue of timing because markets are dynamic. I have been a bird lover since I was very young and could not imagine ever shooting a gun at a bird. However, when my wife and I were invited by my advertising agency to an afternoon of clay pigeon shooting I was interested. Clay pigeons are actually plate-like discs of clay that are fired into the sky at different angles. The shooter has to aim and fire his shotgun in the twinkling of an eye. At first I was missing regularly until I worked out that the disc was moving fast through the air and so I needed to aim my shot in front of the disc and wait for the disc to arrive where my shot would be. This proved much more successful.

So it is with marketing. We have to aim our shot (brand proposition) at the target (consumer) where we think it will be at the time our Product reaches the market. Once again we can see the importance of timing in marketing. By the same token we need to keep our market analysis and Positioning statement up to date because the markets – and the brands in them – will surely evolve in different directions over time.

This is especially true if a brand goes through changes of ownership. Pentland enjoyed massive success in repositioning the Reebok brand. It had bought a controlling interest for $77,000 and then sold it 10 or so years later for US $777 million, one of the deals of the century. With the proceeds it started buying up other well-known sports brands that had fallen into disrepair. One such was Speedo, originally an Australian brand of swimwear that had gone through various changes of ownership and also sub-licensing agreements, which meant that by the time I was responsible for the brand on a worldwide basis its Positioning varied hugely around the world. The brand was now run from Nottingham, hardly famous for its beaches, and so the centrally directed brand Position was a performance brand underpinned by sponsoring Olympic swimmers and seeking to dominate the league table of swimming medals every four years. Meanwhile, some of its leading licensees Positioned it as a beachwear brand, almost entirely at the opposite end of the spectrum. Its leading markets included Brazil with its famous Copacabana beach, Australia (Bondi), the United States (Malibu), France (St Tropez) and so on. It was hard to reconcile these differences in a single tight Positioning and this acted as a brake on the development of the brand.

Repositioning a company

In volatile markets, it can be necessary – even urgent – to rePosition an entire company, rather than just a Product line or brand. For example, Nokia began life in 1865 as a wood pulp business. From here it went into manufacturing paper. In 1898, Eduard Polón founded Finnish Rubber Works, manufacturer of galoshes and other rubber Products, which later became Nokia's rubber business. In 1902, Nokia added electricity generation to its business activities. In 1912, Arvid Wickström founded Finnish Cable Works, producer of telephone, telegraph and electrical cables and the foundation of Nokia's cable and electronics businesses. Shortly after the First World War, the Nokia Company was nearing bankruptcy. To ensure the continuation of electricity supply from Nokia's generators, Finnish Rubber Works acquired the business of the insolvent company. In 1922, Finnish Rubber Works acquired Finnish Cable Works. The three companies, which had been jointly owned since 1922, were merged to form a new industrial conglomerate, Nokia Corporation, in 1967 and paved the way for Nokia's future as a global corporation. The new company was involved in many industries, producing at one time or another paper Products, car and bicycle tyres, footwear (including Wellington boots), communications cables, televisions and other consumer electronics, personal computers, electricity generation machinery, robotics, capacitors, military communications and equipment. Eventually, the company decided to leave consumer electronics behind in the 1990s and focused solely on the fastest growing segments in telecommunications. Nokian Tyres split from Nokia Corporation to form its own company in 1988 and two years later Nokian Footwear, manufacturer of rubber boots, was founded. During the rest of the 1990s, Nokia divested itself of all of its non-telecommunications businesses to focus exclusively on telecommunications and became the dominant manufacturer of mobile telephone handsets for a period. Even now it is further repositioning itself as primarily a software company, adding value to its handsets through multiple applications such as satellite navigation. In September 2013 Microsoft acquired its mobile handset business.

Managing such a process of constant change is very demanding. The expectations of investors, employees, clients and, in a small country like Finland, even politicians and regulators, all need to shift and each company will need to influence how these Perceptions change. Doing so involves rePositioning the entire firm.

This is especially true of small and medium-sized firms, many of which often lack strong brands for individual Product lines. In a prolonged recession, business approaches that were effective during healthier times often become ineffective and it becomes necessary to change a firm's Positioning. Upscale restaurants, for example, which previously flourished on expense account dinners, bonus-fuelled celebrations and snazzy corporate events, may for the first time need to stress value as a sales tool.

RePositioning a company involves more than a marketing challenge. It involves making hard decisions about how a market is shifting and how a firm's competitors will react. Often these decisions must be made without the benefit of sufficient information, simply because the definition of 'volatility' is that change becomes difficult or impossible to predict.

The 22 immutable laws of marketing

Messrs Trout and Ries insist that some laws of marketing are immutable. In *The 22 Immutable Laws of Marketing* (1993), a best-selling follow-up to their work on Positioning, they describe the 22 laws as follows:

1. The Law of Leadership: It is better to be first than it is to be better.
2. The Law of the Category: If you can't be first in a category, set up a new category you can be first in.
3. The Law of the Mind: It is better to be first in the mind than to be first in the marketplace.
4. The Law of Perception: Marketing is not a battle of Products, it's a battle of Perceptions.
5. The Law of Focus: The most powerful concept in marketing is owning a word in the prospect's mind.
6. The Law of Exclusivity: Two companies cannot own the same word in the prospect's mind.
7. The Law of the Ladder: The strategy to use depends on which rung you occupy on the ladder.
8. The Law of Duality: In the long run, every market becomes a two horse race.
9. The Law of the Opposite: If you are shooting for second place, your strategy is determined by the leader.
10. The Law of Division: Over time, a category will divide and become two or more categories.
11. The Law of Perspective: Marketing effects take place over an extended period of time.
12. The Law of Line Extension: There is an irresistible pressure to extend the equity of the brand.
13. The Law of Sacrifice: You have to give up something to get something.
14. The Law of Attributes: For every attribute, there is an opposite, effective attribute.
15. The Law of Candour: When you admit a negative, the prospect will give you a Positive.
16. The Law of Singularity: In each situation, only one move will produce substantial results.

17 The Law of Unpredictability: Unless you write your competitor's Plans, you can't predict the future.

18 The Law of Success: Success often leads to arrogance, and arrogance to failure.

19 The Law of Failure: Failure is to be expected and accepted.

20 The Law of Hype: The situation is often the opposite of the way it appears in the press.

21 The Law of Acceleration: Successful programmes are not built on fads, they're built on trends.

22 The Law of Resources: Without adequate funding, an idea won't get off the ground.

The 'law of line extension' to which Trout and Ries refer depends on clear Positioning. A well-Positioned brand can be extended into quite far-reaching, even unlikely scenarios, if it is well-Positioned and the new line fulfils the same Positioning. The Virgin brand is an example of both how to do it and how not to do it. The brand stands for upstart, challenging the established players in the space. It was first coined as a 'virgin' doing battle with the well-established and, by implication, unexciting music publishers in the recording music industry such as EMI. The brand has been extended to cover retail, brides' wear, cosmetics, soft drinks, vodka, health clubs, mobile phones, air travel, rail travel and many others. Some of these have worked famously. Virgin Atlantic has been a constant thorn in the tail of British Airways, even adopting its flag-carrier tail fin when BA monstrously abandoned this in favour of a bizarre foray into world art. But when Virgin took on some of the rail franchises, the incumbent British Rail disappeared and so there was no longer an established brand for Virgin to challenge.

Unique selling Proposition

A celebrated corporate slogan at Sony was 'We do what others don't'. This was an obvious effort to distance ourselves from competition but also an instruction to all of us as to how we should behave, always seeking that point of difference. This was an example of a unique selling proposition (USP). The USP was first developed by Ted Bates advertising agency, coincidentally the first advertising agency I worked with in the 1970s. The Bates brand was born in 1940, when Ted Bates opened his first office, Ted Bates Inc., in New York. Bates eventually built his company into the world's fourth largest agency group and expanded his business for 26 years without losing a single client.

Ted Bates's creative partner was advertising maverick Rosser Reeves. Reeves was an advertising original; he pioneered the TV commercial, crafted one of the most popular brand slogans of all time (M&Ms 'melt in your mouth, not in your hand'), wrote the first best-selling book on advertising, *Reality in Advertising* (1961), and created the famous 'unique selling proposition' that is still used by marketers today. A key point about a USP is that it may not be strictly unique: you just have to say it first in such a way that you own the proposition.

> When I moved to the United States with Mars Inc. in 1980 I visited Ted Bates in New York City and saw the entire showreel of M&M candies, among others. By now they were being advertised as fun Products to be shared, but in the post-war years when they were newly launched – and for some time after – the advertising was very prosaic, very hard-hitting with men in white coats advocating M&Ms because they were the chocolate that 'melts in your mouth, not in the hand' because of its sugar-shell coating. And then to emphasize the point, the doctor-like figure would hold up the palm of his hand and pronounce 'No chocolate mess!' Thus Reeves established the USP in the conscience of a whole generation.

Copywriting

These two industry pioneers – Ted Bates and Rosser Reeves – believed that advertising exists for only one purpose: to sell the client's Product. To quote David Ogilvy, founder of Ogilvy & Mather, 'Rosser taught me my trade… and that the real purpose of advertising was to sell the Product'. Their edict of effectiveness continues to inspire (or at least it should) all advertising agencies. The art of copywriting is one of the most important in all of marketing. Many People who became famous in other walks of life, particularly writing fiction, began their careers writing advertising copy. Here is a list of some of them:

- Helen Gurley Brown – worked for Foote, Cone & Belding advertising agency as a secretary. Her employer recognized her writing skills and moved her to the copywriting department where she advanced rapidly to become one of the nation's highest-paid advertising copywriters in the early 1960s. In 1959 she married David Brown who would become the film producer of *Jaws*, *The Sting*, *Cocoon*, *Driving Miss Daisy* and others. In 1962, at the age of 40, Brown authored the best-selling book *Sex and the Single Girl*. In 1965 she became editor-in-chief of *Cosmopolitan* and reversed the fortunes of the failing magazine.

- Peter Carey – one of only three authors to win the Booker Prize twice with *Oscar and Lucinda* (1988) and *True History of the Kelly Gang* (2001). In 1962 he began to work in advertising. He worked at various Melbourne advertising agencies between 1962 and 1967, and worked on campaigns for Volkswagen and Lindeman's Winery, among many others.
- Don DeLillo – author of *Underworld* (1997), worked for five years as a copywriter at the agency of Ogilvy & Mather on Fifth Avenue in New York City, writing image ads for Sears Roebuck among others, before leaving in 1964.
- Kenny Everett – comedian and radio DJ. After schooling he worked in a bakery and in the advertising department of *The Journal of Commerce and Shipping Telegraph*.
- F Scott Fitzgerald – after getting engaged to Zelda in 1919, Fitzgerald moved into an apartment at 1935 Lexington Avenue in New York City to try to lay a foundation for his life with her. Working at an advertising firm and writing short stories, he was unable to convince Zelda that he would be able to support her, leading her to break off the engagement.
- Terry Gilliam – director and animator and member of the *Monty Python* team. After finishing college, Gilliam worked briefly for an advertising agency before he was offered a job at *Help!* magazine.
- Alec Guinness – actor. Sir Alec first worked writing advertising copy.
- Dashiell Hammett – author. After contracting tuberculosis during the First World War Hammett turned to drinking, advertising and, eventually, writing such classics as *The Maltese Falcon* (1930).
- Hugh Hefner – publisher (*Playboy*). Worked as a copywriter for *Esquire*, but he left in January 1952 after being denied a $5 wage increase.

- Joseph Heller – author of *Catch-22* (1961). He briefly worked for Time Inc. before taking a job as a copywriter at a small advertising agency, where he worked alongside future novelist Mary Higgins Clark.
- Elmore Leonard – writer of westerns such as *3.10 to Yuma* (1957). A year before he graduated, he got a job as a copywriter with Campbell-Ewald advertising agency, a Position he kept for several years; he did his own writing on the side.
- Ogden Nash – poet. His first job in New York was as a writer of the streetcar card ads for a company that previously had employed another Baltimore resident, Scott Fitzgerald. Nash loved to rhyme. 'I think in terms of rhyme, and have since I was six years old,' he stated in a 1958 news interview. He had a fondness for crafting his own words whenever rhyming words did not exist, though admitting that crafting rhymes was not always the easiest task.
- Bob Newhart – comedian and actor. In 1958, Newhart became an advertising copywriter for Fred A Niles, a major independent film and television producer in Chicago. He and a co-worker would entertain each other in long telephone calls, which they would record then send to a radio station as audition tapes.
- Alan Parker – film director of *Fame* (1980), *The Commitments* (1991), etc. Parker started out as a copywriter for advertising agencies in the 1960s and 1970s and later began to write his own scripts for television commercial. His most celebrated and enduring advertising work was when he worked for famed London agency Collett Dickenson Pearce, where he directed many award-winning commercials, including the famous Cinzano vermouth advertisement, starring Leonard Rossiter and Joan Collins.
- Salman Rushdie – author of *Midnight's Children* (1980). He worked for two advertising agencies (Ogilvy & Mather and Ayer Barker) before becoming a full-time writer. He is reputed to have coined the famous 'Naughty but nice' for the Milk Marketing Board's advert for cream cakes.
- Dorothy L Sayers – author of the *Lord Peter Wimsey* series of crime novels, Sayers' longest employment was from 1922–31 as a copywriter at S.H. Benson's advertising agency in London, forerunner of Ogilvy & Mather. Sayers was quite successful as an advertiser. Her collaboration with artist John Gilroy resulted in 'The Mustard Club'

for Colman's Mustard and the Guinness 'Zoo' advertisements, variations of which still appear today. One famous example was the Toucan, his bill arching under a glass of Guinness, with Sayers' jingle:

If he can say as you can
Guinness is good for you
How grand to be a Toucan
Just think what Toucan do

Sayers is also credited with coining the phrase 'It pays to advertise'. She used the advertising industry as the setting of her novel *Murder Must Advertise* (1933).

- Murray Walker – motor racing commentator. He was employed by the Masius advertising agency, with clients including Mars, Vauxhall Motors and British Rail. He did not retire from this until the age of 59, long after he was renowned as a commentator. Murray is often wrongly attributed with having invented the famous slogan 'A Mars a day helps you work rest and play':

> [it] was something that I administered, but I never invented it. I'll tell you how it got ascribed to me. It got put into an obituary file, maybe all of my obituary files, and I can't get rid of it. It's amazing the way it sticks.

Murray did, however, create the slogan 'Trill makes budgies bounce with health' – a famous advertising slogan for bird seed in the 1960s, and one that I was still using as its brand manager in the late 1970s.

- Fay Weldon – author. In order to support herself and her son, and provide for his education, Weldon started working in the advertising industry. As head of copywriting at one point she was responsible for publicizing the phrase 'Go to work on an egg'. She once coined the slogan 'Vodka gets you drunker quicker'. She once said in a *Guardian* interview: 'It just seemed… to be obvious that people who wanted to get drunk fast, needed to know this.' Her bosses disagreed and suppressed it.

Advertising slogans

Advertising slogans are not the same as Positioning statements but if crafted carefully can express a Positioning statement or at least part of it. 'Go to work on an egg' was a highly effective and memorable advertising slogan but clearly not intended to express the whole Positioning of an egg. Rather it was intended to remind people to have a cooked breakfast, with an egg as an integral part of it, when the trend was more towards convenient cold cereals etc. An effective slogan usually:

- states the main benefits of the Product or brand for the potential user or buyer;
- implies a distinction between it and other firms' Products;
- makes a simple, direct, concise, crisp and apt statement;
- is often witty;
- adopts a distinct 'Personality' of its own;
- gives a credible impression of a brand or Product;
- makes the consumer feel 'good';
- makes the consumer feel a desire or need;
- is hard to forget – it adheres to one's memory (whether one likes it or not), especially if it is accompanied by mnemonic devices such as rhymes, jingles, ditties, pictures or film.

Here are 20 examples of famous advertising slogans. All are memorable but not all effectively express the Positioning of the brand:

- *Andrex, 'Soft, Strong and Very, Very Long'* – replaced in 2004 after a very long and successful campaign that put Andrex as a perennial entrant in the top 10 grocery brands.
- *Audi, 'Vorsprung durch Technik'* – literally 'Progress through Technology': the great Bartle Bogle Hegarty campaign that emphasized the German engineering credentials.
- *British Airways, 'The World's Favourite Airline'* – this is sophistry as it was justified by the fact that BA flew more international passengers than any other airline, though some US carriers flew greater overall totals. It implied that more people preferred it though smaller airlines such as Singapore Airlines and Cathay Pacific were preferred in research. Prior to this, BA advertising slogans included:

  – *The World's Best Airline*;

  – *We'll Take More Care Of You*;

  – *Fly the Flag*.

- *Cadbury's Smash, 'For Mash get Smash'* – in 1974 came the TV debut of toy Martians advertising Cadbury's instant mashed potato.

This ad got so much fan mail that the agency behind it, BmP had to prepare special literature to send out in reply. In 1999 it was voted advert of the century by a panel of industry experts, for its creativity and effectiveness.

- *Cadbury's Dairy Milk*, '*A glass and a half of milk in every half pound*'.
- *Carlsberg*, '*Probably the best beer in the world*' – created in 1973 by Saatchi and Saatchi for the UK market. It began to appear in company corporate ads around the world from the 1980s onwards. The voice-over for the original ad in 1975 was by actor Orson Welles.
- *Coca-Cola*, '*It's the Real Thing*' – a rare example of a successful global advert for a truly global brand. Right on the money for the Positioning.
- *Gillette*, '*The best a man can get*'. Perhaps!
- '*Guinness is good for you*' – my mother used to believe it as she was anaemic and was told by the doctor to drink a daily glass of Guinness because of its iron content.
- *Hamlet*, '*Happiness is a cigar called Hamlet*' – a memorable campaign from the great days of Collette Dickenson Pearce, but probably failed to convince most of its admirers to buy the Product.
- '*Heineken refreshes the parts other beers cannot reach*' – an amusing campaign with the great Victor Borge as the voice-over.
- *Kwik Fit*, '*You Can't Get Better Than a Kwik Fit Fitter*' – first shown in 1984, the famous adverts made the company into a household name. The fitter returned to TV in 2008 with the '*You'll Be Amazed at What We Do*' campaign.
- *Nike*, '*Just Do It*' – iconic.
- *Orange*, '*The Future's Bright, the Future's Orange*' – created by advertising agency WCRS along with the now famous advertising.
- '*Persil washes whiter*' – consistent advertising over many years.
- *Ronseal*, '*It does exactly what it says on the tin*' – marvellously apposite copy but to understand the Positioning you would have to look at the tin.
- *Tango*, '*You know when you've been Tangoed*' – the now-common catchphrase produced by advertising agency HHCL.

- *Thomas Cook Group, 'Don't just book it – Thomas Cook It'* – one of Thomas Cook's most famous advertising campaigns from the 1980s, recently revived after a bewildering gap.
- *Wonderbra, 'Hello Boys'* – probably caused more traffic accidents than any other poster campaign.
- *The Woolwich, 'I'm with the Woolwich ...'* – in the 1980s one of the UK's then largest UK building societies was famous for its entertaining TV advertising incorporating this slogan.

An industry that uses advertising slogans or taglines with particular effect is the film industry. Catchy, enticing short phrases are used by marketers and film studios to advertise and sell a movie, and to sum up the plot, tone or themes of a film. Composing ad copy for posters and trailers is generally the first step in marketing a film and setting a strategic direction for the Product. These 'soundbite' epigrams are often placed on either film posters (above or below the film's title) or on the merchandise itself (DVD or Blu Ray etc), to reinforce what the film is all about. Some taglines are quite obscure, unrecognizable and forgettable. Often, the best taglines are for very inferior films. Examples of famous movie taglines are:

'Garbo TALKS!' *Anna Christie* (1930)

'The story of the strangest passion the world has ever known!' *Dracula* (1931)

'They're dancing cheek-to-cheek again!' *Top Hat* (1935)

'Garbo LAUGHS!' *Ninotchka* (1939)

'There NEVER was a woman like Gilda!' *Gilda* (1946)

'What a glorious feeling' – 'MGM's technicolor musical treasure!' *Singin' in the Rain* (1952)

'It is REQUIRED that you see Psycho from the very beginning!' *Psycho* (1959)

'And remember, the next scream you hear may be your own!' *The Birds* (1963)

'The happiest sound in all the world!' *The Sound of Music* (1965)

'A long time ago in a galaxy far, far away…' *Star Wars* (1977)

'Just when you thought it was safe to go back in the water…' *Jaws 2* (1978)

'In space no one can hear you scream.' *Alien* (1979)

'Where no man has gone before.' *Star Trek* (1979)

'Thank God it's only a motion picture!' *Airplane!* (1980)

'Be afraid. Be very afraid.' *The Fly* (1986)

As in much of this book, my examples are largely drawn from the world of consumer goods marketing but these rules and principles are likely to apply very much more widely. Positioning your brand is something that every charity, university, business of every kind needs to do. I have personally advised two charities and a university on their Positioning and in each case it led first to a repositioning of the brand, then a rebranding exercise and finally a significant and Positive increase in revenues. Consumer goods may have shown the way. But the message can be even more Powerful in other sectors. As Robert Mighall pointed out in a fine article in *Times Higher Education* in July 2009 '"Just Do It" can have a very different resonance when education is the Product.'

Summary

In this chapter we have sought to describe the Product Positioning process. We have:

- referred to the importance of correctly defining your market;
- covered the rePositioning of a company;
- considered the role of Positioning in line extension and sub-brands;
- discussed the concept of the unique selling proposition (USP);
- explained the importance of copywriting as evidenced by examples of copywriters who later found fame as novelists etc;
- quoted famous advertising slogans for consumer Products and movies as examples of successful Positioning.

We have now completed the second section of the book on actions. In the next chapter we will introduce the third group of metrics, starting with *Profit*, which many will say is the most important P of all.

Further reading

As well as the works of Ries & Trout I recommend *Blue Ocean Strategy: How to create uncontested market space and make the competition irrelevant* by W. Chan Kim and Renée Mauborgne published by Harvard Business School Press (2005).

I was privileged to hear Professor Kim lecture on the themes in this book and he takes the concept of Positioning to a highly specialized level. As a sample: 'Do not focus on beating the competition. Instead you should make the competition irrelevant.'

PART THREE
Measurements

Profit

11

It is the socialist idea that making Profits is a vice; I consider the real vice is making losses. WINSTON SPENCER CHURCHILL

A new client had just come in to see a famous lawyer.
'Can you tell me how much you charge?' said the client.
'Of course', the lawyer replied, 'I charge £1,000 to answer three questions!'
'Well, that's a bit steep, isn't it?'
'Yes it is', said the lawyer, 'and what's your third question?'

A distinguished marketer with whom I used to work at Mars Inc. told me that 'You can only make a Profit if you sell water, air or a promise.' It may seem a slightly cynical view but there is a lot of truth in it. Water and air, of course, allow Product managers to design their Product to give the appearance of greater substance than perhaps it really has. Perfume comes to mind as a Product that uses both, water in the Product itself and air in the packaging. But it is surely *the promise* that sells the perfume and allows a *Profit* to be made.

Charles Dickens described the essence of Profitability through the mouthpiece of Mr Micawber in *David Copperfield*: 'Annual income twenty pounds, annual expenditure nineteen pounds nineteen and six, result happiness. Annual income twenty pounds, annual expenditure twenty pounds ought and six, result misery.' If we can more than cover our costs we make a Profit. If we earn less than our costs we make a loss. This has the advantage of simplicity but it is not enough. We also need to know the cost of capital employed and then set out to make a Profit in excess of that, otherwise we might show a Positive bottom line in a simple statement of Profit and loss but we will not have made a sufficient return on our investment.

There are three basic ways that we can set out to improve Profitability:

- increase turnover;
- increase Prices;
- reduce costs.

Increase turnover

Provided that our costs remain the same an increase in turnover will increase Profitability by the marginal balance of Profit. Some of our costs are fixed and some are variable. The variable costs will go up with volume increase but the fixed costs will not and so our overall margin is improved and certainly our net Profit will be higher.

Increase in turnover can come from a variety of sources but it is imperative that the marketing manager has a Plan to do this. If managers instruct their sales force to simply increase turnover without a Plan it is quite probable that volume will increase but Profitability will actually reduce, as the sales force may chase the volume through less Profitable channels.

It is also essential that the marketing manager has a good understanding of such issues as channel and account Profitability so that the volume sales increase can be targeted at the most Profitable channels. They should pay particular attention to variable discounts that may have been achieved. I have often witnessed last-minute heroics by sales teams that actually reduced Profitability because the end-of-year orders took the customer through some threshold whereby they earned additional retrospective discounts on the whole year's volume, not just the orders rushed through at the year end.

Increase Prices

This is probably the method least used and most effective. Marketing managers are often afraid to increase Prices and they are right to be so if their Product has no USP and has high Price elasticity. But a strong, confident brand should be prepared to show Price leadership and seek to set the pace in the market. Some of the proceeds from such an increase should be invested in increased marketing support to help cement the Price increase in the market.

As Product Manager for Trill I increased the Price ahead of inflation and also increased the marginal balance earned on the brand from 48 per cent to 50 per cent. Customers of Trill were very loyal, believing it to be superior to any other similar Product on the market. There was no decline in volume and all of the additional two points of margin went straight to the bottom line.

Reduce costs

Of the three alternatives this tends to be the one on which most marketing managers seem to concentrate – and for me it has the most dangers. Reducing costs is very often code for reducing quality. Of course at the strategic level it is right to seek ways of doing more for less and all good managers do this. But the danger is that under pressure for results, unable to increase volume in the short term, afraid to increase Prices – all the effort goes into ways of reducing costs and this is actually achieved by reducing the specification of the Product in some way.

However, I advocate working closely with suppliers to Plan for long-term reduction in costs that can benefit both parties. I will consider this in more detail in the next two chapters on *Productivity* and *Partnership* respectively.

In considering my 20 Ps of marketing I almost included *procurement* as it is so important. When I was in charge of Green's of Brighton for the Pillsbury Corporation, which had a constant eye on the expectations of Wall Street, I was blessed with an outstanding Procurement Director who, anticipating my regular requests for Profit improvement, worked closely with his suppliers to be ahead of the game and be ready to contribute savings when they were needed. On one occasion when I walked into his office to explain the latest demand from head office, he reached into a drawer and pulled out a cheque that he had stored for such a time!

If you set out to reduce costs in a company I recommend you involve your staff. You will be amazed at the ideas they will come up with. When the Minnesota-based Mayo Clinic found that its 2008 expenses were far exceeding income it turned to its employees for their ideas on where to cut costs. The not-for-Profit group did this by setting up a website where each member of staff could suggest ways of reducing expenditure. One department saved nearly $900,000 per year by turning off non-essential computers when offices were closed. Another suggested separating hazardous waste, which is more expensive to dispose of, and another department dropped printed employee directories in favour of an online version, saving more than $100,000. As a result, the Mayo Clinic found savings of close to $154 million. And the spin-off benefit was that staff felt more engaged in the company.

The relationship between marketing and finance

In this process marketing managers will inevitably engage with their opposite numbers in the Finance Department. The relationship between marketing and finance Professionals is not always a harmonious one. The Marketing Department looks at the Finance Department and sees a bunch of 'bean-counters' only concerned with numbers and restricting efforts to grow the business by taking a short term and negative outlook. All too often, finance personnel look at marketing personnel and see unqualified romantics who like to swan around having expensive lunches with their friends in advertising agencies and who have little grip on the harsh realities of life. Both of these are caricatures, but I imagine readers will recognize the types. In the best companies a close relationship is fostered and I understand that in Procter & Gamble the marketing and finance People now sit close together to maximize their mutual approach to making Profits.

Early on in my time with Sony I was privileged to hear Akio Morita, the charismatic founder of Sony, give the inaugural Innovation Lecture at the Royal Society in London. The event was organized by the Department for Trade and Industry. There were many leading scientists in the audience, including several Nobel Prize winners, but Morita-san soon had them eating out of his hand. He started by saying how much he admired the British. We were the nation that gave the world Newton and Faraday and so much more. However, he had one question: *Why did we allow our accountants to run our public companies?* The audience roared with laughter and even the few accountants in the room had to smile because of the charming way in which Mr Morita made his point. This does seem to be a particular issue in the UK: as already mentioned, for example, Britain has 13 times as many chartered accountants per capita as Germany.

My own relationship with the Finance Department at Sony was excellent. We worked together to achieve a set of steady results with annual increases in sales while also achieving corporate Profit targets. In fact, when I asked my Finance Director what was the Profit, he countered by asking me what I wanted it to be! However, overall corporate Profits at Sony were probably not commensurate with the world class reputation of the brand. Professor Hugh Davidson is one of the marketing academics I admire most, not least for his long track record in a successful brand management career before he turned his hand to writing a series of iconic and iconoclastic books on marketing. He interviewed me for one of these, *The Committed Enterprise* (2002), which is about 'vision' and 'values' and how to make them work. But I recall his pointed criticism of Sony's low Profitability. Hugh's first book was the best-selling *Offensive Marketing* (1972) and then in the sequel, *Even More Offensive Marketing* (1997), he proposed a new acronym for marketers to remember, POISE, which stands for:

Profitable

Offensive

Integrated

Strategy

Effectively Executed

In his emphasis on Profit Professor Davidson shows that there needs to be a proper balance between a firm's need for Profit and the customer's need for value. Those who define marketing as meeting customer needs at a Profit are nearly right but they need to recognize that there may be a very real conflict between meeting consumer needs and making a Profit. Every company has to do both in order to survive, but how should it strike a balance between the two? Davidson shows how *offensive* marketers maximize Profitability by matching their assets and competencies to the most appropriate opportunities for their companies or brands. Efficient matching of the two enables companies both to provide superior customer value and to generate superior Profits.

Another leading marketing academic is Professor Tim Ambler of the London Business School, now retired, who also passes my test of a good marketing academic because he enjoyed a distinguished business career at IDV, part of Grand Metropolitan, predecessor of Diageo, where he founded and fostered many of the famous drinks brands in its portfolio. I was also interviewed by Tim when he was Joint Managing Director of IDV but I didn't get the job! Nevertheless, he has done invaluable research on the measurement of marketing performance and brand equity. With this behind him he has done more to throw light on the problem that boards routinely devote 90 per cent of their time to spending and counting cash flow without wondering where it comes from and how it could be increased. Some years ago leading marketing figures in the UK formed the Marketing Council with the view that good marketing underpins shareholder value creation. I contributed in a modest way to their investigations and Tim Ambler articulated their findings in a book called *Marketing and the Bottom Line* (2000) in which he set out the metrics of corporate wealth, not just Profit but the contributors to Profit. Professor Ambler summarizes his key metrics as shown in Figure 11.1 and Figure 11.2:

FIGURE 11.1 Standard P&L metrics

Actual Metric	% Compared with Plan	% Compared with Competition	Board Review Frequency
sales	volume/value	market share	monthly
marketing investment	period costs	share of voice	quarterly
bottom line	eg Profit	share of Profit	half-yearly

FIGURE 11.2 General brand equity metrics

Consumer Metric	Measured By
relative satisfaction	consumer preference or satisfaction as per cent average for markets/competitor(s); the competitive benchmark should be stated
commitment	index of switchability (or some similar measure of retention, loyalty, purchase intent, or bonding)
relative Perceived quality	perceived quality satisfaction as per cent average for market/competitor(s); the competitive benchmark should be stated
relative Price	market share (value)/market share (volume)
availability	distribution, eg weighted per cent of retail outlets carrying the brand

Profit impact of market strategy

In Chapter 6 (Planning) I briefly referred to Profit Impact of Market Strategies (PIMS). It is appropriate here to develop this concept further. The Profit Impact of Market Strategies database was developed with the intention of providing empirical evidence of which business strategies lead to success within particular industries. Data from the study are used to craft strategies in strategic management and marketing strategy. The study identified several strategic variables that typically influence Profitability. Some of the most important of these were market share, Product quality, investment intensity and service quality (all of which were found to be highly correlated with Profitability).

According to Lancaster, Massingham and Ashford in *Essentials of Marketing* (2001), PIMS seeks to address three basic questions:

- What is the typical Profit rate for each type of business?
- Given current strategies in a company, what are the future operating results likely to be?
- What strategies are likely to help improve future operating results?

Dibb, Simkin, Pride and Ferrell, in *Marketing Concepts and Strategies* (2000), list six main areas of information that PIMS holds on each business:

- characteristics of the business environment;
- competitive position of the business;
- structure of the Production process;
- how the budget is allocated;
- strategic movement;
- operating results.

The PIMS project was initiated by senior managers at General Electric who wanted to know why some of their business units were more Profitable than others. With the help of Sidney Schoeffler they set up a research project in which each of their strategic business units reported their performance on dozens of variables. This was then expanded to outside companies in the early 1970s.

The initial survey, between 1970 and 1983, involved 2,600 Strategic Business Units (SBUs) from 200 companies. That has since grown to nearly 4,000 observations. Each SBU gave information on the market within which it operated, the Products it had brought to market and the efficacy of the strategies it had implemented.

The PIMS project analysed the data they had gathered in order to identify the options, problems, resources and opportunities faced by each SBU. Based on the spread of each business across different industries, it was thought that the data could be drawn upon to provide other businesses in the same industry with empirical evidence of which strategies lead to increased Profitability. Its primary conclusion was that businesses with large market shares (50 per cent plus) had rates of return more than three times greater than small-share businesses (10 per cent or less) for a given level of quality. Overall, 37 variables were identified that accounted for the majority of business success. Of these Dibb, Simkin, Pride and Ferrell chose the following as the most important strategic marketing variables:

- a strong market position;
- high quality of Product;
- lower costs;
- lower requirement for capital investment.

Lancaster, Massingham and Ashford have a slightly different list:

- market share;
- image;
- investment intensity;
- market growth;
- life cycle stage;
- marketing expense to sales ratio.

While these may seem obvious, PIMS provides empirical data that define quantitative relationships and support what some may consider to be common sense. This can be helpful, because in my experience common sense is not common!

Clearly it could be argued that a database operating on information gathered in the period 1970–83 is outdated. However, data continue to be collected from participating companies and PIMS replies that it provides a unique source of time-series data, the conclusions from which have proven to be very stable over time. It has also been suggested that PIMS is biased towards traditional, metal-bashing industries such as car manufacturing, which would not be surprising considering the era in which the original surveys were carried out. In fact, the nearly 4,000 businesses contained within the database cover the consumer, industrial and service sectors.

It is also heavily weighted towards large companies at the expense of small and medium enterprises. This resulted from the data collection method used. Generally only larger firms are prepared to pay the consulting fee, provide the survey data, and in return have access to the database in which they can compare their business with other large businesses or SBUs. Mintzberg (*Strategy Safari: A guided tour through the wilds of strategic management*, 2002) claims that because the database is dominated by large established firms, it is more suitable as a technique for assessing the state of ‘being there rather than getting there’.

A more serious theoretical criticism might be that an empirical correlation does not necessarily imply cause. There is no way of knowing whether high market share caused the high Profitability, or whether high Profitability caused the high market share. Or even more likely, a different factor such as Product quality could have caused both high Profitability and high market share.

In an article in *Sloan Management Review* Tellis and Golder ('First to Market, First to Fail: The real causes of enduring market leadership', 1996) claim that PIMS defines markets too narrowly. Respondents described their market very narrowly to give the appearance of high market share, a danger I described in the last chapter. They believe that this self-reporting bias makes the conclusions suspect. They are also concerned that no defunct companies were included, leading to 'survivor bias'.

The essence of PIMS is the importance of market share in determining Profit. I recall first coming across the theory in the mid-1970s at Mars where we sought to relate it to our business. However, when I joined Sony in the late 1980s I benefited from the teachings of a brilliant engineer, Mr Nobuo Kanoi, who when he took on a new responsibility would insist on lecturing his new charges on Lanchester theory.

Lanchester's laws

Lanchester's laws are mathematical formulae for calculating the relative strengths of a predator/prey pair. In 1916, during the height of the First World War, Frederick Lanchester devised a series of differential equations to demonstrate the power relationships between opposing forces. Among these are what is known as Lanchester's Linear Law (for ancient combat) and Lanchester's Square Law (for modern combat with long-range weapons such as firearms). Lanchester based his studies on the Zulu wars, but they were adapted to great effect in the Second World War to help the Allies win the aerial war. In the post-war era they have been further adapted to apply with some success to the business world – and so we can assert that PIMS at best validated century-old military theory.

The Profit zone

In *The Profit Zone* (1998) by Adrian J Slywotzky and David J Morrison the authors argue that market share is dead. They go on to say:

> In the classic Product-centric age, the key question was: How can I gain market share, increase unit volume, and gain scale economies? In the new age of rapidly shifting market value that commenced in the mid to late 1980s the questions are different:
>
> - 'Where will I be allowed to make a Profit in this industry?'
> - 'How should I design my business model so that it will be Profitable?'

They go on to describe 11 Profitability models, each of which has different business patterns and strategies to move a company into the 'Profit zone'. These can be broadly summarized as:

1. customer development/customer solutions Profit (eg GE, Nordstrom);
2. Product pyramid Profit (eg SMH (Swatch), Mattel);
3. multicomponent system Profit (eg Coca-Cola, Mirage Resorts);
4. switchboard Profit (eg Schwab, CAA);
5. time Profit (eg Intel, Sony);
6. blockbuster Profit (eg Disney, NBC);
7. Profit multiplier model (eg Virgin, Honda);
8. entrepreneurial Profit (eg ABB, 3M0);
9. specialization Profit (eg EDS, Wallace);
10. installed base Profit (eg Microsoft, Otis);
11. de facto standard Profit (eg Microsoft, Oracle).

In identifying these 11 models they prefer them to at least as many others with well-known practitioners.

Good management have their eyes all the time on the contributors to Profit. When they make decisions they understand what will be the impact on the bottom line. This does not mean that their *only* concern is Profit. As Henry Ford said: 'Business must be run at a Profit, else it will die. But when anyone tries to run a business solely for Profit ... then also the business must die, for it no longer has a reason for existence'; and on another occasion: 'A business that makes nothing but money is a poor kind of business.' Indeed, when I was Managing Director of Sony UK I asked my boss, Jack Schmuckli, CEO of Sony Europe, what did he want me to achieve. Was it sales growth or customer satisfaction? Brand image or market share? Management development or Profit? His answer was 'Yes!'

Corporate social responsibility

Perhaps Mr Ford meant more even than this – what today we call corporate social responsibility (CSR) (as discussed in Chapter 8). Ideally, CSR policy would function as a built-in, self-regulating mechanism whereby business would monitor and ensure its adherence to law, ethical standards and international norms. Businesses would embrace responsibility for the impact of their activities on the environment, consumers, employees, communities, stakeholders and all other members of the public. Furthermore, business would promote the public interest by encouraging community growth and development, and voluntarily eliminating practices that harm the public sphere, regardless of legality. Essentially, CSR is the deliberate inclusion of public interest into corporate decision making, and thus the observing of a three-way bottom line: People, planet, Profit.

The practice of CSR is subject to much debate and criticism. Proponents argue that there is a strong business case for CSR, in that corporations benefit in multiple ways by operating with a perspective broader and longer than their own immediate, short-term Profits. Critics argue that CSR distracts from the fundamental economic role of businesses; others argue that it is nothing more than superficial window dressing; others still argue that it is an attempt to pre-empt the role of governments as a watchdog over Powerful multinational corporations. To some extent all these views have merit and CSR has certainly been redefined throughout the years. My own view is that it is an inevitable part of running a business, as Henry Ford said a century ago. A business must recognize its corporate social responsibility, and if it does so energetically and with enthusiasm it will find it an aid to an organization's mission, as well as a guide to what the company stands for and will uphold to its consumers.

Mutuals

Not all organizations are set up with a view to make a Profit. There are several other business models that have validity for different purposes. In the 19th century the Co-operative movement emerged and developed into a powerful wholesale, retail and political movement, offering services literally from cradle to grave. Indeed the Co-operative movement was at one time the largest supplier of funeral services. Surpluses were distributed to members in the form of dividends – my grandmother used to like collecting her dividend stamps at her local Co-op branch. The Co-operative movement has declined as a power and lost massively its market share, but it continues, and some examples of its influence can still be seen in, for example, its more ethical banking services. However, while not seeking to make a Profit, the Co-op is seeking to make a surplus that can be returned to members. There may be good political and ethical arguments that can be brought to bear, but while the motives may be different the actions should not be. A marketer employed by the Co-op still needs to compete effectively and show that surplus.

Of similar structure is a mutual organization, especially in financial services. Banks, building societies, insurance companies have all benefited from mutual status and it is perhaps a sorry fact that many of these have been sacrificed on the altar of free market deregulation. Great building societies that used to collect savings from investors, which were then lent to borrowers for the building and purchase of homes, were an admirable institution that benefited many in society. Within a generation nearly all of the most famous and solid of these have been wiped out in senseless mergers and by poor risk management. But some remain and it is to be hoped that more will be founded and revived. Here marketers do have a different responsibility. They need to balance their desire to grow with a proper understanding of the risks on both sides of the balance sheet. They need to build and nurture a reputation for trust and solidity. Clearly there have been massive failures in this area.

Charities

Charities are organizations that benefit the public in a way that the law agrees is charitable. The law was modified in the 2006 Charities Act, which came into force over the following years. Charities are regulated by the Charity Commission. They do not seek to make a Profit but will have to account for their expenditure, and donors will want to feel that the bulk of their donation goes to the cause itself rather than to the administration of the charitable organization. In that sense charities do well to have a keen focus on at least two of my three prescriptions for improving Profitability: increasing revenue and reducing cost. Many large charities operate in the quasi-commercial field with extensive chains of shops competing for attention on the high street. They have sophisticated marketing departments who have usually received their training in the commercial arena.

Not-for-Profit companies

The Companies Act (2006) allows for the creation of companies limited by guarantee. These are set up not with charitable purpose but to perform some public good, perhaps in research; their membership agrees to guarantee the company's debts to a nominal amount. Such companies are not allowed to earn Profits or distribute dividends, but their management will do well to remember Mr Micawber's shrewd analysis and that even in such circumstances they will not survive if income does not exceed expenditure.

There are many organizations in the public sector that are set up with purposes similar to commercial enterprises but without a Profit requirement. The most famous and perhaps controversial of these is the British Broadcasting Corporation. The BBC was actually set up in 1922 by the leading manufacturers of radio equipment. Prior to that there had been an almost entire ban on radio-telephony broadcasts by the Post Office. The manufacturers successfully lobbied to change this and they became the initial members of the BBC, a company limited by guarantee. They provided the capital to build the radio masts and listeners paid a 10*s* (50p) licence fee to listen on equipment that had to be made by a British manufacturer. Half the licence fee went to the BBC.

Over time the charter has been changed so that the BBC is now a public body, independent of government and industry but still financed by a licence fee. It is no longer necessary to buy a licence to listen to the radio but it is a legal requirement if you want to watch a television, even if you claim that you never watch the BBC's own channels. The BBC now gets the entire licence fee as its income (at the time of writing £145.50 per household for colour, £49 for black and white) and this has usually been increased annually for inflation. Not only does this mean that the BBC effectively receives a poll tax on most households in the country, which is perennially increased by an inflation factor, but it also increases as households fragment and the population grows. No business has both protection against inflation and benefits from household growth, yet the BBC executives pay themselves as if they were an international business rather than a public servant. Some 39 of them earn more than the Prime Minister's £197,689 salary and 80 are paid more than the £144,000-a-year Culture Secretary, whose departmental brief includes the BBC. With this unfair advantage of guaranteed income, enforceable by law, the BBC competes directly with commercial enterprises, particularly in the provision of an outstanding website that is free to use while competitors must finance theirs through advertising or subscription. If the Competition Commission were to investigate it would have to find that this is a monopoly against the public interest. But then there is only one Competition Commission.

Some businesses go off the rails because they become distracted from their principal purpose. Sir Kenneth Cork was a famous liquidator who drew up a list of evidence that businesses were likely to be in trouble. This included such extravagances as spanking new head offices with more than likely fish tanks in the head office reception! Andrew Bentley, chairman of the Board of Governors of the University of Bedfordshire where I used to be a governor, tells the story of an eminent lady he used to work with who called this syndrome 'The Edifice Complex'! Great business leaders do not suffer such aberrations. They focus on their business objectives of which the principal one is to make a return on the shareholders' investment while also keeping a weather eye out for other legitimate claims of the community of other stakeholders. The market will allow the good marketer to earn his or her Profit.

Summary

In this chapter we have:

- looked at the three basic ways to improve Profitability:
  - increase turnover,
  - increase Prices,
  - reduce costs;
- learnt from Professor Hugh Davidson that there must be a proper balance between a firm's need for Profit and the customer's need for value;
- reviewed Professor Tim Ambler's metrics of good marketing that underpin shareholder value creation;
- studied the pros and cons of PIMS;
- outlined the lessons of Lanchester theory;
- discussed the views of Slywotzky and Morrison that Profitability comes through the design of the business model;

- considered corporate social responsibility;
- summarized some of the not-for-Profit models.

In the next chapter we will develop the theme of metrics in marketing by examining *Productivity*.

Productivity

12

Never try to teach a pig to sing. It wastes your time and annoys the pig. **GROUCHO MARX (1895–1977)**

In the last chapter we saw that the good marketing manager must manage the key drivers of Profit. One of these is *Productivity*, the subject of this chapter. In business, resources, both human and monetary, are always limited by definition. The most successful, most Profitable business in the world does not have unlimited resources or time. So we must try our very best to get more out of the available resources, more bang for our buck.

This is obviously a responsibility of any manager, not just a marketing manager, but the marketing manager does have a special responsibility for improving Productivity. That is because part of their responsibility, the Planning and procurement of marketing communications, is guaranteed to waste money. Remember the words attributed to John Wanamaker, a US department store merchant, quoted in Chapter 4 (Promotion): 'Half the money I spend on advertising is wasted; the trouble is I don't know which half'. If we parse this we find that there are two kinds of waste.

The first is inevitable. When I place an advertisement in the newspapers I am theoretically buying readership of X thousand. However, less than X thousand will actually see the advert as not every reader reads every page. Even if they see the page they may not bother to read the advert. So there is inevitable waste in any advertising campaign. The same applies to any other media. There is some evidence that in online advertising, where clicks are involved, an assumption can be made about accurate recording of actual visits to a site and payment can be restricted to this. But there is still much wasteful expenditure on online advertising – and certainly all other forms of media are inefficient in this sense.

The second kind of waste is avoidable with skill and judgement. It is that the advertising must be effective. Anyone with any longevity in advertising, either as client or agent, knows that they have been responsible for considerable waste by Producing or signing off advertising that simply did not work. It did not achieve its goal. It made no difference to sales. It did not enhance brand image. Or worse, it may have had a deleterious effect on both.

Zero-based Planning

To avoid waste we have to start as always with Planning, as discussed in Chapter 6. Most organizations these days will go through some kind of Planning process; indeed, some I've known never get out of it. They might be familiar with the idea of resource Planning from a zero base but few ever really do this. The concept is that you start with a blank piece of paper and then Plan the resources required to deliver on your objectives, rather than starting with your existing resources and Planning the inevitable incremental cost increases for inflation and expansion and career development, which customarily produces an unacceptable result.

Proper zero-based Planning starts with that legendary blank piece of paper and involves a serious intellectual challenge right from the start. Why? Because the first thing you realize is that you have taken yourself off the page, along with everyone else. One of the reasons why there is such little Productivity improvement in the public sector is that no one ever does this. They receive the instruction to cut overall costs by 10 per cent and then pass it on down the line. Everyone in succession gets the same instruction. Finally there is no choice but to cut so-called 'front-line services'. But every politician says he won't cut front-line services! So no cuts are made at all! This is why half the money spent on education goes nowhere near the schools. This is why half the money spent on the health service goes into inefficient administration. The answer? The blank piece of paper.

It is no bad thing to ask yourself if your business can afford you. It is no bad thing to get someone else, perhaps your friendly financial controller, to validate your cost effectiveness against external benchmarks. When you have done this it is much easier to ask others to do the same.

Once you have gone through this step you continue to Plan the organization and its resources that are necessary to deliver on your objectives. Then a reorganization of these resources might be required (we deal with some of the human factors involved in that in Chapter 16 on People). I have gone through this process many times and often with very Positive results. But on occasions I have been forced into it by the performance of the business, sometimes through external factors and sometimes through factors that should have been more under my control.

As I briefly explained in Chapter 6 (Planning), in Chile I faced external factors of bewildering strength. I ran a business for Mars that imported its Products from the United States. The Chilean peso had been fixed at 39 to the US dollar for three years. Effectively this had the result of squeezing local manufacturers, as world-class manufacturers like us could import our goods. There was a tariff but it was only 20 per cent and even with the cost of freight we could still compete effectively in the local market. Then in the space of less than three months the currency was devalued on six occasions and the rules for buying dollars were also changed. The rate of exchange went from 39 pesos to the US dollar to 90 pesos to the dollar. The Chilean economy was going through a recession that would prove to be the seventh most severe in modern world history. Our business became impossible to maintain because we imported in dollars, sold in pesos, and then when we went to the market to collect our debt one or two months later our pesos were devalued and insufficient to buy the dollars to pay our external debt.

My management and I considered all the possibilities. I even took myself off the blank page and did not put myself back on. As outlined in Chapter 6, finally I concluded that there was no choice but to recommend closure. After going through all the alternatives, Forrest Mars, one of the three owners of the Mars Corporation in Brazil, accepted my recommendation, but he had three conditions:

1. I was to lose no money.
2. I was to keep the brands alive, because they would be back.
3. I was to look after the People I had hired because he liked them.

Obviously the first was impossible for the reasons I have explained above, but I achieved it in the sense that I had no bad debt and so lost no money locally. I had only sold against personal cheques, because I had discovered that passing a bad personal cheque meant an automatic jail sentence. I had a special safe built in my office to which only I had the key in which I kept these cheques. If someone could not settle I might allow them to roll over a new cheque by 30 days but I always collected the debt.

The second I achieved by selling our existing stock on consignment to a local distribution company. And Forrest was right. Mars went back a few years later and have full distribution today in a much more prosperous Chile.

And on the third I did my best, although my sales manager had had enough and returned to his native Argentina. My other Chilean staff all found jobs and two went on to become very successful businessmen in Chile.

Decision making

Not all decision making is painful but good decision making is at the heart of achieving good levels of Productivity. The decision-making style of gung-ho leadership can often lead to considerable inefficiencies. Such leaders do not pay enough attention to detail and give unclear signals. Their staff then take considerable time to understand the mission and such wasted time leads to wasted resources. I have worked for US and Japanese companies and have learnt from both, but I have sometimes observed the excessive US style leading to a situation where leaders cry 'Follow me!' and their colleagues are left bewilderingly asking each other 'What was all that about?' The Japanese style is famously characterized as being more consensual and in some ways this may be right. But I think it is more subtle than that. Consensuses seem somehow democratic, but my first Japanese boss, Nobu Watanabe, who recruited me to Sony, was at pains to explain that this was not democracy. He asked me to imagine that I was the chief executive of a company, chairing a meeting where the decision was whether to launch a new Product. A presentation is made by the marketing team recommending the launch and then you ask each member of the management team what is their view:

- You start with the marketing director whose team has just made the presentation. Not surprisingly, the launch is favoured because market share has been slipping and it is felt that this new Product can revive that lost share and put the company back on a growth track.
- The sales director supports this as dealers are getting concerned about lost sales. The sales force needs this new Product to get back the initiative.
- The manufacturing director is in favour because of lost Production efficiency and the possibility of having to lay off some staff. This new Product will help with labour recovery.
- The finance director is in favour because lost sales means lost Profits and the new Product should restore that. What is more, a lot of money has already been spent in developing this new Product, which will be written off if the Product is now abandoned.
- The human resources director is concerned about morale and recruitment and supports the launch to address those issues.
- And then you turn to ask the last person on the team, the research and development director, who expresses a preference for more time to test the Product.

And so, in a democracy, your decision is clear. It is overwhelming, with five directors in favour and one asking for a delay. You decide to launch the Product and you have just launched Thalidomide. The point is that you have to give proper weight to each person contributing to the decision. All the arguments are valid but, for example, in a drug company there is nothing more important than safety.

New Product development

Not all new Product development turns out to be so catastrophic but much is highly inefficient. The great majority of new Products fail, many because they are not tested sufficiently or because they are simply not good enough. The marketing manager is, or should be, responsible for this process as they should represent the voice of the consumer, who ultimately decides whether a Product is good enough. One particularly common fault is to run a test market with considerable focus and support and then not reproduce that on a national scale. What the hot-bed nature of the test tells us is irrelevant unless it is reproduced nationally. Sometimes this is simply impossible as where, for example, additional sales resource is flooded into the test market to ensure distribution levels are high and then the sales resource is not available on national roll-out.

I wrote in Chapter 1 of the failure of some firms to operate to their own standards of testing the acceptability of Products. In fast-moving consumer goods your ultimate sales levels are a function of the following formula:

Propensity to purchase

x levels of awareness

x trial

x levels of repeat purchase

x frequency of purchase

All of these variables are predictable in established markets and can be influenced by pulling different levers from the marketing armoury. But there are minimum standards below which a Product will not be sustainable. It will be discontinued by a retailer if it does not earn its keep. It will be costly to manufacture if it does not maintain a minimum volume. It might go off the salesperson's radar if the level of repeat purchase falls away and he or she loses confidence in the Product. So for all these reasons it is vital to maintain standards – or the resulting loss of Productivity can be enormous.

Lessons from engineering

I am not an engineer but I have had the opportunity to manage a factory at Pillsbury when the manufacturing director left for another Position. Until a successor was recruited I took the role myself. As a marketing man who had benefited from the experience of training at some world-class companies I was impressed with the greater levels of measurement that the manufacturing staff brought to the job. 'Labour recovery' is an accounting term to allow you to plan the efficient use of human resources in the factory and then manage the variances that inevitably result. But why is such labour recovery only used in manufacturing? Meanwhile, office staff get through a workload that is seldom measured and where variances are never reported. What I am advocating is that colleagues can learn from each other in improving Productivity. Manufacturing staff can teach marketing staff about efficient work flows, because they are measured on such things and so often think about ways to improve them. Over time many of these processes become automated and considerable gains in Productivity are made. As far as I know, such gains are rarely made in the world of marketing. I think the credibility of the marketing profession would be greatly enhanced if there was a wider commitment to achieving such Productivity gains.

I have observed attempts to include this kind of thinking in sales force management. At Pedigree Petfoods we employed a sales engineer whose job was to measure sales force Productivity and recommend improvements. The problem was that his principal method of operation was little more than time and motion study and so focused on activity rather than results and effectiveness. What is needed is a range of measures that look at both inputs and outputs, with more weight given to outputs.

Measuring outputs

In relation to sales I believe the most important contribution to Productivity is to measure sell-through data, not sell-in data. As discussed in Chapter 9 (Push-pull), the desirable state is one where Products are pulled through retail distribution by consumer demand rather than pushed through by expensiveP stimuli. The efficiency comes not only from the improved use of marketing expenditure but more importantly from the management of inventory. During my time at Sony I was particularly disappointed with the analysis of some of the factories with whom we dealt, who seemed to think that once the Product had been shipped it had been sold. I used to tell them it was not sold until the consumer had bought it and was delighted with the experience.

Similar shortcomings can be seen in the measurement of media buying effectiveness. This has changed dramatically over my career, from the days when advertising agencies were usually one-stop shops that both produced creative work and bought media, and made fortunes by earning their income through charging a fixed commission on the value of the media they bought.

There was no relationship between the income generated in this way and the cost of actually producing great advertising, but that was the system for many years. It has rightly been broken up and replaced by a system where media is bought professionally by independent specialist agencies while creative shops charge fees for their work. Much greater Professionalism is brought to the procurement of the two separate functions. Nevertheless, there is still considerable room for improvement in the measurement of effective advertising.

Key to the management of Productivity is accountability. If responsibilities are clearly identified and individuals are both accountable but also empowered to manage their responsibilities and implement solutions to problems they identify, then Productivity will be enhanced considerably. I have observed the identification of problems by individuals who call a meeting of those managers involved in order to review the problem. Considerable discussion then ensues on what the problem actually is and what might be done to solve it or prevent it recurring. Usually there will be recriminations about possible causes of the problem and fancy footwork by those distancing themselves from the problem. Finally, the individual who had originally identified the problem is charged with going away to solve it! Much of these wasteful meetings can be avoided if these responsibilities are clearly identified in the first place.

Mars Inc., with whom I spent seven good years in the UK, United States and Chile, lives by the 'five principles': quality, responsibility, mutuality, efficiency and freedom. Regarding the principle of efficiency they make the following statement:

> Efficiency
>
> We use resources to the full, waste nothing and do only what we can do best.
>
> How is it possible to maintain our principles, offering superior value for money and sharing our success? Our strength lies in our efficiency, the ability to organise all our assets – physical, financial and human – for maximum Productivity. In this way, our Products and services are made and delivered with the highest quality, at the least possible cost, with the lowest consumption of resources; similarly, we seek to manage all our business operations with the most efficient processes for decision making. http://www.mars.com/global/who-we-are/the-five-principles.aspx

This is an excellent statement of purpose in managing Productivity and is applicable to all the processes of marketing. I also believe that Mars strives very hard to live up to it.

However, when I was at Crombie Eustace, a start-up brokerage in which I was a partner, we used to laugh at one Mars company that was a client of ours. They had produced at some expense a pencil holder for managers' desks, which had the word 'efficiency' stamped upon it. We, on the other hand, stored our pens in the bottom of a Fairy Liquid bottle that we had cut up in true Blue Peter fashion!

Personal Productivity

I now turn to personal Productivity. Ren McPherson, chairman of Dana Corporation Systems says:

> When you put on the hat of manager for the first time in your life, you give up honest work for the rest of your life... you no longer drive forklifts, open the mail, answer the phones or do anything of any direct economic value to the enterprise... Given that is the case, the only thing you have left is... the way you spend your time.

Each individual manager has the responsibility to manage their own personal Productivity in the best way they can. This is not confined to marketing managers but, for the reason stated above, marketing has a particular need to demonstrate its commitment to this principle. This has been drummed into me ever since I was first trained at Procter & Gamble as a sales representative and was taught that my objectives were to:

- sell volume;
- improve distribution;
- build goodwill;
- *operate efficiently and economically.*

Over the years I have, like everyone else, attended courses on time management; like everyone else I have been sold expensive stationery to assist my time management; like everyone else I have learnt to make lists of actions and how to prioritize them; and so on. But the most effective teachers I have had in this area have not talked of time management, which seems an ever-losing battle because in the end time cannot be managed. It wins. It is irrepressible. Instead, what you must manage is your own effectiveness and efficiency or, in a word, Productivity.

Most senior marketers will have developed and practised line management skills and these need to be well rounded to be able to manage the performance and needs of a great variety of individuals. A general manager, managing director or chief executive will need both a high degree of *task orientation* to get the job done, and a high degree of *relationship orientation*, working with colleagues to get the job done. Robert Blake developed a two-dimensional model to plot how these behaviours apply. But the late Bill Reddin of Magill University had the insight to add a third dimension, that of *effectiveness*.

As a young sales manager with Pedigree Petfoods I was fortunate to be sent on a training course taught by Reddin, based on the 3D Theory of Management Effectiveness. An effective manager developed the situational analysis to determine what type of behaviour is called on from him in any particular situation. Different individuals require different management techniques and the good general manager is adept at both knowing which and knowing how to apply them. He or she will also focus on outputs rather than inputs. Ultimately every job can be measured in terms of outputs (in the last chapter I listed the metrics on which Tim Ambler recommends the marketing director to focus).

My other great teacher in this regard was Jay Hurwitz of the Institute for Business Technology, who worked with me when I was at Sony. Jay is an American based in the UK with a particularly effective technique. He got me to focus on Productivity rather than time management. This was in the days before e-mail was rife and certainly before I was using it. So there was still a lot of paper correspondence that came in to my in-tray on a regular basis. He grabbed each piece of paper from the in-tray in turn, jabbed it in my face and said, 'What are you going to do with this?' Depending on what it was I might say, 'Oh! That's something I need to discuss with Steve.'

> JAY: 'When are you going to see Steve?'
>
> DAVID: 'I have a meeting with him on Friday.'
>
> JAY: 'So, what are you going to do with this now?'
>
> DAVID: 'I guess I'll leave it in a pending tray.'
>
> JAY: 'And when you see Steve, how will you remember where it is, and even that you have it? Why don't you create a Speak-To file for Steve, and all your other reports, and when you have your one-on-one regular meetings you can bring out your Speak-To files and deal with all the pending papers at one go.'

And so I did and continued to do so. It was a highly effective way of reducing the number of times you handle a piece of paper. I think of it like football when it is well played. The best players have good first touch and usually only need one or two touches to control the football and move the game on. That is how it should be with a piece of paper. Deal with it immediately if you can. If it can or should be delayed only touch it once more. Don't put it back in your in-tray. So how does that change with e-mail? I have not discussed it with Jay but I imagine his advice would be the same. Deal with it once, immediately, or if you leave it for a later time, deal with it only once more and then delete it or archive it where you can easily find it if you need to.

Jay also taught me how to Plan my time so that I really prioritized the important actions. He asked me how many hours per week I worked, not including travelling time. I told him. It was a big number though not as big as some workaholics I have known. He then asked me if I was content with this. I answered that yes, I was broadly happy. It was a long working week but I recognized that I was in a Position of considerable responsibility and so accepted the workload. He then asked me to come up with about six to eight broad headings for the types of work I did, including the routine areas. This might have been something like: corporate, customers, People, strategy, Planning, review and administration. He then asked me to allocate a percentage of the agreed number of hours to each of these with the whole adding up to 100 per cent. This might have looked as follows:

- corporate – 20 per cent;
- customers – 20 per cent;
- People – 20 per cent;
- strategy – 10 per cent;
- Planning – 10 per cent;
- review – 10 per cent;
- administration – 10 per cent.

Then the trick was to allocate blocks of time in my diary that corresponded to each of these items, starting with the most important. I was employed by the corporation and had a duty to respond to its requests to attend meetings in Tokyo, Cologne or wherever and that had to fit in the first 20 per cent. Then I allocated one day per week on average to spend out in the field. And then I allocated one day per week on average to work with my direct reports and other colleagues on leadership, coaching and mentoring. And then I fitted the other items in around this Plan. This was a quite different approach to that which I, and I suspect most others, had taken before – that is to allow the diary to fill up with meeting requests and other administrative duties and thus the really important area of seeing customers and listening to your People got restricted.

Jay also encouraged me to book meetings with myself for thinking and planning. My PA was instructed to guard my door on these occasions. So I operated an open-door policy except it was sometimes closed. I went further and started to go to the gym during the working day. I wanted to set the example to say that this was okay. It was not necessary to only work-out outside working hours. Because I believed, and believe, that a fit person will in any case be more Productive than an unfit one.

Tony Schwartz, president and CEO of The Energy Project, has written of *The Productivity Myth*. Ben Bernanke, chairman of the US Federal Reserve Bank, in testimony to the US Senate in 2010 stated that Americans were working 10 per cent fewer total hours than they did before the recession, due to layoffs and shortened workdays, but were Producing nearly as many goods and services as they did back in the full employment days of 2007. Bernanke called these gains in Productivity 'extraordinary' and 'unforeseen'. Schwartz, however, believes that this is simply because those in work are afraid of losing their jobs and so work that much harder. But this is not necessarily a good thing. It can lead to problems of health, particularly if it is sustained. He concludes an excellent Harvard Business Review (HBR) blog by saying:

> We need a better way of working. It's not about generating short-term, superficial Productivity gains by using fear as a motivator and then squeezing People to their limits. Rather, it depends on helping leaders to understand that more is not always better, and that rest, renewal, reflection, and a long-term perspective are also critical to fuelling value that lasts.
>
> If you're a leader, here's where you need to start: Stop measuring your People by the hours they put in, and focus instead on the value they Produce. Make that your primary measurement. Then encourage your People to intermittently renew during the day (and on weekends, and over vacations), so that when they're working, they're really working.
>
> That's the path to true Productivity. http://www.linkedin.com/e/avn/126953700/2146335/EML_anet_nws_c_ttle-0Ut79xs2RVr6JBpnsJt7dBpSBA/

Summary

In this chapter we have covered the following:

- demonstrated the importance of Productivity in the marketing mix;
- shown that this starts with good resource Planning;

- covered the significance of decision making and clear accountability in the process;
- questioned what marketing can learn from colleagues, especially those in manufacturing;
- described the contribution of a Professional procurement function;
- outlined methods of improving personal effectiveness and efficiency.

In the next chapter we will tackle the important subject of *Partnership*.

Partnership

13

The ideal committee is one with me as the chairman, and the other two members in bed with the flu. **LORD MILVERTON**

The secret to a successful marriage is separate bathrooms.
SIR MICHAEL CAINE, INTERVIEWED ON *DESERT ISLAND DISCS*, DECEMBER 2009

In this chapter I want to consider the role of Partnership in the marketing mix. Partnership can mean many things, not least a legal status. That is not what is intended here but rather the development of successful, long term, strategic relationships based on achieving best practice and sustainable competitive advantage. These relationships can be formed between individuals or organizations for the creation of a new enterprise.

Examples of successful marketing Partnerships include the following:

- A joint venture between two or more entities to pool their resources in bringing a new technology to market.
- A closer relationship between suppliers and their customers in bringing innovative improvements to the customers' Products and services.
- Collaboration between two or more normally non-competing parties to solve a technological challenge and prepare for market entry.
- A consortium of organizations bidding for public funds to develop and test an innovation in the event of a market failure.
- A service provider working with a content owner to drive traffic to a website and build awareness of the content.
- Joint selling where two or more Partners share account intelligence and seek to integrate the value chain.
- A franchise where a brand owner benefits from low-cost market entry into new territories while operators can run independent businesses with proven models and brands.

Business Partnering can create, organize, develop and enforce operational (short-term), tactical (medium-term) and strategic (long-term) Partnerships.

Benefits of business Partnering

The benefits of business Partnering are legion and include the following:

- Reduction of general costs. Business Partnering can be cheaper and more flexible than a merger or acquisition, and can be employed when a merger or acquisition is not feasible.
- Business Partnering increases the 'competitive advantage' (Porter, *Competitive Advantage*, 1985). This comes from cooperation and identification of better opportunities of revenues and investment in the market sector.
- Partnering takes an innovative approach to achieving business objectives. It replaces the traditional customer–supplier model with a collaborative approach to achieving a shared objective; this may be to build a communications network, improve an existing service contract or launch an entirely new programme of work. Essentially, the Partners work together to achieve an agreed common aim whilst each participant may retain different motivations for achieving that common aim.

There is nothing new about Partnership and indeed it has a venerable history over many centuries. Machiavelli said that every prince needs allies, and the bigger the responsibility the more allies he needs. The richest man in the world today, Carlos Slim, has followed that lesson and says: 'In this new wave of technology, you can't do it all yourself, you have to form alliances.' Recall in Chapter 5 (Packaging), I discussed the famous Partnership of Rolls-Royce, where the salesmanship and the financial resources of Charles Rolls perfectly complemented the engineering of Henry Royce to found one of the most famous of all marques.

Procter & Gamble

My first employer, Procter & Gamble, was formed by the Partnership of James Gamble and William Procter who were both immigrants to the United States from the British Isles in the early 19th century. James was the son of an itinerant Methodist minister from Northern Ireland who took his wife and family across the Atlantic to find a better life in Illinois. By the time they reached Pittsburgh they had all but exhausted their funds. The only accommodation they could afford was space on a flat boat sailing down the Ohio

River. Young James, aged 16, became violently ill. At the next stop his desperate parents rushed him ashore to find a doctor. They found themselves in Cincinnati and decided to stay. Cincinnati was by then a thriving city, but there was little demand for another clergyman so George opened a 'greenhouse'. After a short time working there James apprenticed himself to an established soap maker, William Bell. After eight years of learning the trade he set up his own soap and candle shop with a friend, Hiram Knowlton. At the age of 30 he married Elizabeth, the daughter of Alexander Norris, a respected local candle maker.

William Procter opened a woollen goods shop in London but the next day was wiped out by the burglary of all his stock. He decided to rebuild his life in the United States and by coincidence took his wife, Martha, in the same direction as the Gamble family. On a similar flat boat on the Ohio River, Martha fell ill with cholera. They also stopped at Cincinnati but this time the doctors could not save her.

Devastated, Procter looked around for some way to pay off his creditors. In his youth he had been apprenticed to a general store where he had learnt to make dip candles, so he set up in the candle trade. He met Olivia Norris at his local church and asked her to marry him. So James Gamble and William Procter became brothers-in-law married to two sisters. Both were buying the same animal fats for their respective businesses and were therefore effectively buying competitors. Their mutual father-in-law, Alexander, persuaded them to go into Partnership. This took several years but in 1937 James Gamble ended his Partnership with Hiram Knowlton and moved his share of the inventory into Procter's premises. At this stage no written contract had been signed but the two now regarded themselves in Partnership and set out to complement each other's efforts. The company that still bears their names is now one of the largest and most successful consumer goods companies in the world.

But when I joined it in 1971 its culture was less inclined to the concept of developing Partnerships. Its processes were secretive and internally driven; it only promoted management from within; it rarely sent delegates to conferences for fear of leaking confidential information. That has been transformed, particularly under the inspirational leadership of AG Lafley. During his period in office as chairman of the board, president and CEO, sales doubled, Profits quadrupled, and P&G's market value increased by more than US $100 billion. A major contributor to this success was merging P&G's internal resources with outside 'open' innovation. As much as 50 per cent of P&G's innovations were sourced from suppliers and other external agencies.

M&Ms

There is a lot of mythology about the origin of M&Ms, the world's most successful candy. The truth is that one of the *Ms* stands for Mars – Forrest Mars Sr – for whom this was the first breakthrough Product since he had left his father's business; the other stands for Murrie, as in R. Bruce Murrie, the son of William Murrie, long-time president of the Hershey Chocolate Company and a traditional competitor to Mars. R Bruce Murrie was originally Forrest's Partner in the M&M business and there are people who say the initials stood for Murrie and Mars. Hershey machines were modified for the first M&M plant in Newark, New Jersey. The two companies were competitors, but it was wartime and the army wanted supplies of chocolate that could withstand heat. M&Ms with their sugar-shell coating are ideal in that regard.

Perhaps it was because of this early experience of mutual cooperation with others, even a competitor, that Forrest Mars developed *mutuality* as the third of his five principles. Mars Inc. now state it as follows:

> Mutuality
>
> A mutual benefit is a shared benefit; a shared benefit will endure.
>
> We believe that the standard by which our business relationships should be measured is the degree to which mutual benefits are created. These benefits can take many different forms, and need not be strictly financial in nature. Likewise, while we must try to achieve the most competitive terms, the actions of Mars should never be at the expense, economic or otherwise, of others with whom we work.
>
> http://www.mars.com/global/who-we-are/the-five-principles.aspx

I tried to put this into practice as I travelled round the world building and developing Partnerships for Mars subsidiary Kal Kan based in Los Angeles. I sought to set up mutually rewarding relationships and, for me, a key part of this was that the distributor needed to understand our philosophy and subscribe to it. I was approached by one company who wanted to represent us in Mexico. At that time, 1980, US Products could only be imported into a few duty free areas, including one across the border from San Diego in Baja, California. Over dinner Gil offered to drive me to Tijuana to see the opportunity and I accepted. Gil picked me up from the factory one day and we drove the 120 miles from Los Angeles to San Diego and then across the border to Tijuana. This is one of the busiest borders in the world but most of the traffic is northbound. Once in Tijuana, Gil showed me around a few supermarkets and I was impressed by the number of displays of dog food. But I saw no people walking their dogs in the street. I asked Gil some questions about dog ownership and how people looked after their dogs. What types of breed were popular and so on. Gil could not give an answer to any of my questions. And gradually the penny dropped. Gil had no interest in importing my company's dog food Products for sale to pet owners. He saw them as a cheap type of meat that could be prepared in tortillas, tacos and enchiladas. With enough chilli sauce no one would know the difference and we would clean up. I told him that it was not part of our mission to compete with human food and that we could only work with distributors who would help us build a good awareness of the brand among dog owners who cared about the nutritional needs of their pets. The journey back to Los Angeles was somewhat quiet.

North of the border there was a different problem. Canada had tough tariff barriers that made it almost impossible to import from the United States. Mars business was managed by Effem Canada, a marketing unit headed up by a charismatic marketing professional, Eric Morris. I flew to Toronto to see him and his staff to explore the possibilities of dealing with these barriers.

Afterwards he wrote the following to the President of Kal Kan, John Barrow:

Letter to John Barrow, President of Kal Kan from Eric Morris, President of Effem, Canada. October 3rd 1980.

Dear John

Just a note.
Had our visit with David yesterday, and I was greatly impressed and so was everyone else with whom he had any converse.

We had an intelligent interchange: he understands we prefer doing business with other companies in the group. We understand that much has happened at Kal Kan to trim costs and be competitive. One day, surely it will be feasible and viable for both of us to get together.

When that day dawns it will be because of the sort of enlightened connection made by David.

Regards,
Eric

Sony

I saw some remarkable examples of Partnership during my time at Sony. I joined the company soon after the debacle of Betamax. The general view of the world is that Sony lost the format war against JVC's VHS – and this is true as far as it goes but it is not the whole story. The lesson that Sony learnt from this experience was that it needed more influence over the software, as consumers did not only make their decision to buy on the quality of a format but also on its utility. JVC had done a better job in signing up content owners so that consumers could buy pre-recorded movies. The offer on Betamax was much more limited even if to the practised eye the picture resolution was superior.

Sony then made two significant acquisitions, CBS Music, which became Sony Music, and Columbia Pictures, which became Sony Pictures. Sony had managed a joint venture with CBS Music to effect its distribution in Japan for many years and so had a good understanding of the business. It helped that the President of Sony, Norio Ohga, had a musical background having studied under Herbert Von Karajan in Berlin in his youth. This acquisition was relatively easy to manage and gave Sony new insight into the software side of the equation. But it took on a particularly innovative nature when the corporation decided to enter the computer games market in competition with Nintendo. It formed a new joint venture between Sony and Sony Music. By this time Sony owned 100 per cent of Sony Music so this may seem unnecessarily complicated, but it meant that the new company reported directly to Ohga outside the main divisions of Sony and that it could develop its own culture.

Once the first Playstation was developed I argued along with my colleagues on the hardware side of the company that we should have the responsibility for distributing it. President of Sony Europe, Dr Ron Sommer, asked me to write a paper detailing all the arguments in favour of this. I stated that we had the infrastructure, the relationships with the retail trade, were the custodians of the brand, and had successfully established new markets in the past and so on. Fortunately, I and my colleagues lost the argument. What top management understood, still bearing the scars of the Betamax defeat, was that the synergy of hardware and software was all important. Indeed the Playstation was more like a Gillette razor blade system. It was vitally important to rapidly establish a population of owners who would then buy the more Profitable games. These games were more like the CDs of the recorded music industry, hence the role of Sony Music. This Partnership was to build a brand new, highly Profitable business for Sony that would contribute up to 40 per cent of its Profits over the next 10 years.

Sony and its competitors also learnt from the Betamax and VHS shoot-out when it came to develop a digital disc format. There were long and difficult negotiations with many confusing announcements but finally a new set of standards were agreed between a number of leading consumer electronics companies, including Sony, Toshiba and Philips, in which the Digital Video (or Versatile) Disc (DVD) was born. The standards were agreed in such a way that several rights holders saw some of their Intellectual Property Rights incorporated in the format and so had a legitimate claim to a share of the royalties. Although the standards took years to agree, once they were agreed the clarity of communication to the public was helpful and the new format took off in one of the fastest-growing consumer electronic businesses. It was a pity that the lessons were again forgotten in the fight to establish a higher density format with Blue Laser and its rivals.

Sky

Japanese companies including Sony largely missed out on the new consumer electronic business driven mainly by content, that of satellite broadcasting. In the late 1980s Astra 1A was the first satellite launched and operated by Société Européenne des Satellites (SES), now SES Astra. The satellite provided television coverage to Western Europe and was revolutionary as one of the first medium-powered satellites, allowing reception with smaller dishes than before. Among the channels carried in the first years was Sky Television (later British Sky Broadcasting, after the merger with rival British Satellite Broadcasting on the Marcopolo satellite). Astra 1A began television broadcasts in 1989.

Sky was the brainchild of Rupert Murdoch and he approached Japanese companies, including Sony, to ask them to manufacture and distribute a satellite receiver and set top box. The key to this would be Pricing, and Murdoch believed that this needed to be no more than £200 at retail. Sony managers explained to Murdoch that this was not how markets were created. First Products were bought by early adopters and then over time prices came down as the mass market developed. Murdoch countered that this was not the way this market would work as he could not afford to pay the satellite broadcasting costs while the market slowly grew. Instead he went to Alan Sugar, owner of Amstrad, who knew something about low-cost Production. Sugar went to Mark Souhami, deputy chairman of Dixons Stores Group, and the largest consumer electronics retailer in the UK, and asked him for a forward order of 200,000 pieces. Souhami gave him the order and with this Sugar went to his supplier in China and commissioned design and the opening order. Thus the market was created by a three-way Partnership of broadcaster, manufacturer and retailer, each taking a share of the risk and each contributing an essential component of the mix: desirable content, Product to access it, and distribution to the public.

Sky has gone on to be a huge success and subscribers pay up to four times the cost of their annual TV licence fee in subscriptions, plus occasional subscription premium for new movies or live sports matches. In addition, Sky television carries paid advertising.

Cellnet

Another example of the disruption of the conventional business model of consumer electronics came in the development of mobile telephones. Initially this was primarily a B2B application but in the early 1990s Cellnet, then the number two operator in the UK behind Vodafone and the forerunner of 0_2, decided the time was right to open up the consumer market more aggressively. They approached us at Sony as they recognized the power of our brand, but saw that while we had a Position in telephony in Japan we had not thus far entered the UK market. In fact, we had tried a Product but in small volumes and so were open to the approach. We thrashed out a deal where we would source a Sony-branded cellular phone pre-registered with a Cellnet number and for every phone that Cellnet connected they would pay us a fee. Our first mobile phone was much smaller than any other on the market, a typical Sony design, which I christened the Mars bar phone. We introduced Cellnet to our dealership. The then MD of Cellnet was the late Stafford Taylor who was to go on to become Managing Director – Personal Communications for British Telecom, one of the joint venture owners of

> As the business with Cellnet developed I realized that unlike our other Products, where we had a relationship with the consumer, here the network controlled that relationship with monthly billing and we were subordinate to the networks in the hierarchy of relationships. I also discovered that the network operators were obliged to advise their service providers with Pricing information. So I recommended that Sony form a service provider and participate in this business. We set up Sony Cellular Services, which built up a network of subscribers and some years later was sold for a substantial return on investment for the corporation.

Cellnet with Securicor. He forged a Partnership with Dixons Stores Group that led to the opening of a chain of jointly owned stores branded The Link, concentrating on the fast-developing mobile telephone sector.

NXT

NXT followed the business model successfully pioneered by Dolby of licensing its technology to all parties and insisting that the licensees used the NXT logo on their Products. However, it proved to be a difficult model to implement and some of the early Products on the market were of poor quality. We decided to influence this by developing our own Product concepts and offering them to licensees with good brand names and distribution. One of our first Partners in this enterprise was TDK, the Japanese brand famous for its leadership of recording media but not well known for hardware. However, it had considerable success with a set of loudspeakers we developed for use with a PC. I still have a set on my desk as I write this. Two slim, stylish but unobtrusive speakers sit at either side of me while a powerful sub-woofer is out of sight at my feet. Another brand with which we Partnered was Brookstone, the US-based novelty retailer. Brookstone with a turnover of US $350 million owned 245 stores, which tended to be in 'high end' shopping mall and airport locations. Its Positioning was that: 'Brookstone is a nationwide specialty retailer offering an assortment of consumer Products that are functional in purpose, distinctive in quality and design, and not widely available from other retailers.' We designed a micro system known as the 'CD Wafer' system because of its very slim speakers. Brookstone sold over 100,000 of these systems, clearing more than US $20 million at retail. At NXT I tried to follow the advice of the Brazilian entrepreneur, Ricardo Semler, author of *Maverick!*:

- Never stop being a start-up.
- Don't be a nanny.
- Let talent find its place.
- Make decisions quickly and openly.
- Partner promiscuously.

There are many examples of famous business Partnerships: Marks and Spencer, the Wright Brothers, Hewlett-Packard, to name just a few. Bill Gates and Paul Allen wrote the first programmes that became Microsoft; Gates would later say, 'Our success has really been based on Partnerships from the very beginning.' But the most intriguing Partnerships are those where the parties deliberately provided different qualities, as with Rolls-Royce. Here are a few more examples.

Edison

Thomas Edison would not have been able to exploit his invention of the light bulb without financial backing. Throughout the 1870s and 1880s, Edison received funding from a group of wealthy investors, including J.P. Morgan and the Vanderbilt family, laying the foundations for what later became the Edison Electric Light Company. In 1879, Edison demonstrated the incandescent electric light bulb to his backers and launched it publicly shortly thereafter. Three years later, the first commercial central power system was installed in Manhattan. Within five years, 121 Edison central power stations spanned the country.

Chanel

In 1921 Coco Chanel created Chanel No. 5, which quickly became popular. But she lacked the capital to exploit it. In 1924 Théophile Bader, the founder of the Galeries Lafayette department store, introduced her to Pierre Wertheimer, owner of Bourjois, the largest cosmetics and fragrance firm in France. Together they established Parfums Chanel. Wertheimer took a 70 per cent stake in the new company, Bader 20 per cent and Chanel received 10 per cent. Chanel became rich as well as famous but tried to restructure the deal in her favour and finished losing all her shares. Today, the Wertheimer family owns 100 per cent of the company, including worldwide rights to the Chanel name. Chanel No. 5 became one of the best-selling perfumes in history.

Apple

Steve Jobs and Steve Wozniak met in the early 1970s when Jobs was attending lectures at Hewlett-Packard, where Wozniak worked. The two experimented with hardware and software in Silicon Valley. The pair blended Wozniak's computer and software prowess and Jobs's marketing genius to build the first Apple personal computer in Jobs' family garage in 1976. In 1980, the company went public, making both men multimillionaires. By 2013 Apple had become the largest technology company in the world valued at over US $400 billion and best known for its innovative Products, ranging from the Macintosh to the iPod to the iPhone to the iPad.

Mergers and acquisitions (M&A)

Mergers might be thought to be the ultimate example of Partnership and some have been very successful. However, in researching this chapter I looked at several pieces of analysis conducted over the last 15 years or so that showed this not to be the case. Here are some quotes about different pieces of research:

- 'However, approximately two out of every three M&As fail to achieve the intended goals which were the stated reasons for the business deal.'
- 'At the same time, the success rate of M&As has been poor. Some estimates put failure rates as high as 60–70 per cent.'
- 'Some studies show that 50–70 per cent of mergers fail, in that they don't live up to their financial promise.'
- 'The stats on M&A failure, in fact, might be gloomier than the American divorce rate. Depending on whether success is defined by shareholder value, customer satisfaction, or some other measure, most research places the merger failure rate somewhere between 50 per cent and 80 per cent.'

One piece of research by KPMG International, the accounting, tax and consulting firm, found that 83 per cent of corporate mergers and acquisitions fail to enhance shareholder value. In the report 'Unlocking shareholder value: the keys to success', KPMG analyzed the 700 most valuable international deals in the years 1996 to 1998. 'More than 8 in 10 deals fail to enhance shareholder value because of poor planning or execution or both, yet, by contrast, most of the executives interviewed (82 per cent) believed their deals were successful,' said Donald C Spitzer, the United States national Partner in charge of the Global Financial Strategies practice of KPMG. 'This is an extraordinary finding, and noteworthy because transactions remain the most dynamic driver for growth among corporate executives,' said Spitzer.

It is particularly interesting that firms like KPMG made such findings because they also have a pecuniary interest in promoting M&A. M&A is stimulated not only by the ambitions of overly optimistic senior executives but also the armies of accountants, the battalions of bankers, the legions of lawyers, and the platoons of PR advisers who earn vast fees advising both sides of the transaction. Of course, the transaction that failed to enhance shareholder value to the acquiring company may well have added shareholder value to the benefit of the acquired company's shareholders. In other words, the common failure is to pay too much.

The KPMG research conducted interviews with 107 executives of the subject firms and identified a combination of six 'keys', three hard keys and three soft keys, which were necessary for a deal to succeed. The three 'hard keys', pre-deal business activities that had a tangible impact on the ability to deliver financial benefits, were:

- synergy evaluation (business fit);
- integration planning;
- due diligence.

The three 'soft keys', human resources issues that must be examined even before a deal is announced, were:

- management team selection;
- cultural issues;
- communications with employees, shareholders and vendors.

I have not found any research indicating that a majority of M&A transactions were successful. All the research points to at least 50 per cent failure and much of the analysis points to much higher levels of failure. What is not clear from the research is whether this applies equally to mergers and to acquisitions. They are not the same. A merger takes place when two companies agree to go forward as a single new company rather than remain separately owned and operated. This is more likely to take place when the firms are about the same size. Both companies' stocks are surrendered and new company stock is issued in its place. For example, in the 2000 merger of Glaxo Wellcome and SmithKline Beecham, both companies ceased to exist at the time of the merger and a new company, GlaxoSmithKline, was created.

However, this kind of transaction is quite rare. Usually, one company will buy another, but to save the face of the acquired party it will be announced that a merger has taken place. This may be desirable in helping to address one of KPMG's soft keys, but unless the other keys are also addressed it won't be enough to guarantee the success of the merger. An example of a transaction that was described to the world as a 'merger' was the takeover of Chrysler by Daimler-Benz in 1999, which went on to fail several of the KPMG success criteria.

A purchase deal will also be called a merger when both CEOs agree that joining together is in the best interest of both their companies. But when the deal is hostile – that is, when the target company does not want to be purchased – it should always be regarded as an acquisition.

Over the years, strategies have changed in building large firms by acquisition. There was a fashion to grow companies by acquisition in different industries as a way of diversifying risk. It was thought that companies could ensure that they were not exposed to cyclical downturns if they had assets in different cycles. However, this also ensured that they were more likely to be exposed to some downturn and so were at best offering mediocre returns. While they had expertise in financial engineering there was no other common expertise in the business and so added little value to the component firms. Hanson Trust was a well-known example of such a firm, which grew by acquiring firms with interests in basic commodities that it was thought would always be in demand, such as bricks.

More common today is the consolidation of companies operating in the same markets, but even here executives should be looking for more than just loose references to synergy, which in my experience is a highly elusive benefit. I would recommend that the following characteristics should be present for a merger to be likely to succeed in adding shareholder value:

- *Compatibility of direction.* Compare the two companies' mission statements, business plans and purpose, and if they are compatible then the first building block of a successful merger may be in place.
- *Growth.* The merger should be directed from a desire to grow more quickly than would be possible organically. If the other party offers entry into a new market or removes a barrier to growth then a merger may make good sense.
- *Economies of scale.* Some larger firms lose their flexibility and the ability to adapt and respond to changes in market conditions. Economies of scale are not always beneficial. It is salutary, for example, to see how often customer service has suffered when merged companies merge the back office function and so reduce their ability to respond to customer demands.
- *Common culture.* Compare the two companies' cultural styles. If one party is highly competitive with a strong hire-and-fire element, and the other is more sympathetic with a no lay-off policy, it will be difficult to create a happy marriage.
- *Geography.* Cultures also vary greatly by geography. If the headquarters of the two entities are close it will be much easier to maximize the return on investment, finding the best employees from

either side. If they are remote then the communication problems will be particularly challenging. This is particularly true if the two parties are based in different countries.

It should be possible to articulate the positive effect of a merger clearly and concisely and in such a way that most employees will welcome it. Remember that the majority of M&A fail to achieve the objectives set – attempts to merge the number two player with the number three or four, to create a new number one, instead often finishes with a new number three. All too often mergers are driven by a philosophy of doing something for the sake of it. Growth comes from hiring good people, building a consensus for growth based on integrity and openness and empowering them to release their creativity and innovation. If a merger will enhance this process then go for it. If it will distract your people then forget it.

Alliances

If most acquisitions fail, what is the alternative? In 1998 Yves Doz and Gary Hamel wrote an important paper published by Harvard Business School Press, 'Alliance Advantage: The Art of Creating Value through Partnering'. They argued that, to date, most intercompany collaborations have involved the setting up and management of joint ventures in well-circumscribed areas. In most areas, these ventures are designed to contain and share known risks, not to create an expansive future. These risks are well understood, and the strategic foundations of the joint venture are clear to the Partners, whose managers focus most of their attention on the economics and contractual design of the agreement. Once agreement is reached, one of the Partners usually assumes operating responsibility and, for all practical purposes, runs the operation as if it were the sole owner. This arrangement lacks the dynamism, collaboration and mutual learning characteristic of successful strategic alliances. The strategic alliance, in contrast, is characterized by the following:

- There is greater uncertainty and ambiguity.
- The manner in which value is created – and the way in which Partners capture it – is not preordained.
- The Partner relationship evolves in ways that are hard to predict.
- Today's ally may be tomorrow's rival – or may be a current rival in some other market.

- Managing the alliance relationship over time is usually more important than crafting the initial formal design.
- Initial agreements have less to do with success than does adaptability to change.

They went on to say that business Partnering has gained significant momentum and focus within leading global businesses, as 'a medium for achieving significant revenue growth'. A recent example of an unlikely alliance was that of YouTube and *Monty Python*. As the younger generation discovers the delights of *Monty Python's Flying Circus* they post their favourite extracts on YouTube. At first, the stars and creators of the show objected on the grounds of copyright. But then they were persuaded to cooperate on joint promotion. The result, *Monty Python* DVDs have returned to the best-seller lists as the new generation wants to own the DVDs for repeat play.

We can see that Partnering requires all Partners to transform their businesses in terms of relationships, behaviours, processes, communications and leadership. Neither participant can succeed without the other, so the recommended approach is to implement the transformation as a joint activity wherever possible.

Summary

In this chapter we have:

- seen how Partnership involves the development of successful, long term, strategic relationships based on achieving best practice and sustainable competitive advantage;
- considered the benefits of Partnership;
- described examples of Partnership;
- looked at the challenges involved in mergers and acquisitions;
- reviewed the thinking on alliances.

In the next chapter we will address the question of *Power* in marketing.

Power

14

Suppliers and especially manufacturers have market Power because they have information about a Product or a service that the customer does not and cannot have, and does not need if he can trust the brand. This explains the profitability of brands. **PETER DRUCKER**

In marketing one of the objectives must be to achieve a position of *Power* over the competition in order to improve Profitability. This may be expressed in *Pricing Power*, where an organization has the ability to increase its Prices without undue concern over competitive reaction. This may also be expressed in *distribution Power*, where retailers feel obliged to stock an item in order to satisfy their customers. Conversely retailers obtain a position of Power over the supply chain in which they can largely dictate the terms of trade. This latter trend has been a constant over the past 40 years in the UK, where retailer distribution has become increasingly concentrated. Tesco now has a market share of 30 per cent of grocery distribution and about £1 in £7 of all retail spending in the UK. Grocery sales in the UK are dominated by Tesco, Asda and Sainsbury's. These 'Big Three' had a combined share of 64.9 per cent of the UK grocery market in the 12 weeks ending 23 December 2012.

Power brands

I first came across the concept of Power in marketing at Pedigree Petfoods. Tony Hallett was the divisional manager in charge of marketing our canned brands. These were very much the core Products of the company's success and the biggest and most Profitable of them; Tony designated Pedigree Chum for dogs and Whiskas for cats as *Powerbrands*. His strategy was to dominate the market by positioning these Products as premium brands supported by heavyweight advertising almost all year round. Product strategies were carefully honed over several years and Product quality was maintained most rigorously. Pedigree Chum returned over 30 per cent Return on Total Assets, and Whiskas was earning over 40 per cent. Similarly their market shares were in the same sort of ratio, around 30 per cent for Chum and over 40 per cent for Whiskas. The advertising for Chum ran for many years with the claim that 'Top breeders recommend (it)'. Top breeders were defined as those whose dogs were rated best of breed at the annual breeders' show Crufts. The assumption left for the average dog owner to make was that if Pedigree Chum was good enough for top pedigree dogs it was good enough for their pooch. There was a whole department dedicated to driving this strategy, which required establishing relationships with virtually all the breeders who were likely to win these competitions. Each year a new advert would be shot in order to show the relationship between the winning dogs and their diet of Pedigree Chum.

Whiskas was built on a claim that it was the preference of most cats. The actual claim was based on what the cat's owner said, so 'Eight out of ten cat owners said their cats preferred Whiskas.' The subtle difference in cats' actual preference and the owners' perception of that preference was often the subject of satire, but nevertheless it supported a Powerful business proposition for many years.

Such strong sustained performance can only be maintained for long periods with great discipline over all parts of the marketing mix, most crucially Product quality. The risk is that claims made on quality may be undermined over time because of the sheer size of the volume produced. A newer competitor with smaller volumes might be able to make a superior Product simply because they can afford to source smaller volumes of higher quality materials. However, they will still have the challenge of overcoming the perceptions built up in the marketplace (we will deal with the issue of *perception* in more detail in the next chapter).

Lessons from the military

To strive for a position of Power involves much of the marketing mix that we have already considered. It is often likened to military affairs. Much of the vernacular of the military has spilled over into marketing. We develop *strategy* and *tactics* to beat the competition. We plan a *campaign*. We deploy our sales *force* in the *field*. We set *targets* for them to hit. Sponsors fear *ambush* by those who don't pay the costs of sponsorship. Some marketers fight with *guerrilla* tactics. An aspiring marketer would do well to read some of the works of the great military strategists such as Sun Tzu, a Chinese general, who wrote *The Art of War* in the 6th century BC. It has long been celebrated as a work of military strategy but many marketers believe it has lessons for them as in, for example, recommending awareness of and acting on strengths and weaknesses of both a marketer's organization and that of an opponent. This lesson has been valid throughout history.

Of even greater influence has been Carl von Clausewitz who joined the Prussian Army at the age of 12, in 1792, just before it invaded France after the beginning of the French Revolution. He later fought in the Napoleonic wars, rose to the rank of Major General, married well and became highly thought of. He also fought for the Russians and helped negotiate the alliance between Russia, Prussia and Great Britain, which led to the downfall of Napoleon. Von Clausewitz is best known for his work *On War*, in which he set out to explain war in rational analysis rather than by previous ideas that it was little more than chaos. His famous aphorism that 'War is a mere continuation of politics by other means' needs to be understood in context because von Clausewitz subscribed to the dialectical view of history and so this statement is the antithesis of a previous statement that 'War is nothing more than a duel (or wrestling match).' His synthesis is resolved in his 'fascinating trinity', a dynamic, inherently unstable interaction of the forces of violent emotion, chance and rational calculation. This has influenced not only famous Prussian generals such as Moltke but also Lenin and Mao Tse-tung. Moltke said, 'No campaign Plan survives first contact with the enemy', and it is this recognition of the friction of conflict that has relevance in business. We can write, prepare and approve our perfect Plans but we must recognize that once in the field we will encounter the enemy or competition and everything starts to change.

In pursuing the military analogy with marketing we would do well to remember the dialectic. Hugh Davidson wrote of *Offensive Marketing* (1972); Nick Heptonstall of *The Will to Win* (1999). Fiona Gilmore describes *Brand Warriors* (1999), and her opening line is 'Business is war; the objective is competitor destruction through superior industrial economics.' But she goes on to say:

> Brand warfare is different: the brand warrior identifies the key conquest as the customer, not the rival. Beating the rival follows inexorably from winning over the customer's heart and mind, so the process of nurturing a brand is a crucial aspect of the warrior's attack. (*Brand Warriors: Corporate Leaders Share Their Winning Strategies*, 1999)

She may have had Victor Hugo in mind when he said, 'A stand can be made against an invasion by an army; no stand can be made against an invasion by an idea.' It is the Power of the idea that we are really trying to control and unleash. Peter Drucker said that this Power was derived from knowledge of the Product or service that was not known to the customer, and hence the ability to earn a Profit. Jack Welch of General Electric thought it was primarily about customers. He said: 'There are only two sources of competitive advantage: the ability to learn more about our customers faster than the competition and the ability to turn that learning into action faster than the competition.' So the dialectic is that in order to have Power over our competitors we must have Power over our customers and that comes from knowledge.

Intellectual property

A particularly effective form of exerting Power is to control a vital component or ingredient through intellectual property. When compact cassettes were introduced for home recording they suffered from tape hiss. Several companies tried to solve this problem. Ray Dolby, an American educated in Cambridge, was the first to establish a reputation for a successful solution. Gradually all the manufacturers of recording equipment fell into line to use the Dolby system He had obtained a position of Power over the market even though at that time he was not the manufacturer.

When I was chief executive at NXT, which had a similar ambition for our flat loudspeaker technology, I had the pleasure of meeting Ray Dolby at the Consumer Electronics Show in Las Vegas. We demonstrated a car fitted with our speakers, which not only gave a terrific audio performance but also saved valuable weight and space in the vehicle. Ray listened to the demonstration and then told me 'Yes, that could be a solution.' It was praise indeed and gave us encouragement on a path that led to the fitting of such speakers to Toyota cars and other vehicles.

At NXT I also had dealings with 3M, one of the companies I most admire. 3M was founded in the 19th century as Minnesota Mining and Manufacturing. It began life extracting minerals from the state of Minnesota and then went into aggregates for the construction industry. Over time it diversified into a huge range of different Products but more importantly upmarket in terms of complexity and uniqueness. I had the opportunity to see a selection of the Products in the 3M museum in its head office in St Paul and could not resist buying a stethoscope from the staff shop there, as 3M is the largest manufacturer of stethoscopes in the world! Now it seeks to control markets by having its corporate finger on the critical pulse. Thus it has a patent on a key component in the ink cartridges that are used in all inkjet and laser printers. It is said that the most valuable liquid in the world is the printer ink in the cartridges. On a cost per litre basis it is more costly than champagne or petroleum or any other liquid you might care to mention. But this is not strictly accurate because you don't just buy a liquid per se, but a complex delivery mechanism. And part of that mechanism is the contact point, the part covered up by a strip of sticky paper when you open the cartridge. That is patented by 3M and thus it exerts market Power without needing to invest in the manufacture of the printers or the distribution of the inks.

The British technology company ARM has a similar position in mobile phones. While not having an exclusive, its chips are so much in demand that essentially every smartphone or tablet (with a few exceptions) runs on an ARM-based chip. The company has been able to grow with the growth of the mobile phone market, to the point where virtually 100 per cent of the world's population own a mobile phone. Sir Robin Saxby, founder chairman of ARM, once explained to me that while his first 12 employees were engineers hired to design and build the semi-conductors, soon after that he set out to find and hire very competent globally experienced sales and marketing people to build the equally valuable relationships with key customers.

W.L. Gore has a similar position in outdoor clothing. Its Gore-tex fabric, which is waterproof but still permeable to air, is used in a wide range of outdoor clothing and footwear. It is seen as superior to its competitors and has widespread recognition by regular users of this sort of gear. Thus it can obtain market shares well in excess of that possible if it chose to enter the market directly as an apparel manufacturer.

Legal restrictions

In seeking to obtain and exert Power there are dangers, both in legal and in cultural terms. The legal risk is that while the logical extension of a desire to obtain Power is to obtain a monopoly, there are several legal restrictions on such outcomes and therefore on some of the efforts to achieve them. Under Article 102 of the Treaty on the Functioning of the European Union (TFEU) – which succeeded the Treaty of Rome, the founding treaty for the European Community, now the European Union – if an enterprise has a dominant position in a market, which does not serve the public interest, then the commission has many remedies including the ability to fine the enterprise up to 10 per cent of its worldwide turnover. This eye-watering threat has been used on many occasions and is certainly not idle. For example, in February 2008 the EU fined Microsoft €899 million for abusing its dominance of the market.

The tests are complex. We have to define 'the market', which may not always be straightforward. We also have to define 'the public interest'. One risk that an enterprise would be wise to mitigate, therefore, is seeking to 'dominate a market'. It will be much harder in the future to defend one's position and deny that you have a dominant position if there is a long list of e-mails and messages to the sales force stating one's intention to dominate, or congratulating oneself on achieving a dominant position.

Cultural risks

The cultural risk will again be familiar to students of history. The great British historian Lord Acton famously said, 'All Power tends to corrupt; absolute Power corrupts absolutely.' Acton was clearly writing of political Power, so does his aphorism apply to market Power? I believe so, having observed the arrogance that can come with strong, even dominant positions. At Sony we were sometimes accused of arrogance and I worked hard to drive out of our minds and our behaviour the arrogance of being number one. We were number one but only by the acceptance of our customers, both dealers and consumers. In the trade press there was a well written, if pseudonymous series of articles by one 'Ray Muttley'. I know who 'Ray' is but it must remain his secret. In the summer of 1997 a service conference was organized by the retailers with support from some but not all manufacturers. 'Ray' had occasion to write as follows:

> I know we harbour a certain apathy when it comes to service, but what stood out at the conference was a real desire and enthusiasm by a great many people to try to do something, and I unashamedly single out Sony as one manufacturer that comes across as wanting to get it right. My, how that organisation has changed over very recent times from the toffee-nosed to the sort of People you would like to have living next door! From me – one of their biggest critics over the years – that's praise you can't buy...

'Ray' was an independent dealer, but one encountered very different attitudes from some of the largest retailers. One very large grocery company wanted to deal in our goods. They invited our national account managers to meet with their buyers and discuss the possibilities. They opened with the following charming remark: "We're ****, We f*** the a*** off brands." Our people responded that we were Sony and we only dealt with people who respected our brand – and so no business was done. I have no idea if the senior management of that company knew that is how their buyers behaved, but I do know that some of their buyers got promoted to positions of senior management.

Retailer Power

The abuse of market Power by major retailers is so prevalent that it is simply accepted as a fact of life by most suppliers. Some large suppliers, particularly those with a global footprint, have the resources to deal with it and are capable of looking after themselves. But other smaller suppliers find it very difficult to survive on the thin margins left them by unscrupulous buyers who are themselves under tremendous pressure to produce short-term results and are themselves likely to face attrition. Retailers now demand allowances for listing a Product, allowances for continuing to list a Product and allowances for having listed a Product. You pay going in, you pay while you're there and you pay going out. From time to time, when their own shareholders or top management are putting the buying department under renewed pressure, they will write to suppliers demanding some new allowance for having the effrontery to have an account with them.

The competition authorities are there to deal with such abuses of Power, but despite regularly investigating the supermarkets they never find evidence of such abuse. This is predictable because few if any suppliers have the courage to blow the whistle on a customer on whom they depend. Turkeys and Christmas come to mind. The competition authorities have been responsible over many years for the gradual destruction of the British high street, which used to typically feature a variety of skilled retailers, local businessmen and women who made and reinvested their Profits in the community. They have been replaced by chains of charity shops, while the supermarkets have sucked the trade out of town and the profits out of the region altogether and down (or up) to their head offices in London or Yorkshire.

The supermarkets have also successfully defended themselves against such charges by saying that it is the consumer who decides and it is the consumer who gets a good deal. And here they have a point. It is the consumer who decides, though I suspect that most have little idea of the damage their collective decisions have done to the local economy and to the British way of life. The Law of the Commons prevails. Further, the consumer has benefited from many of the innovations that the better retailers have brought, including the variety of goods, the range of Pricing alternatives, the introduction of healthier foodstuffs and the internationalization of the grocery basket. The reader may recall from the Introduction that my first work experience was to fill shelves in a supermarket. At that time, the refrigerator was full of lard and margarine made from animal fats; very little cooking oil was on sale. Now huge numbers of oils, including the best virgin olive oils, are in abundance and there is little lard to be seen. I have no doubt that this is primarily down to the supermarkets.

One should also note that the big four supermarket chains that have prevailed – Tesco, Asda, Sainsbury's and Morrisons – have seen off significant competition. They have prospered while Alldays, Bejam, Carrefour, David Greig, Europa, Fine Fare, Gateway, Hillards, International Stores, Jacksons, Keymarkets, Lipton's, MacFisheries, Norman's, One Stop, Presto, Quality Fare, Richway, Safeway, Templeton's, Victor Value, Wm Low and countless thousands of others have been swallowed up. In prospering it is their shareholders who have benefited with very high net margins when compared with other international players. There was a time in the 1980s and 1990s when the leading supermarket chains were reporting up to 7 per cent net profits (though this is less today), an extraordinary level in a business primarily based on selling food and other necessities. I suspect the supermarkets have learnt that this was unwise and now reinvest their Profits in aggressive competition, acquiring landbanks and overseas expansion. The first might be deemed desirable if the only test is Price competitiveness, but the Price is not only the Price of goods in the supermarket trolley but also the Price of ever-diminishing alternatives, unhealthy concentration of Power and loss of capacity at the supplier level.

Some years ago I joined a small food brokerage business. Our model was to use our skills to help manufacturers, both British and overseas, achieve distribution through the Powerful supermarket chains. We represented toiletries companies that had distribution in the traditional chemist outlets but wanted to expand through grocery distribution. We represented a manufacturer of pet accessories that had distribution through the traditional pet trade but wanted to expand through the grocery outlets, and so on. It was remarkably easy to make significant increases in their business in this way. But, of course, in the long term such actions were feeding the Power of the monster at the expense of these traditional outlets. I recall a sales manager at Procter & Gamble boasting to me that he held the company record for the highest single order of Daz. He had 'sold' 8,000 cases to a relatively new discounter called Kwik Save. Such orders no doubt gained a little in efficiency for P&G, but not that much. However, it gave Kwik Save an edge over its local rivals and over time helped put these rivals out of business. Thus, the inappropriate targeting of one sales manager and his ilk contributed to the demise of hundreds and thousands of retailers and, ironically, of many sales managers – as such large forces are no longer required by the likes of Procter & Gamble.

Because the UK has an unhealthy level of retail concentration our balance of payments as a nation is unduly affected, with considerable damage to the competitiveness of our economy. If a Japanese manufacturer, for example, wants to introduce its Products here in the UK then its efficiency as a manufacturer will be combined with the efficiency of the British retail distribution, and the Product in question will reach the British customer quickly and efficiently. Try to reverse the process – and the inefficiency of the British manufacturer combined with the inefficiency of the Japanese distribution, which is labyrinthine in complexity, means the British Product has very little chance of reaching the Japanese home. In recent years this model has expanded to cover most of the Far East, with South Korea, China and several other nations queuing up to siphon their Products through the efficient British retail trade. No wonder Napoleon called us 'A nation of shopkeepers'.

Consumer Power

The customer has the ultimate Power. The money comes from the market and it is a foolish marketer who forgets that. Whatever position one holds in the value chain, the cash flows up the chain from the final customer. There are many ways to influence that customer and this book is dedicated to that process, but finally the customer decides. One of the most effective of all marketing techniques is the one that is most difficult to control, that of word of mouth. Jeff Bezos, the founder of Amazon, says: 'If you do build a great experience, customers tell each other about that. Word of mouth is very Powerful.' A market where word of mouth has always been amazingly Powerful is that of recorded music. Early adopters hear a new piece of music on the radio or over the internet. They buy the record in store or download the track from a web-based supplier such as iTunes. Then they play it to their friends who follow suit. If the process happens quickly enough – and there is sufficient energy in the system for this to take place usually – then the track becomes a 'hit'. As an example of the remarkable Powers of penetration that the best of recorded music can achieve, consider that, at one point, one in four British households owned a copy of Pink Floyd's *Dark Side of the Moon*.

Market-derived Power

Some markets by their nature confer Power on the companies that come to dominate them. The convergence in information technology of computers, communications, consumer electronics and content has produced companies with extraordinary Power and influence over all our lives. In *Waves of Power* (1997), David C. Moschella wrote: 'During the 1980s, the IT industry's centre of gravity shifted from mainframes to PCs. Today, the PC is giving way to a new network-centric era. Network capacity has already replaced microprocessor performance as the key market driver.' He argues that the doubling of semi-conductor performance every 24 months, predicted by Moore's law that had driven the hardware industry for three decades, would continue to do so, and he has been proven right in that. But he went on to say that Metcalfe's law, which states that the value of a network increases exponentially as the number of users increases, while network costs rise only linearly, would be the real driver of the upcoming network-centric industry. Therefore, tapping into the Power of network economics would be the key to next-generation financial success. And so it has proved, as Google, Facebook and the rest have risen from nowhere to dominate today's information technology industry. Such companies are not even a footnote in Moschella's book, published just 16 years ago.

In this chapter we have focused primarily on the Power an organization seeks to exploit externally over its customers, its suppliers or its competitors. However, it is also important to consider the Power we can exercise through, or internally to, the organization. As John Kotter, professor of leadership at Harvard Business School, says: 'The most fundamental leadership challenge is unleashing the energy potential in enough people to create the Power, if you will, to make organizations leap and dodge.' That Power comes, I think, from understanding that leaders need to articulate a vision, engage their colleagues in committing to that vision and, above all, deliver with enthusiasm and precision. They need to align their colleagues with the vision, empowering them to deliver. This particularly involves clarity of accountability with the responsibility to deliver. There is no point in making someone accountable if they are not also fully authorized to take all decisions relating to their remit.

Summary

In this chapter we have:

- described the concept of Power brands;
- looked at the lessons for marketers in military strategy;
- considered examples of Power through intellectual property;
- reviewed the legal and cultural risks from excessive market Power;
- analysed the pros and cons of concentration of Power in retailers;
- observed that ultimate Power lies with end users;
- emphasized the importance of empowerment of employees.

Perception

15

Perception is all there is.

TOM PETERS

Humankind cannot bear very much reality.

TS ELIOT, 'FOUR QUARTETS'

Perception is the act of recognition or comprehension by the observer. It may come through the senses or the mind. It may not be correct but it is what matters. How a customer *Perceives* the Product or service they are being invited to buy is all important. The good marketer understands that it is not the message but what is received that counts. This is not only about communication but about all the ways in which a Product is presented to the market. In today's world of instant feedback on Twitter and Facebook it is even more important because carefully crafted communication strategies can fall at the first hurdle if a different Perception develops in the market.

Facts are secondary to Perception. As has been said many times by many commentators, Perception is reality. As Oscar Wilde said, 'Believe nothing of what you hear and absolutely nothing of what you see.' Here are a few facts that may surprise:

- In Italy, until recently, it was not possible to get a haircut on a Monday.
- Rents in central Manchester are 40 per cent higher than in central Manhattan.
- 24 per cent of the world's construction cranes are operating in Dubai.
- Lauren Bacall and Shimon Peres are first cousins.
- There are half a million semi-automatic machine guns in Swiss homes.
- The percentage of Nigerians living on less than US $1 per day has risen from 32 per cent in 1985 to 71 per cent today.
- A study of the 101 known suicide bombers in Iraq from March 2003 to February 2006 found that only seven were from Iraq. Eight were from Italy.
- More Ethiopian doctors are practising in Chicago than in Ethiopia.

- Israelis own 10 per cent of the private land on the moon.
- The British rail system receives almost £5 billion per year in public subsidy – almost four times as much as it did when it was privatized in 1994.
- One in every 3,400 Americans is an Elvis impersonator.
- More than half of the London Underground network is over ground.
- Britain has 13 times as many chartered accountants per capita as Germany.
- More houses in China have a DVD player than running hot and cold water.

Take a common Perception that people have of Britain. Britain is a rainy country. It always rains there. In fact, annual rainfall is higher in Istanbul, Rome and Sydney than in London. This is not so much a factor of climate change but a factor of what lies behind a Perception. If the Perception was that Britain is a cloudy country that would be accurate because there are fewer hours of sunshine in London than Istanbul, Rome and Sydney, but when it rains in those cities the rain is heavier and so adds to the depth of annual rainfall that is measured.

Fairy Liquid is a Product developed by Procter & Gamble to help, which I used to sell during my time there. It has been brand leader for many years but has been sold on a twin strategy of appealing both to emotions and to reason. The emotional appeal is that Fairy Liquid is formulated to be 'kind to hands' that by implication will be coarsened by using other brands of harshly formulated detergent. It is worth remembering that prior to the creation of this category customers would do the washing up with a sprinkle of laundry detergent, which probably was harsh in usage. The fact that the customer can use rubber gloves for washing the dishes is almost irrelevant here, as many can't be bothered to do this. The rational appeal is that although Fairy Liquid is more expensive than most other brands it is concentrated and less is required to do the same amount of washing up. For many years the British film actress Nanette Newman would demonstrate this in TV commercials by showing many table loads of dishes washed in Fairy Liquid compared with just a few tables covered in dishes washed in Brand X. Consistent advertising over many years has built a Perception that Fairy Liquid is both safe to use and economical, despite its higher shelf Price. These are the Perceptions that are lodged in many consumers' minds. The facts may now be different. Other brands may have adopted safe formulations. Other brands may offer concentrated detergents that are even more economical than Fairy. But that powerful Perception is hard to dislodge – particularly if the brand values are maintained, the communication has remained consistent and the customer does not experience any dilution in the brand experience.

A more recent example of the same phenomenon is the iPod. Introduced by Apple in 2001 the iPod gave the consumer a chance to store recorded music in a compressed way using MP3 technology and listen to this on the move, much as previous generations had enjoyed the Sony Walkman, which could only access one tape at a time. The iPod also was linked to an innovative method of accessing music tracks over the internet called iTunes and downloading these to the iPod to add to the store of music. It took off as a global craze and quickly outsold all its rivals. But there were many brands of these music players and some of them had features that might have been seen to be superior. Some, for example, had significantly more memory and could store thousands more tracks than the iPod, while many others were considerably cheaper. But the design of the iPod marked it out as the must-have accessory and the market Perception was that it was superior in every way.

Personality endorsement

In Chapter 5 (Packaging) we discussed how endorsement by leading personalities can add to the attractiveness of a Product. At Pentland I had the great privilege to work with two distinguished sportsmen who influenced our Product marketing and thus enhanced the Perceptions felt by the end users in the market. The late Chris Brasher was one of the pacemakers in the famous four-minute mile won by Roger Bannister at Iffley Road stadium in Oxford in 1954. He won a gold medal in his own right in the steeplechase at the Melbourne Olympics in 1956. He later founded the London Marathon. As well as his athletic achievements he enjoyed a successful career as a journalist and TV personality and also worked in the athletic footwear business. With this experience he set up his own brand of hiking footwear – and I still wear Brasher boots to this day. Chris sold 75 per cent of the firm to Pentland but continued to chair the board of Brasher Boots and I was fortunate to also sit on that board representing Pentland's interest. Chris personally tested every variety of boot on stiff walking tours of the Scottish Highlands. He would also test all the other accessories and clothes items that were sold under his name. In this case, the Perception in the market – that if it was good enough for a great athlete and experienced hiker like Chris Brasher it was good enough for the weekend walker – was based on fact. It was good enough for Chris because he made it his business to be – and put his own name on it.

Sir Chris Bonington played a similar role for Berghaus, another Pentland outdoor brand. Chris was non-executive chairman of Berghaus, which was also a brand for which I was responsible at board level in Pentland. The brand had been founded by outdoor enthusiasts in the north-east of England who tested everything themselves in tough outdoor conditions. However, to gain greater credibility in the highly competitive outdoor market they recruited a number of well-known mountaineers who then tested the gear in the most extreme conditions. Of these none was more famous than Chris, who was and probably remains Britain's most famous mountaineer. He led several expeditions to the Himalayas, including tough assaults on Everest, and on some of these he wore and used Berghaus equipment. Again, the Perception in the market – that if it was good enough for Britain's greatest mountaineer then it was good enough for my weekend camping in the Lake District – was based firmly on fact. In this case, fact and Perception coincided.

Conor Dignam on Perception

As his first editorial in what he described in 2000 as the new millennium Conor Dignam, the then editor of *Marketing* magazine, wrote on the theme 'Why Perception is now marketing's most important "P"'. He wrote:

> The traditional 'P's of marketing – Product, Price, Promotion and Place – will continue to have an impact upon business as much as ever. But a new and powerful 'P' must now rate as crucial to any brand's success: Perception. A poor image with the public isn't something you can tell the boys in the PR office just to sort out. It can be damaging, if not terminal, to a brand's health. Those that have failed the Perception test in the past – Camelot, Shell, Sainsbury's – are working hard to turn around their image. Those which have traditionally enjoyed strong public support and brand Perceptions – Virgin, Body Shop, Boots – will fight to retain their position and standing. Public Perception of a brand in this consumer-savvy, message-saturated age has found its way into concrete form. So the decline of Sainsbury's and Marks & Spencer in recent years has been exacerbated by the dissatisfaction of staff who no longer take pride in wearing the retailer's uniform, by customers who feel they are no longer getting the best choice or Price, and a general feeling that what's being offered is 'second best'. Similarly, the Perception of 'Rip-Off Britain' has hit the UK car

> market. In relative terms, car Prices in the domestic market are no higher than they have ever been, but now potential buyers feel there is more on offer, that they can afford to wait, and that eventually the manufacturers will cave in and Prices will tumble. That is the reality for marketers in the new age of consumer sovereignty, where the buyer has more information on Price, performance and alternatives than ever before. Perception does not just reflect performance, it influences it.

More than 10 years on from Dignam's editorial it is instructive to reflect on the truth in his argument and what has happened since. Companies have worked hard to turn around their image not by simply adjusting their communication strategies but by working very hard on Product range in the case of M&S and Sainsbury's and working even harder on their customer service and other employee programmes. Rip-off Britain is not so much in the headlines these days but this is largely because of massive deflation in Prices of clothing and other consumer goods imported from China. Car manufacturers have also had to work extremely hard to keep Prices down, and anyone working for a car manufacturer who proposes a Product development that might increase the cost of manufacture by £1 per vehicle is not doing their career prospects any good. Dignam's point that the consumer had more information than ever before is even more the case 10 years on, when the majority of consumers are able to compare online Prices of most categories of goods.

Problems of Perception

Advertising man Rory Sutherland, former president of the Institute of Practitioners in Advertising (IPA), notes that most problems are problems of *Perception*. He thinks that many problems in life can be solved by addressing Perception rather than going through the pain of trying to change reality. He quotes the example of Eurostar, whose engineers proposed to improve the journey by spending £6 billion on some additional high speed capacity and thus shortening the journey time from London to Paris by 40 minutes. He muses that a better use of the investment would be to employ the world's best supermodels, male and female, serving Château Petrus throughout the journey. In such a case he suggests people would ask for a longer journey time and there would still be change out of the £6 billion!

But he also quotes real-life examples of such lateral thinking. King Frederick the Great of Prussia wanted to introduce the potato to the

Prussian diet as an alternative source of carbohydrate to wheat, and thus diversify the risk of food failure. At first he tried to enforce this view with quite draconian rules but the Prussian peasants refused to adopt the potato, which they said was not good enough for their dogs. So Frederick tried a different tack. He decreed that the potato was a royal vegetable and only the royal family could consume it. He limited its culture to a royal garden, which was to be guarded day and night by the royal guard. Except that his orders to the guard were not to guard it very well. Sure enough a commodity that was exclusive to royalty was soon in demand and quantities of potatoes were stolen and soon grown throughout the kingdom.

Sutherland extrapolates from these imaginary and historical examples to show how problems have been solved or brands have been built based on embracing Perception as the central element to be improved.

The law of Perception

In Chapter 10 (Positioning) I quoted the chapter headings of Ries and Trout's book *The 22 Immutable Laws of Marketing* (1993). Chapter 4 is entitled 'The Law of Perception' in which they set out to demonstrate that marketing is not a battle of Product. It is a battle of Perception. They assert that marketers who are obsessed with establishing facts to make sure that truth is on their side are deluded:

> There is no objective reality. There are no facts. There are no best Products. All that exists in the world of marketing are Perceptions in the minds of the customer or prospect. The Perception is the reality. Everything else is an illusion.

They root this assertion in observations of human nature. They argue that most people think they are better Perceivers than others. Consequently truth and Perception become fused in the mind, leaving no difference between the two. Marketing people focus on facts because they believe in objective reality. But the trap here is that you only have to alter slightly your own Perceptions to believe that you actually have the best Product. Changing the Perceptions of others is altogether more difficult.

The famous example of New Coca-Cola, which I touched on briefly in Chapter 1 (Product), is an example of how this can go wrong. For many years Pepsi Cola had a successful campaign based on blind tests. In blind tests fractionally more people preferred Pepsi to Coke because it is slightly sweeter and so more people with their sweeter tooth prefer it. So the executives at Coca-Cola reformulated their Product to be even sweeter than Pepsi.

Sure enough, in research it was preferred. But not in the marketplace because it was not the traditional Coke that most people Perceived that they preferred. Fortunately for Coca-Cola shareholders the mistake was recognized quite early and Classic Coke was restored, even though in blind tests it was the least favoured Product.

The psychology of Perception

The problem with Ries and Trout's approach is that it might lead the marketer to neglect Product design and quality in order to concentrate entirely on trying to manage Perceptions. In my view, you need to do both. I favour those kinds of marketing that concentrate on both rational and emotional arguments for buying a Product. My favourite examples that I have quoted in this book do both. They work on both sides of the brain. But I use this expression loosely because the degree to which different sides of the brain control different behaviours, such as creativity or logic, is greatly exaggerated in the popular literature.

Brain function lateralization is evident in the phenomena of right- or left-handedness and of right or left ear preference, but a person's preferred hand is not a clear indication of the location of brain function. Although 95 per cent of right-handed people have left-hemisphere dominance for language, only 19 per cent of left-handed people have right-hemisphere dominance for language function.

In psychology, Perception is the process of attaining awareness of or understanding information. The word 'Perception' means 'receiving, collecting, action of taking possession, apprehension with the mind or senses'. Perception is one of the oldest fields in psychology. What we Perceive is a result of connections between experiences and knowledge, including one's culture, and the interpretation of the Perceived. If we cannot relate what we see to what we have experienced before, or have some knowledge of, then we are unlikely to Perceive it.

We can distinguish two types of consciousness that enables Perception. First, any occurrence that is both observable and physical, which is known as phenomenal. The second is psychological. The first is simply a matter of opening one's eyes and seems to be entirely a matter of sight. Thus it is usually not present in the absence of sight. But some of us can visualize objects in our mind's eye; however, this is much less likely if we do not have prior experience of seeing the object. Thus the process of Perception alters what we see. If we have preconceived ideas they influence what we *Perceive* we see. We are unable to comprehend new information except through the prism of our existing knowledge. This is why in my opinion so much of recent educational theory has gone off the rails. If we allow children to simply follow their own ideas of what to learn they are restricted by their limited state of knowledge. The teacher should stretch the child by constantly opening up new lines of inquiry but always linking them to the existing roots of knowledge. When we see unfamiliar objects we try to make sense of them with our existing state of knowledge. This is the principle behind camouflage, which we find in nature and mimic in battle conditions. Preconceptions can influence how the world is Perceived. For example, one classic psychological experiment showed slower reaction times and less accurate answers when a pack of playing cards reversed the colour of the suit symbol for some cards (eg red spades and black hearts). Often those who are accustomed to driving on the right think it must be very difficult driving on the left, but to those of us who learnt to drive on the left it is normal and we may have difficulty when driving on the right. The reason why the British drive on the left is because they always did, even before the internal combustion engine and tarmac. The probable reason for that is that most people are right-handed and so wanted to be able to defend themselves with a sword against an attack from the other side of the road. There is archaeological evidence that the Romans drove their chariots on the left throughout their Empire. The reason why countries in continental Europe now drive on the right is that they used to drive on the left like us but then Napoleon decided to change it all by decree (as with so much he did). He wanted to show that he had the Power to do such things.

Corporate branding

In 1995 John Balmer published an interesting article in the *Journal of General Management* called 'Corporate branding and connoisseurship'. He observed that the rise of corporate brands in the 1990s should have compelled senior managers to develop a deeper understanding and proficiency in corporate brand management. If effectively managed, the corporate brand could serve as a critical differentiator of the company in a commercial environment that was becoming increasingly competitive. Properly managed corporate brands also result in consistent consumer demand, added-value to Products and services, higher financial margins, protection from competitors and high-quality staff. Corporate brand management could be successful if it was based upon a clear corporate mission and philosophy, an understanding of the corporate Personality and corporate identity, and reliable information pertaining to the Perceptions of stakeholders regarding the organization. It is not my purpose here to go into the issues of corporate branding versus individual Product branding but rather to ask how Balmer's last point about 'reliable information pertaining to the Perceptions of stakeholders regarding the organization' is to be addressed.

Perception management

What is required is Perception management, and one of the techniques of Perception management is perceptual mapping. This is a graphic technique to plot and visualize relative Perceptions. The marketer selects the axes that they wish to plot, say relative Price and relative quality, and then plots the competitive Products on the graph. The marketer can do this to measure their own Product position relative to its competitors or to see where there may be a gap in the market – in which they could position a new Product entry. It is important to remember that in perceptual mapping the marketer is mapping the actual Perceptions of consumers, not their own Perception of how the market is organized. It is a common error to fall into the latter trap and simply convince yourself and your colleagues that all is well. Nevertheless I would still expect the marketing manager in a classically organized company to have insight and appreciation as to what is happening in their market. But I would also expect them to validate their judgements on the basis of evidence. As Scott Bedbury, the branding expert and former top marketing guru at Nike and Starbucks, says: 'It's not enough to have a great Product or service anymore. The world is full of Products and services that work. You have to take stock of how your brand makes consumers feel.'

Another common error is to listen too much to the sales force. The sales force will usually report on competitive activity. This is an important source of useful market data. However, if one relies on it too much it will start to distort behaviour. An example of this is the beer market in Japan. For many years Asahi brand was second to Sapporo. The complaining Asahi sales force would report back to their head office of all Sapporo activities, including their Promotions and discounts and all the other inducements they offered their distributors to stock and recommend their brand of beer. Asahi marketing management would blindly imitate this activity, which of course had the effect of changing nothing. Finally, a dazzling insight came to one of the marketers and he decided to develop a new type of beer. This was launched as Asahi Dry, an inspired piece of lateral thinking in the beer market! The Japanese love innovation and promptly tried the new Product, which tasted not only different but good and became a best-seller. Asahi had changed the market Perceptions of beer and done so by ignoring the advice of their sales force.

Positioning and Perception are essentially two sides of the same coin. It is rather like speech and hearing. Positioning is what I say to the market. Perception is what the market hears. As more marketing communication becomes *received* (as with social media) rather than *directed* (as with advertising) it is increasingly important to recognize the importance of Perception. It remains vital to stay true to the intended positioning – all brand activity must correspond to the positioning model – but it is equally vital to understand changing Perceptions in the market. This is not always a matter for precision but often more a matter of insight.

Summary

In this chapter we have:

- recognized the importance of Perception in the market even when it may not be correct in terms of fact;
- showed how some brands have established unassailable positions by encouraging unique Perceptions of themselves;
- seen how many problems are those of Perception – and it may be easier to change that than to change reality (on the other hand we have also seen how some Perceptions will be very hard to change);
- considered the process of Perception in psychology;
- discussed Perception management and the technique of perceptual mapping;
- looked at the role of Perceptions in building national spirit.

PART FOUR
Behaviours

People

16

If you leave us our money, our buildings, and our brands, but take away our People, the company will fail. But if you take away our money, our buildings, and our brands, but leave us all our People, we can rebuild the whole thing in a decade.

RICHARD DEUPREE, PRESIDENT, PROCTER & GAMBLE 1947

It is not original to state that *People* make the difference but it is nevertheless true. During my time at Sony I had the pleasure to work with a great Japanese boss called Shin Takagi. Shin sadly died in 2009 but he left his mark on many of us. He had unique experience in Sony in that he had held senior positions in Germany, Italy and Spain, where he founded the sales company, the United States and the UK. I asked him why there were so many problems in one particular country. He told me, 'There are no good guys!'

Good People are particularly important in marketing because marketing should take the lead, so it is necessary to find People who can make a difference with their *Positiveness* and *Proactiveness*, their *Professionalism*, their *Passion* and *Pride*, and their *Personality*. These are the qualities on which we will focus in the remaining chapters of the book. In this chapter we will consider how we can find such People, how we assess them, how we train and develop them, how we can build teams around them. We will look at some of the specific skills of marketing as well as some of the general skills that any decent manager must possess or acquire. And we will consider the different types of marketer, because in my experience there are many different types that can be effective.

Recruitment

Whether you make an appointment to a key marketing position from outside or inside your organization you must still go through a programme of recruitment. I don't say this to comply with some employment law or some internal regulation but because it is best practice. The processes should be the same. As in everything the process starts with a plan, in this case a specification for the job to be done, a job description. Next we need a candidate profile. What are the ideal qualities we are looking for? What minimum level of experience is required? Answers to these questions should be thought through and carefully considered. This is a serious matter.

We may wish to advertise the position, or go through a recruitment agency. For more senior positions we may want to use a recruitment consultant, a 'head-hunter'. But in every case the process is broadly the same. We are looking for as much information about the candidate as possible. We can get this information in a variety of ways and we should use as many ways as possible. The candidate's job application should not only present a curriculum vitae but also a statement as to why his or her particular skillset and experience is appropriate to the role. In interviews we should structure the questions in such a way as to probe the candidate's relevant track record and their motivation for doing the job. We may set up group situations to see how the candidates interact with each other in a problem-solving situation. We will seek references from previous employers. And, most important, we will involve colleagues in our decision.

Most of us think we are good judges of People but research actually shows that we are quite likely to make up our minds about someone within a few minutes of meeting them. In recruitment we should resist making decisions too early and let the process unfold of gaining as much information as possible.

We must also remember that this is a two-way process, and the candidate must have as much opportunity to find out whether the job really is the right one for them. They must be able to ask about the company's performance, its prospects for the future. What are their own prospects of further advancement beyond the present role? If the candidate is unsuccessful they should still go away with a positive impression of the company. When I was recruited to join Sony to run its consumer Products business in the UK the recruitment process was drawn out over several months. The head-hunter from Egon Zehnder asked me if I was getting impatient with this. I said no, because I felt that at each meeting both sides made progress. It was like a courtship – and so it proved because I had 10 very happy and successful years there. By contrast, when I have had less happy or successful experiences it has sometimes followed a much shorter period of recruitment in which both sides may not have done adequate due diligence.

I was trained to interview both at Procter & Gamble and then again at Mars. In Pedigree Petfoods a group of sales managers were sent on a course in some personnel management techniques of which interviewing was one.

Our instructor for the day played the role of a candidate for a position as one of our sales representatives. He outlined his fictitious CV on the blackboard and then gave us all a chance to ask him questions. By the time it got round to me all the relevant questions seemed to have been asked so I asked my old standby that I had experienced in my own first job interview for Procter & Gamble: 'What do you do for fun?' Our instructor in a rather offhand and exasperated way said that he liked to go grass track racing, daring me to deduce anything from that. Then he announced that we had all failed because none of us had spotted the two-year gap in his CV and so failed to check what occurred at the time. His fictitious persona had gone to borstal!

Checking information is not always easy. On one occasion I needed to recruit a senior manager in the United States. I briefed a head-hunter based in California whom I met personally when I was attending a trade show in Las Vegas. She produced a shortlist and I flew back to Los Angeles to interview them. One seemed best to me because of the way he picked up on our Product proposition and suggested that his experience selling the added value of a technical component would be of great help to us. I asked him to fly to England, where he met other members of the team and all were impressed. We hired him and then the problems started. He used up a lot of corporate resource but achieved very little. After nine months I decided enough was enough and went over to the United States to terminate his contract. A few weeks later we came across his revised CV that he had inadvertently mailed to his old e-mail addresses. He was now claiming all sorts of success during his brief time with us. I wondered just how much of his original CV had been true.

Assessment

Whether at the recruitment stage or later, we may wish to assess the abilities of an individual. Again, all of us think we are good judges of character or performance. And in the case of performance – well, it's easy isn't it, because we have the evidence of the numbers. Yet it is not easy because there are many factors that can contribute to the numbers and we must be able to assess the individual from a much wider perspective. We again seek a range of information. Some employers seek psychometric evidence at the recruitment stage and this is a good policy provided they have already gone through an exercise of deciding their corporate values and what behaviour and characteristics are deemed appropriate in the delivery of these values. Myers-Briggs is a very popular testing procedure largely based on Jungian analysis. Fundamental to the Myers-Briggs Type Indicator (MBTI) is the theory of psychological type as originally developed by Carl Jung. Jung proposed the existence of two dichotomous pairs of cognitive functions: 1) the 'rational' (judging) functions: *thinking* and *feeling*; 2) the 'irrational' (perceiving) functions: *sensing* and *intuition*. Jung suggested that these functions are expressed in either an introverted or extroverted form. From Jung's original concepts, Briggs and Myers developed their own theory of psychological type on which the MBTI is based.

Jung's typological model regards psychological type as similar to left- or right-handedness: individuals are either born with, or develop, certain preferred ways of thinking and acting. The MBTI sorts some of these psychological differences into four opposite pairs, or dichotomies, with a resulting 16 possible psychological types. None of these types are better or worse; however, Briggs and Myers theorized that individuals naturally prefer one overall combination of type difference. The 16 types are referred to by an abbreviation of four letters. For instance: 1) ESFP – extroversion (E), sensing (S), feeling (F), perception (P); 2) INTJ – introversion (I), intuition (N), thinking (T), judgement (J). And so on for all 16 possible type combinations. This is useful in career planning, team building, leadership assessment and a variety of other situations but it is not generally seen as appropriate in recruitment. It is important to remember that this type of psychometric analysis is not judgemental and there are no winners and losers.

In my opinion a more useful test is offered by Dr Roger Birkman. Birkman flew bomber missions in Europe for the United States Army Air Corps. He began to explore differences between individuals while serving as a pilot and a pilot instructor. The impact of visual and interpersonal misperceptions on pilot performance and student learning abilities led him to the study of psychology. By 1951 he had developed his original 'Test of Social Comprehension'. Birkman developed his testing instrument as a self-report questionnaire eliciting responses about perception of self, social context and occupational opportunities. The test itself was created not from existing psychological theory, but through exhaustive empirical research conducted in the workplace. Birkman was interested in application rather than academic study.

The Birkman Method integrates needs measurements to assess the occupational interests that shape career and job-role fit. As a result, it does not describe an individual in a vacuum but rather in the complex, dynamic reality of the workplace. The unique construction and comparative database of the Birkman Method provides powerful insight into what specifically drives a person's behaviour, creating greater choice and more self-responsibility. Since its introduction in 1950, the Birkman Method has been used by more than 2 million People and 5,000 organizations worldwide, including corporations, not-for-profit organizations, governmental agencies, and individuals in their hiring, retention, motivational and organizational development activities. It has been verified by extensive reliability and validity studies.

I was introduced to the Birkman Method by an old friend, Andrew Austin, himself a former RAF officer who has the representational rights for the method in the United Kingdom. Andy took me personally through the method and then gave me my own so-called Personal DNA Report. This shows my relative strengths in creative planning and design, expediting and technical, communications and marketing, and fiscal and administration. From this I can see specifically my aptitude for different professions. I am glad to say that marketing, sales and employee relations / training appear highly in my list but so do social service and counselling, and artistic careers, while book-keeping and the petrochemical industry are very low down!

Training and development

Once you have made your staff selection and appointed them to the role, the process of training and development begins: it starts with an induction programme. I have often come across what I call 'Friday night salesman–Monday morning manager' syndrome, where internal candidates are promoted because they are seen as excellent in their current roles and so it is assumed that they will make good managers. But there is a world of difference between achieving good results on one's own and achieving them through others. In every case there needs to be a proper assessment made. As the Chinese proverb has it: 'If you want one year of prosperity, grow grain. If you want 10 years of prosperity, grow trees. If you want 100 years of prosperity, grow People.'

Training should begin with an appropriate period of induction. This should encompass a proper explanation of the role; introduction to all reports, peers and other interested colleagues; a session with the person's direct manager in which the key responsibilities of the role are laid out, targets are set and agreed, and ways of working are clarified. At Sony I benefited from an excellent induction set out for me by my first Japanese boss, Nobu Watanabe. After I had been with the company for a few weeks he invited me to spend an entire day with him at the company's flat in London, during which he explained what my objectives were to be in the first three years; how he expected me to behave; what issues he expected me to bring to his attention; and several other valuable lessons to which I will return in a later chapter. I wonder how many bosses are so generous of their time but, of course, it is a good investment of time to spend a day on such issues early in a new relationship and thus avoid many misunderstandings later.

I was further grateful to Nobu a few months later when I was hiring a new sales director. The incumbent had taken one look at me and promptly resigned having been overlooked for my role. At first I ran sales directly myself to get to know my salespeople better and also as many of their customers as possible. But clearly I needed a fulltime Sales Director. After an extensive search I found the individual, Jerry Parker, who I thought would be best able to do the job. Nobu then interviewed him and said he supported my decision but observed that Jerry lacked specific experience of the consumer electronics market and recommended that he should spend some time as part of his induction working with a dealer. Jerry followed this advice and liked to tell the story later of how proud he felt the first day he sold a refrigerator. Once Jerry had completed this part of his induction his launch as the new sales director was far more effective and he went on to enjoy a very successful career with Sony over the next 20 years or so.

Training follows a simple cycle. First, *explanation* – the trainer explains how to do a particular job. Then *demonstration* – the trainer demonstrates the function to the trainee. Then *imitation* – the trainee imitates the trainer and performs the function. Then *consolidation* – if the trainee has shown understanding of what is required then the trainer leaves him or her alone to consolidate this piece of the job before returning at a later date to check that this is still working and, if so, to teach a new skill using the same cycle of explanation, demonstration, imitation and consolidation.

Development consists of giving an individual more and more challenges in order to develop their abilities and confidence. This can be done both on the job and alongside the job. In a large organization there will be many opportunities to test an individual's qualifications for additional responsibility in projects, test markets, etc. In smaller organizations the opportunities come even more naturally as there is more likely to be an attitude of everyone 'mucking in together' and, in such situations, you soon see the cream coming to the top.

In Mars I learnt that the company liked to develop its People by moving them around different functions. Forrest Mars Sr had many strokes of genius but one was to treat all executive functions as equal. This allowed him to swap executives about without getting into difficult discussions about differential compensation. Top management usually came from within and would only emerge after extensive experience of different functions. Thus it was most unlikely that, say, a marketing manager would be able to go up the company to director level without spending a good period of development time in a different function such as procurement or manufacturing. I will return to this theme in Chapter 18 (Professionalism), because I know there are many marketers who are jealous of their professional standards and resent interlopers coming into their field without apparent qualifications. But having seen it work with great success in Mars and having used it myself with similar success in Sony I have huge confidence in this technique of management development.

Team building

An important aspect of management is team building. It is particularly important in marketing, not only because marketing should provide the lead in the company as representative of the market that the company exists to serve, but also because of the wide variety of skills that are needed to run a successful marketing operation. One of my successors at Sony, Steve Dowdle, was a very effective team builder. He would knit together a team using the different strengths of the individuals in the team to complement each other and then provide his own energy and drive to keep the team motivated. I first saw him do this when he ran the audio Product management team at Sony UK, which he called 'The A Team'. While all the individuals in his team had specific Product responsibilities he also assigned each of them a wider role. Thus Geoff Muge, his hi-fi systems Product manager, was also given creative leadership in dealing with agencies. Tim Mahne, his hi-fi separates Product manager, was the most computer literate in the team and looked after all the spreadsheets, tracking forecasting, purchasing, sales margins and inventories. Yoshi Nakamura was the Product manager in charge of personal audio, including Walkman, Discman etc, but Yoshi also took the lead on all communication with the factories in Japan. Carl Rose, who assisted Yoshi on his huge range of Products and looked after the accessory range, was a gregarious character who took the lead in relations with the sales force. The team all understood each other's roles, respected each other, worked and played hard and were highly successful in driving for market leadership in nearly all the categories for which they were responsible. All of them went on to senior roles within Sony.

Linked to this is the need to make sure that credit is shared. One of the finest bosses I ever worked for was John Coady, president of global development when I was at Mars. It was John who asked me to go to Chile and start a marketing company there. He used to say, 'If only we did not worry who gets the credit how much more progress we could make.' Success has many fathers, as they say, while most run away from failure. But this is odd because we learn so much more from failure. Bill Gates, surely one of the most successful businessmen the world has ever known, is reputed to have deliberately set out to recruit some vice presidents who had known their share of failure in their careers; he did this because most of his senior team had known only the extraordinary success of Microsoft. Gates wanted someone around him who would be there if the wheels started to come off and who would say, 'I recognize this problem, I've faced it before and this is what we should do.'

Management

There have been many books written on management and this book is intended for the marketer who wants to understand that there is more to marketing than the four Ps. But if they have ambition to get very far they will have to learn about management. They will need some of the qualities that I am going to describe in the following chapters. One of the most outstanding managers I ever knew was Akio Morita, the co-founder of Sony. He wrote a short pamphlet with his thoughts on management, which is much more valuable in its insights than many of the lengthy books on the subject, in particular his chapter on Positiveness, as Morita thought that this was the first requirement of a manager. He also spoke in an interesting way on 'trust':

> Trust your People. This is a most important rule. Too often, top managers are overly concerned about whether or not they themselves are trusted. But if you want to be trusted, you have to trust your People first. If you trust them they will trust you in return.

> Trusting your subordinates means being magnanimous enough not to give overly detailed instructions. Relations with subordinates may easily become soured if you are overly eager to exert leadership and give exhaustive instructions.
>
> On the other hand, I am always saying, 'Don't trust anybody!' at the company. While it may sound as if I am contradicting myself, my point is that it is very important to follow up and check whenever you give instructions or ask other People to do something for you. You have to get your subordinates in the habit of always reporting back to you. See to it that the 'Plan-Do-Check' cycle is carefully followed.

This ability to hold two apparently contradictory notions in one's head at the same time and resolve them is one of the principal lessons I learnt from the Japanese.

Leadership

We can see from these two contrasting styles – the visionary leadership of Akio Morita versus the deadline, bottom line-driven autocratic management style – the importance of leadership. Yesterday's leadership skills will not work in today's fast-moving and evolving world. Only creative leaders who are visionary and empathetic will succeed. I offer the following suggestions as to what you can do to succeed as a creative leader:

- Instead of commanding, coach your team and organization towards success.
- Don't manage People, empower them. The know-how, experience and solutions are often out there; it's a matter of helping People discover them.
- Cultivate respect by giving it, instead of demanding it.
- Know how to manage both success and failure.
- Show graciousness in your management rather than greediness. Be humble about your successes and, whenever possible, give someone else the opportunity to shine.

Johann Wolfgang von Goethe summed it up when he wrote, 'Treat People as if they were what they ought to be and you help them to become what they are capable of being.'

> The Red Arrows are a famous squadron of performance pilots. Anyone who has ever seen their display cannot fail to have been impressed by their breathtaking, dare-devil acrobatics. I met some of them once and they told me that after every single performance without fail they have a debrief in which they each contribute a verdict on that performance. Starting with the senior officer they will admit to the slightest error and discuss ways in which it can be avoided in future. Such a discipline is no doubt essential in such a dangerous pursuit. But it is still a valuable practice in marketing.

The skills of marketing

There are both general and specific skills in marketing. The general skills that any manager needs include high levels of numeracy and literacy. These are measurable and can be assessed at the time of recruitment. Less easy to assess but also highly important is emotional intelligence, a concept that has come more into fashion in recent years. Someone may have high numerical and verbal reasoning scores but lack insight into human behaviour and not relate well to colleagues. The specific skills of marketing include analysis and the ability to reason. Creativity is highly desirable and, again, abstract reasoning is capable of measurement and can be assessed at time of recruitment. Leadership qualities are essential.

The 10 types of marketer

I have identified 10 types of marketer, some better than others:

- *Cerebral marketer* – highly intelligent and treats marketing as an intellectual exercise. Mainly concerned with strategy and likes to develop theories of how things work. At best can be a very useful member of a team; even its leader provided he or she is surrounded by People who are good at execution and following things through. Drummond Hall, with whom I worked at Mars, was one such marketer and went on to become a highly successful chief executive of Dairy Crest.

- *Competent marketer* – process driven, he or she manages their portfolio in a structured way, primarily focused on the calendar. This type of marketer may lack insight or brilliance but is reliable and will achieve modest success. I have known many such marketers and they are useful to have around but are not leadership material.
- *Cut and run marketer* – primarily focused on their own career development and their horizon is the next job offer. The average length of service of marketing directors in general can be as little as 18 months and this leads to excessive short termism. Another feature of such People is that they seek to develop high profiles outside their own company, appearing frequently in the pages of the marketing press. They often take the credit for celebrated advertising campaigns even though in all certainty the advertising ideas came from their agency.
- *Comptroller marketer* – bottom line driven. Their primary focus is the profit and loss account, and while in itself this is no bad thing it can often be at the expense of building long-term brand equity. Someone who has enjoyed huge success is Sir Martin Sorrell, who turned himself from being Finance Director to the Saatchi Brothers to leading the largest marketing service corporations in the world in his own right.
- *Cowardly marketer* – avoids decisions and keeps their head down. Abdicates the true responsibilities of being a marketer and providing the leadership of market focus. Likely to be managing a portfolio of cash cows and dogs and is temperamentally unable to renew them through innovation.
- *Commercial marketer* – largely sales oriented and spends much of his or her time either with the sales force or even seeing customers on their own. Their approach is more one of trade marketing and they have little concept of developing a consumer proposition. May be found managing a brand that has known better days and now depends for its survival on trade support.
- *Creative marketer* – focused on the marketing communications part of the job and likes to spend his or her time with the agencies developing new campaigns. There have been many successful marketers who began as copywriters and broadened their role either on the client side or on the agency side, eg John Hooper, who began as a copywriter at Procter & Gamble then founded his own

promotional agency with a colleague before spending a distinguished spell as Director General of the Incorporated Society of British Advertisers (ISBA).

- *Cavalier marketer* – a risk taker who wants to be an entrepreneur but takes risks with the company's money. As all gamblers, he or she will enjoy some moments of success but is likely to lose in the long run.
- *Charismatic marketer* – relies on their own personality to lead and inspire others. Sir Richard Branson is the most famous and successful example of this type. I am almost precisely the same age as Sir Richard and have observed that his businesses chime with his age, thus he got into music publishing in his twenties, air travel in his thirties and gymnasia in his forties. When he starts a Virgin funeral business I will start to worry.
- *Champion marketer* – an all-rounder. Well trained at one of the classic business schools of the real corporate world such as Procter & Gamble or Unilever he or she understands all the aspects of marketing and has a range of techniques to call on. Sir Crispin Davies, one-time chief executive of Reed Elsevier, is one who comes to mind. Crispin launched Crest toothpaste in the UK for Procter & Gamble when I had the pleasure to work with him and I have followed his career with interest.

I hope it is clear from this summary that there are several different ways in which someone can be successful at marketing. But common to all of them will be the need for strong roots in one or more of the multifaceted disciplines of marketing, be it planning or copywriting, sales or Product development. Few of us are strong in all the suits – as a bridge player knows, it is impossible: what matters is how you play your hand. There are no supermen, and in any case Superman was vulnerable to Kryptonite.

Summary

In this chapter we have:

- introduced the behavioural element into marketing, starting with People;
- discussed the importance of recruitment;

- compared different methods of assessment, including Myers-Briggs and Birkman;
- explained the cycle of training and development;
- contrasted styles of management;
- emphasized the role of leadership;
- considered the skills required in marketing;
- described the 10 types of marketer.

Positiveness

The meek shall inherit the earth but not its mineral rights.

JOHN PAUL GETTY 1

You gotta accentuate the Positive
Eliminate the negative
Latch on to the affirmative
Don't mess with Mister In Between

JOHNNY MERCER

On landing at Hastings in 1066 William, Duke of Normandy, slipped. Knowing that his men would regard this as a bad omen, he picked up two handfuls of earth and proclaimed: 'See, I have taken England with both hands!' Some People are naturally Positive while others have to work at it. Whichever category you are in, if you want to be successful at marketing you must be *Positive*.

Returning to Akio Morita's thoughts on management:

> The substance of management is organizing as many People as possible to accomplish larger tasks by effectively drawing the best from each one of them.
>
> To do this you require personal magnetism. It is important for you to attract your People, that is, to be attractive enough to magnetize other People so that they willingly listen to you and work for you. To put it bluntly, if you are lacking in this magnetism, you are not going to be qualified for top management in business, no matter how clever you may be.
>
> What then is this 'personal magnetism'? First, you need to be a *neaka* person, a person who responds to things in a Positive way. A negative-minded *nekura* person is not qualified for management.

Mr Morita went on to talk about charisma, honesty about one's own mistakes, magnanimity, recognition and trust. But his first requirement of a top manager was for that person to be '*neaka*' or Positive.

As a young sales representative with Procter & Gamble Positiveness was one of the qualities most highly regarded in a future manager. I still have in my possession my appraisal where I had let things slip. The appraisal reads:

> Good instore but you need to be more influential and forceful in meetings. Your first reaction tends to be negative even though your resulting conclusion may be Positive. This tends to reduce the effect you have on your colleagues.

Six months later these words had had the desired effect:

> Your performance since July has been marked by a good degree of diligence which has brought you the rewards. You are currently the top man in the Unit and this Review is sufficiently satisfactory for you to begin a Section Management Training Programme. Your priorities are now two-fold:
>
> 1 To develop the business man image.
> 2 To remove any doubt that you are the number 1 man in the District producing ideas and imaginative approaches to business.

I was 23 and keen to live up to these expectations. I set out to contribute at least one idea per week while letting all and sundry know about my achievements. Brought up to respect modesty I overcame this and learnt how to 'brag'. It was part of the game. I took on a whole series of additional responsibilities and six months later got my reward in promotion.

Persistence

Persistence was also a quality in high regard at Procter & Gamble and is closely related to Positiveness. Indeed persistence was deeply embedded in the corporate DNA. The research scientists looking for a treatment for dandruff tested 20,000 compounds before settling on zinc pyrithione, the key ingredient in Head & Shoulders shampoo. This calls to mind the dedication of Thomas Edison, the famous US inventor who held over 1,000 individual patents and said 'We now know a thousand ways not to build a light bulb.'

In sales, this quality is particularly valued in negotiation with a customer. The key question is: 'When do you accept the answer "No"?' One story that did the rounds involved an area manager demonstrating persistence to his trainee salesman in a tough part of Liverpool. He chose a particularly difficult traditional grocer and set up his sales tools, his bag of samples etc on the grocer's counter. He went through his presentation and asked for the order. The grocer said he had no intention of buying anything that day as he didn't need anything, had plenty of stock, was too busy and a host of other reasons. The area manager tried to overcome all of these objections but to no avail. The grocer lost his temper, picked up the bag of samples and all the other sales tools and went to the door and threw them into the street. The area manager went into the street followed by his terrified trainee. The manager picked up all his equipment, told the trainee to follow him and mark his words, marched back into the shop, set up all his sales tools once more on the counter and then, leaning across the counter, he smiled at the grocer and said: 'We will have our little joke, won't we? Now how about this suggested order?' He got the order.

So when should you take no for an answer? In my experience the first no may mean no but it may mean you have not done enough to convince me. The second no may mean no but it may also mean I'm still thinking. The third no probably does mean no. Jeremy Paxman may not agree, judging by his famous interrogation of the former Home Secretary, Michael Howard, as to whether he had threatened to overrule Derek Lewis, head of the prison service, after a damaging report on a number of prison escapes. He asked the same question 12 times (14 if you include different wording of the same point earlier in the interview). Howard actually gave quite a lot of information but did not directly answer the question.

Jay Levinson, the advertising guru who was the creative genius behind Marlboro Man and the Jolly Green Giant, and who made a fortune from his book *Guerrilla Marketing* (1984), says: 'the problem with admen today is that they secretly want to be actors or create some lavish piece of artwork rather than make money for their clients, which is what it all boils down to. More important is persistence and finding cheap ways to reach audiences.'

Responsibility

Mars in its five principles specifies *responsibility*, which I think covers related ground, as follows:

> As individuals, we demand total responsibility from ourselves; as associates, we support the responsibilities of others.
>
> We choose to be different from those corporations where many levels of management dilute personal responsibilities. All associates are asked to take

> direct responsibility for results. To exercise initiative and judgement and to make decisions as required. By recruiting ethical People well suited to their jobs and trusting them, we ask associates to be accountable for their own high standards.

George Bernard Shaw put this well when he said: 'People are always blaming their circumstances for what they are. I don't believe in circumstances. The People who get on in this world are the People who get up and look for the circumstances they want and if they can't find them, make them.'

Motivation

At Sony I enjoyed planning our sales conferences, both internal and external. At our internal sales conferences I usually hired a motivational speaker. Some came from the world of sport such as Sebastian Coe, Duncan Goodhew and Will Carling. But one of our most appreciated speakers from the world of sport was not so well known for his own sporting ability but rather as a coach. Frank Dick, a former international athlete, served as chief coach to the British team at four Olympic Games, seven European Cups, three European Championships and three World Championships. It was during this period that the Great Britain and Northern Ireland athletics team rose to become a genuine Power in world athletics, led in particular by male track stars such as Sebastian Coe, Steve Ovett, Steve Cram and Dave Moorcroft, in addition to the double-Olympic decathlon champion Daley Thompson. Daley was coached by Frank and rose to become one of the world's greatest ever athletes. Frank also worked with Boris Becker, Gerhard Berger, Denise Lewis, Marat Safin and Katarina Witt, among other top sportsmen and women. He has gone on to a very successful writing and speaking career and tried to answer the question whether the lessons that work in sport can be applied to the world of business. He concludes that:

> Whatever you do in life it is almost inevitable that your performance will be assessed. To perform you need two basic attributes that when combined and developed make you a winner:
>
> – A desire to achieve
>
> – A set of skills in order to be able to achieve.

Translating this attitude into corporate behaviour it helps if you can instil a culture of self-belief with reinforcing corporate support. The story goes that

> Another brilliant motivational speaker I booked at a Sony sales conference is Christine Harvey. Christine wrote the best-selling books *Your Pursuit of Profit* (1988) and *Secrets of the World's Top Sales Performers* (1989). She has started several successful companies of her own and has travelled the world teaching top-flight executives how to sell, how to manage and how to motivate. She tells the story of how dolphins are trained. Apparently the trainers use a whistle to show approval of when a dolphin has successfully completed the desired manoeuvre such as soaring out of the water to a certain height. This reinforces Positive behaviour. After the conference I asked my friend, the late Jack Taylor, the former World Cup referee, with whom I had worked on a sponsorship deal, which whistle he used. The ACME Thunderer was the answer. I then ordered an ACME Thunderer whistle for each of the delegates to the conference. The sound of whistles went on for days.

in the Middle Ages a traveller came across two labourers hewing rock. He asked them what they were doing. The first said rather rudely, 'What does it look like? We're hewing rock'. He turned to the second and enquired, 'And what about you? Are you hewing rock?' He replied, 'No sir, I'm building a cathedral'.

Some modern businesses get this right. Ritz-Carlton is renowned for its successful employee engagement. To assist staff in delivering its refined, attentive service promise its internal motto is: 'We are ladies and gentlemen serving ladies and gentlemen'. Less successful was United Airlines in 1997 when it tried to reposition as the airline most centred on the passenger with its 'Rising' ad. Discontented flight attendants countered with their own campaign, CHAOS (Creating Havoc Around Our System). According to *USA Today,* the 'Rising' campaign was rated the second worst advertising programme for 1997:

> United officials admitted that the carrier's own customer service falls short of the mark desired by business travellers and announced it has used the findings to develop a new customer-driven initiative it hopes will revolutionize air travel in the next five to 10 years.

A website called 'Untied' was set up to channel complaints about the airline and it suggested: 'Here's a simple initiative we've been proposing: How about listening to your passengers' suggestions and complaints?'

Positive thinking

The most famous book on Positiveness is probably Dr Norman Vincent Peale's book, *The Power of Positive Thinking,* first published in 1952. The book promotes the concept of Positive thinking and while selling in millions has also polarized opinion. It came under strong criticism from mental health specialists, partly because Peale illustrates his thesis with several anecdotes that are hard to substantiate. Others say his techniques are nothing more than concealed hypnosis, while still others say that Peale exaggerates the fears in his readers and this leads to aggression.

But Peale still has his advocates such as Dr Tony Alessandra, another widely published author who writes:

> Positiveness means maintaining a state of Positive expectations about People and situations, including a Positive state of energy in your thoughts and emotional patterns. Dr Norman Vincent Peale's book, *The Power of Positive Thinking*, was published over 40 years ago and it continues to sell well because it contains such a universal truth: the attitudes we hold help to shape the reality we experience.

He states that there are three requirements. Positiveness is built on having your own Positive life philosophy, on knowing what strengths you have, and on surrounding yourself with other sources of Positiveness. It is important to avoid People with negative attitudes who drain your own energy.

Many People reduce this discussion to the hackneyed metaphor of: 'Is the glass half full or half empty?' Positive People, the optimists amongst us, are supposed to see it half full while negative People, the pessimists amongst us, see it as half empty. This is too simplistic. The answer to the question is both. The glass is half full and it is half empty. If I am enjoying a glass of wine and I have drunk half of it then I have enjoyed the experience. And I will enjoy the rest of the wine when I am ready to drink it. What really matters is the size of the glass.

Being Positive does not mean false optimism or unjustified optimism or not being realistic about the potential risks that you face. The Charge of the Light Brigade has gone down in history as a pointless loss of brave lives, thrown away on the altar of excess foolhardiness and rotten leadership. Actually it was a calculated gamble that came off – if you accept a loss of 20 per cent of your forces as worth the price of gaining the ground at the end of the valley and stopping the Russian guns positioned there. The whole Crimean War was pointless when judged against other purposeful wars either fought to defend the nation or its interests or to expand those interests.

The Crimean War was fought to support the Islamic nations of Turkey and its allies against the imperialism of Russia. The overall losses suffered by the British were staggeringly high and the Charge of the Light Brigade was not worse than the rest of the campaign. However, Tennyson wrote his famous poem within months and that is the version of history that most recall.

Negativity

President Bill Clinton said, 'Pessimism is an excuse for not trying and a guarantee to a personal failure.' Negativity is a powerful force that good marketing People seek to avoid and if possible eliminate. It can be useful to have a negative person around to validate ideas, but don't put them in a position of authority over others. Lord Broers, former vice chancellor of Cambridge University, once told me of a colleague he knew early in his long and distinguished career at IBM. If you had a great idea and then sought his views on the idea he would tell you all of the many ways why the idea would not work and also the countless times it had already been tried. Lord Broers, who is a keen sailor, likens such People to the lobsters that you catch on the keel of your boat, which then slow you down.

Writing this at a time of coming slowly out of a deep and painful recession I am reminded of an article I wrote in *Marketing* magazine in December 1992, also a time of recession:

> The other day in a meeting with a group of electrical retailers, I was asked how long I thought the recession would continue. 'As long as we keep talking about it,' I replied. The recession has taken over from the weather as Britain's favourite topic of conversation. How long will it continue? How deep will it go? When was it last as bad as this? What will the Government do about it?
>
> The sameness of these questions is particularly depressing. The weather is at least infinitely variable in Britain, which is why we take such perverse pleasure in discussing it. But the weather is a natural set of phenomena over which we have no control. The economy is at least partially the aggregate of a set of transactions over which all of us have significant influence.
>
> Marketing is sometimes defined as 'meeting customer needs', but it is very much more sophisticated than that. We need to eat, but we do not need to go out to a new fancy restaurant that was reviewed in the Times. A child needs to play but not to buy the latest Nintendo Gameboy. A business man needs to travel but not to fly first class. We all need to rest, but not to take an expensive holiday in Mauritius.

> The consumer's decision to engage in these added value and therefore premium priced transactions is entirely voluntary, and will be largely shaped by his/her degree of confidence. The economy could be a tenth the size and still everyone's basic needs could be comfortably accommodated.
>
> But who inspires this confidence? Do we rely wholly on the Government, or cannot we in business at least set out to share this responsibility? After all, as David Ogilvy implied in a different context, we are all consumers.
>
> Marketing sets the agenda in most companies. It is our role to define the vision, quantify the objectives and prepare the strategy to achieve these objectives. If you downsize your organization or, to use that other abominable euphemism, 'dehire', then it is a self-fulfilling prophecy.
>
> When you reduce your marketing investment you send very large smoke signals to your customers and your own workforce that you are not confident. Your customers will increase demands for discounts, and your sales People will become dispirited. You have then kick-started the negative spiral and will find it very slow and expensive to reverse.
>
> 'Ah,' I hear you say, 'that's all well and good, but the media will get in the way of my Positive upbeat message to the consumer'. Yes, the media does insist on seeing the glass as half empty not half full: we have 10% unemployment, not 90% employment.
>
> But we have influence. Why don't you give up listening to the eternally depressing Today programme as you drive to the office and listen to Mozart's Clarinet Concerto instead? Reach the office in a good mood.
>
> Remember, every time you pass on a piece of bad economic news, you are making your personal contribution to the delay in recovery.

More than 20 years on I am comfortable with most of this though I see I fell into the trap of the half-and-half glass. I've gone back to the morning ritualistic masochism of the *Today* programme and I think I would say that marketing is more about satisfying wants rather than needs, which is the whole point.

Advertising slogans

But Positiveness is not just an attitude of mind; it's also a *must* in communication. Let's consider advertising slogans. A slogan is a way of summarizing the central positioning of a brand. Table 17.1 lists some of the most memorable in the English language from the post-war era in the UK and the United States, with my own ratings for Positiveness.

TABLE 17.1 My ratings for positiveness of well-known slogans

Brand	Slogan	Positiveness Rating
American Express	'That will do nicely.'	***
Avis Rental Cars	'We're number two; we try harder.'	****
Charles Atlas	'You too can have a body like mine.'	***
Barnum & Bailey's Circus	'The greatest show on earth.'	****
Bounty	'The taste of paradise.'	***
British Airways	'The world's favourite airline.'	****
BMW	'The ultimate driving machine.'	*****
Cadbury's Milk Tray	'And all because the lady loves Milk Tray.'	***
Carlsberg	'Probably the best lager in the world.'	*****
Camay	'You'll be a little lovelier each day, with fabulous pink Camay.'	***
Coca-Cola	'It's the real thing.'	*****
De Beers	'A diamond is forever.'	*****
Eggs	'Go to work on an egg.'	**
Esso	'Put a tiger in your tank.'	***
Gillette	'The best a man can get.'	*****
Guinness	'Guinness is good for you.'	***
HSBC	'The world's local bank.'	**

(*Continued*)

TABLE 17.1 *(Continued)*

Brand	Slogan	Positiveness Rating
Haig Scotch Whisky	'Don't be vague. Ask for Haig.'	*****
Heinz baked beans	'Beanz Meanz Heinz.'	***
Hoover	'It beats as it sweeps as it cleans.'	**
The Independent	'It is. Are you?'	***
Intel	'Intel inside.'	**
Kellogg's Frosties	'They're grrrreat!'	***
Kentucky Fried Chicken	'Finger lickin' good.'	**
Kitkat	'Have a break – have a Kitkat.'	**
L'Oreal	'Because I'm worth it.'	****
M&Ms	'The milk chocolate that melts in your mouth – not in your hand.'	**
Mars bar	'A Mars a day helps you work, rest and play.'	***
Milk	'Drinka pinta milka day.'	***
Nike	'Just do it!'	*****
Orange	'The future's bright – the future's Orange.'	*****
Polo	'Polo – the mint with the hole.'	***
Remington	'I liked it so much I bought the company.'	*****
Singapore Airlines	'Singapore Girl, you're a great way to fly.'	****

(Continued)

TABLE 17.1 *(Continued)*

Brand	Slogan	Positiveness Rating
Tango	'You know when you've been Tango'd.'	*
Toyota	'The car in front is a Toyota.'	****
US Army	'Be all that you can be.'	*****
Johnny Walker	'Keep Walking.'	**
Yellow Pages	'Let your fingers do the walking.'	***
Zanussi	'The appliance of science.'	**

All of these slogans worked or they would not have been used for so long and become so memorable. But while some worked well on their own others only really worked with the visual image. The Tango advertising was very popular in the 1990s and the expression 'You know when you've been Tango'd' entered the vernacular, just as Courage's 'It's what your right arm's for' did in the 1960s. But these amusing campaigns are not really strong in Positive communication, rather they help People find their brands through joining some kind of club. Others communicate more of a technical benefit, which may be relevant but does not create the same Positive halo. BMW's 'The ultimate driving machine' encompasses a superlative, ie the most Positive rather than a comparative such as Toyota's 'The car in front is a Toyota', which tries to say the same thing but just falls short. Some just make a straightforward memorable brand statement in an assertive way. Haig's 'Don't be vague – ask for Haig' is a splendid, specific call for action, as is Nike's 'Just Do It'.

Perhaps the best of all is Viktor Kiam's long-running campaign for Remington shavers: 'I liked it so much I bought the company'. What stronger statement could anyone make? Phineas T. Barnum's 'The greatest show on earth' is also an extremely strong statement – but in the end it is a matter of opinion and many would not have agreed. British Airways' 'The world's favourite airline' was also an exceptionally strong claim and this was backed up by statistics, but they were somewhat spurious. As already mentioned, BA justified its claim on the basis of flying the most passengers *internationally*.

There were US airlines flying more passengers but domestically within the United States. Research into attitudes to airlines at that time would have showed a number of airlines that were *preferred* to BA, including Singapore Airlines, who appear in this list with a more subtle campaign based on their famous standards of service.

This brings us back to the issue of spin. It is normal human behaviour to present one's best side. Politicians have always been prone to exaggeration and even distortion of the truth, but recently we have seen the rise of spin doctors, Professional communicators who seek to ensure that their masters' words are always presented through the media in a more Positive light, thus putting a Positive spin on something. Such spin doctors justify their behaviour by saying that in a world of 24-hour media they have no choice but to counteract the cynicism of the media by presenting their masters' words in this way. They perhaps have a point because the media are cynical. Each side seems to bring the other to the point of cynicism and there is a race to the bottom. However, if you read newspapers from the late 19th century you will see that little has really changed.

Positiveness in social networks

The world is learning new forms of communication through social networks and any self-respecting brand now needs a strategy to manage the brand within the most popular of these, Facebook, Twitter and so on. But the old rules of communication still apply. Where social networks can be particularly useful to the brand manager is as a source of information about customer perceptions of their brand. The marketer's role is as much about bringing information from the market to the company and sharing it with colleagues as it is about sending messages to the market. But social networks can be used to reinforce Positive messages; there is no sense in advertising your troubles. There's no market for them.

Conclusion

Winston Spencer Churchill became Prime Minister at a time of desperation for Britain. Following the Dunkirk evacuation he used these words in the House of Commons:

> We shall not flag or fail. We shall go on to the end, we shall fight in France, we shall fight on the seas and oceans, we shall fight with growing confidence and

> growing strength in the air, we shall defend our Island whatever the cost, we shall fight on the landing grounds, we shall fight in the fields and in the streets, we shall fight in the hills; we shall never surrender.

He understood the power of a supremely Positive message to lift the spirits of the British People and rouse them to exceptional efforts. For this extraordinary achievement he is routinely described as Britain's greatest citizen. Nicholas Soames, his grandson, told me the following story he recalled from his youth. As a little boy he crept into his grandfather's bedroom and climbed up on the bed where Sir Winston was sitting smoking a cigar and dealing with his papers. Nicholas said: 'Grandfather, is it true that you are the greatest man in the world?' 'Yes,' said Churchill, "now push off!".

Perhaps Steve Radcliffe (see www.futureengagedeliver.com) had Churchill in mind when he developed his three simple principles of leadership:

1. Future: you've got to be good at imagining the future.
2. Engage: you need other People to want to build the future with you.
3. Deliver: you've got to make stuff happen.

And finally, on this theme, consider that Martin Luther King did not inspire People by saying 'I have a nightmare'.

Summary

In this chapter we have:

- considered the need for Positiveness in marketing;
- discussed the complementary roles of persistence and responsibility;
- underlined the vital role of motivation;
- evaluated the pros and cons of Positive thinking;
- described the alternative of negativity;
- outlined how advertising slogans use positivity;
- looked at Positiveness in social networks.

Professionalism

Sir,
I see that Hugo Rifkind describes Maria Eagle as a "qualified" solicitor ("Name that Eagle", Oct 12). Would that be as used in a "qualified success", implying somehow not complete?

I recall that after a road accident at which I offered help, my local newspaper reported that "luckily, a Professional anaesthetist was in the next car to arrive". I spent some time reassuring worried friends that, to my knowledge, there are no amateur anaesthetists practising in the UK.

DR NICK GROVES, CARDIFF, LETTER TO *THE TIMES*, 13 OCTOBER 2010

Marketing is not a *Profession* in the strict sense of the word. My online Oxford dictionary defines the word Profession as follows:

noun:

1. a paid occupation, especially one that involves prolonged training and a formal qualification: *his chosen Profession of teaching, a barrister by Profession*

   [treated as singular or plural], a body of people engaged in a particular Profession: *the legal Profession has become increasingly business-conscious*
2. an open but often false claim: *his Profession of delight rang hollow*
3. a declaration of belief in a religion; the declaration or vows made on entering a religious order; [mass noun] the ceremony or fact of being professed in a religious order: *after Profession she taught in Maidenhead*

Thus while marketing is a paid occupation, so is road sweeping. What distinguishes teaching and the bar as Professions is that both involve prolonged training and a formal qualification. There are many practitioners of marketing who have undergone prolonged training and received a formal qualification but they are not requirements to practise marketing. Many distinguished marketers have found their way into marketing almost by accident and then gone on to make their fame and fortune. This is frustrating to those who argue that marketing should be a Profession but I'm afraid the cat is out of the bag, the genie out of the bottle and the ship has left harbour.

The reason for this is largely historical. Guilds and Professions have an ancient history. Evidence of guilds and of craftsmen can be found in India, Egypt, Persia and Greece before the Christian era. They were formed and managed by the craftsmen themselves to act as a protective barrier against competition. They set out to enforce standards and would train successors but withhold secrets from them until they had proved loyal by years of service. European guilds emerged in the Middle Ages and evolved a set of characteristics that were common across Europe. Guilds were led by the master craftsmen, those who had mastered all of the skills of a craft. They trained apprentices who after a long period of apprenticeship working on the basic skills would develop into journeymen. A journey is literally the distance a man could travel in a day and thus the journeymen could spread out from the home town to get work. Only the best of them were let into the inner secrets of the master craftsmen to secure succession of the guild. It is no accident that the word 'mystery' is derived from the Latin word for a Professional skill. At their best the guilds looked after the weaker members of their movement, the poor, destitute, old and infirm. At their worst they acted as a closed shop keeping prices high and competition restricted.

Over time the guilds became controlled by the state through the use of letters of patent or royal charter. In England the livery companies emerged in the 12th century and received a royal charter to protect their craft or Profession. Thus they were monopolies and eventually the liveries fell into decline and were replaced by a more open market system. Philosophers as diverse as Rousseau, Adam Smith and Karl Marx all criticized the guilds.

The livery companies live on today but in a largely ceremonial way, although all of them have retained their philanthropic role. Livery companies will seek chartered status after reaching maturity and this involves a decision of the Privy Council. Her Majesty's Most Honourable Privy Council is a body of advisors to the British Sovereign. Its members are mainly senior politicians, who were or are members of either of the Houses of Parliament. The Privy Council was traditionally a Powerful institution, but its policy decisions are now made by one of its committees, the Cabinet of the United Kingdom. It advises the Sovereign on the exercise of the royal prerogative, government regulations and appointments where such matters are delegated to the council under the specific authority of Acts of Parliament. The council advises on the issuing of royal charters, which grant special status to incorporated bodies, and city and borough status to towns, and 'chartered' status to certain Professional or educational bodies.

> In 2010 my livery company, the Worshipful Company of Marketors, received its royal charter. In a flamboyant ceremony in the Guildhall, HRH the Duke of Edinburgh, the company's first Honorary Freeman, presented the charter to the Master. Mr Alex Galloway CVO, former Clerk of the Privy Council, gave us a short exposition of the history of the royal charter and what it meant for the company. He described the conditions that were necessary for a royal charter to be awarded to a Professional association. The Chartered Institute of Marketing is such an association and I am proud to be a Fellow. But I did not have to take any exams to achieve this status.

My father held Professional status as a chartered surveyor. He practised as a quantity surveyor for a national firm that he joined straight from school and retired as its senior partner after over 50 years' service, interrupted only by the war years that he spent in the army in Madagascar, Burma and Germany. After the war he worked hard to qualify, studying for his exams late at night. He qualified first as an Associate of the Royal Institute of Chartered Surveyors (ARICS) and later as a Fellow of the Royal Institute of Chartered Surveyors (FRICS). I remember his great chagrin when the institute decided, for mysterious reasons, to merge its interests with estate agents. Thus someone who had just set up shop in the high street to sell flats appeared to have the same Professional status. It is a minefield.

By contrast, the more established Professions insist on exams and a homogeneous membership and limit their membership accordingly. It is generally agreed that the three original Professions were divinity, medicine and the law. To this day membership of these Professions is controlled. Only the Church can ordain its members, and in the Roman Catholic Church and its offshoots such as the Anglican Church there is an unbroken apostolic succession back to the founders, the apostles. In the medical Professions there is very strong control over who can practise as a doctor or surgeon and in the UK there is a single association to which all belong. The British Medical Association is one of the most formidable trade unions in the country. The law is similarly controlled with access to the bar, controlled by the Inns of Court through the Bar Association. Only barristers can practise in most courts but the general public bring their grievances to court through solicitors who are all registered by the Law Society, another monopoly. In the United States each state has its own bar association and only those it recognizes can practise law. In Japan access to this Profession is controlled by the national government, which used to set the pass level at just 3 per cent in order to keep numbers low to avoid the development of a litigious society as they perceived the United States to be.

Having established that marketing lacks the historical status or rigour of more established and regulated Professions then why do I insist on Professionalism as one of the 20 Ps of marketing? I do so because I am looking for the highest Professional standards in marketing. Let us consider what academic study determines as Professional standards. I am grateful to the British Computer Society for their analysis of this in seeking to answer the question, 'What is a Profession?'. Their conclusion was that a review of current literature suggests that there is no hard and fast definition for defining a Professional. Often, doctors, lawyers and architects are used as paradigms. They considered work by Abraham Flexner, Ronald Pavalko, Jennifer Davies and Deborah Johnson.

In 1915 Dr Abraham Flexner described the criteria of a Profession, developed initially for the American Medical Association:

- A Professional possesses and draws on a store of knowledge that is more than ordinary.
- A Professional possesses a theoretical and intellectual grasp that is different from a technician's practice.
- A Professional applies theoretical and intellectual knowledge to solving human and social problems.
- A Profession strives to add to and improve its body of knowledge through research.
- A Profession passes on the body of knowledge to novice generations, for the most part in a university setting.
- A Profession is imbued with an altruistic spirit.

In 1988 Ronald M Pavalko described certain qualities that are attributed to Professions:

- A unique knowledge base justifying the claim to special expertise.
- A long training period requiring specialized knowledge and indoctrination into the occupational subculture.

- Relevance of work to social values.
- Occupational autonomy. The Profession is self-regulating and self-controlling. Only members of the Profession judge and certify who is competent to practise.
- A strong sense of commitment and loyalty to the Profession.
- A strong sense of common identity resulting in a significant subculture.
- A code of ethics and system of norms that are parts of the subculture, reinforcing motivation, autonomy and commitment.

According to Jennifer Davies, in order for an occupation to be defined as a Profession it should possess five traits:

- A body of specialized knowledge upon which practice is based.
- A code of conduct that emphasizes public duty. This is established and maintained by a Professional association.
- A high degree of autonomy, ie self-governing. The Professional association controls entry to the Profession and training.
- A sense of dedication.
- The Professional body is established either by royal charter or Act of Parliament (statute). It is a criminal offence to pretend to be a member of any Profession licensed under statute. Under royal charter, an imposter would have to be sued by the Professional body itself, rather than prosecuted by the Crown Prosecution Service.

Deborah Johnson suggests that the following list of characteristics is often associated with Professions:

- Professions require mastery of an esoteric body of knowledge, usually acquired through higher education. Only members of the Profession possess this knowledge.
- Members of Professions typically have a good deal of autonomy in their work compared to other occupations in which members simply act on orders given.
- Professions usually have a Professional organization, recognized by state government, which controls admission to the Profession and sets standards for practice.
- Professions fulfil an important social function or are committed to a social good, for example, 'health' as in the case of medicine.

Deborah Johnson proposes other characteristics sometimes associated with Professions. These include that: a Profession has a division between those who are practitioners and those who do research; members of Professions are bound by a code of Professional conduct or ethics; and members are seen as making a life commitment to the field of their Profession. A rational appeal is made to these characteristics to justify the higher salaries associated with these special Professions.

Pavalko argues that because of these attributes, Professions are perceived to exhibit that high quality of work in terms of requisite expertise, experience and dedication to service, which justifies public respect and trust.

In this analysis I think we can see where marketing really starts to depart from the accepted norms of a Profession. Marketing demands the profit motive to be successful, as we demonstrated in Chapter 11. Even when marketing is enrolled in a not-for-profit purpose it must still use the characteristics of a businesslike, competitive stance. Perhaps if marketing were to take on these more altruistic characteristics it might be more acceptable as a Profession. I will return to this theme in the Conclusion. But in the meantime I wish to emphasize that it is still a requirement to adopt a Professional attitude, use Professional methods and meet Professional standards. At least some of the attributes identified by Flexner, Pavalko, Davies and Johnson are desirable – as Table 18.1 demonstrates.

In this analysis, as far as marketing is concerned only the possession of and drawing on a store of knowledge that is more than ordinary seems to fit the requirements to be Professional, but we could probably say the same about plumbers and I suspect that more of the requirements listed above would be essential for them. We must rely on the more vernacular understanding of Professionalism. Let me give some examples of what I mean:

- When the marketing manager makes a recommendation to his board to launch a new Product the board members should expect that this recommendation is firmly evidence-based and that the Product has been well conceived, designed, tested and prepared for launch. The recommendation will include a well-prepared financial statement on the return on investment that the new Product is likely to achieve, taking into account any cannibalistic effect on existing Products in the portfolio as well as the likely competitive response.
- When the account manager of an advertising agency presents a new creative idea to a client, both parties will have contributed to a well-written brief based on a proper analysis of the market, the current performance of the brand and the desired outcomes.

TABLE 18.1 Study by the British Computer Society by Flexner, Pavalko, Davies and Johnson

Writer	Feature	Essential	Desirable	Not Required
Flexner				
1	a professional possesses and draws on a store of knowledge that is more than ordinary	√		
2	a professional possesses a theoretical and intellectual grasp that is different from a technician's practice		√	
3	a professional applies theoretical and intellectual knowledge to solving human and social problems			√
4	a profession strives to add to and improve its body of knowledge through research		√	
5	a profession passes on the body of knowledge to novice generations, for the most part in a university setting			√
6	a profession is imbued with an altruistic spirit			√

(Continued)

TABLE 18.1 *(Continued)*

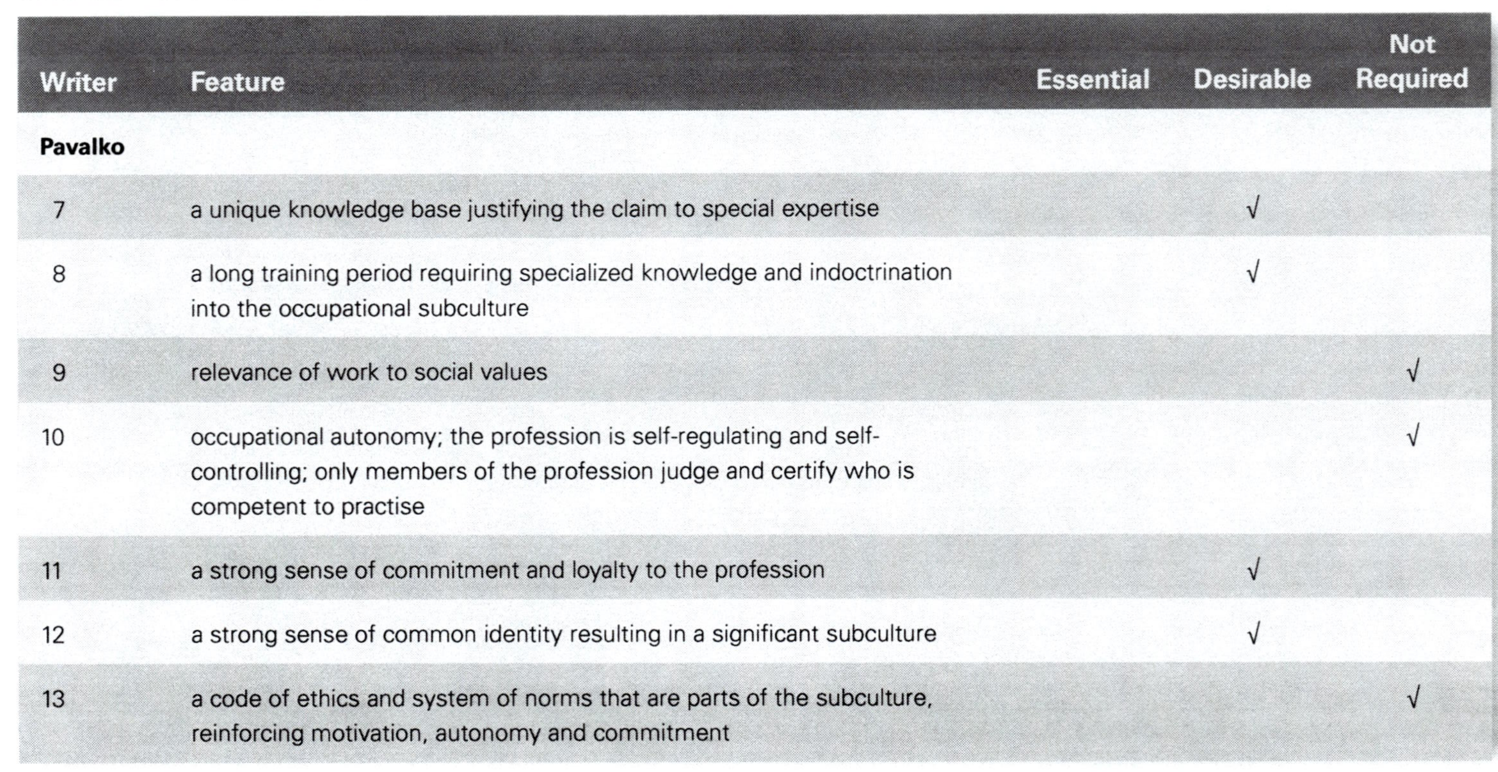

Writer	Feature	Essential	Desirable	Not Required
Pavalko				
7	a unique knowledge base justifying the claim to special expertise		√	
8	a long training period requiring specialized knowledge and indoctrination into the occupational subculture		√	
9	relevance of work to social values			√
10	occupational autonomy; the profession is self-regulating and self-controlling; only members of the profession judge and certify who is competent to practise			√
11	a strong sense of commitment and loyalty to the profession		√	
12	a strong sense of common identity resulting in a significant subculture		√	
13	a code of ethics and system of norms that are parts of the subculture, reinforcing motivation, autonomy and commitment			√

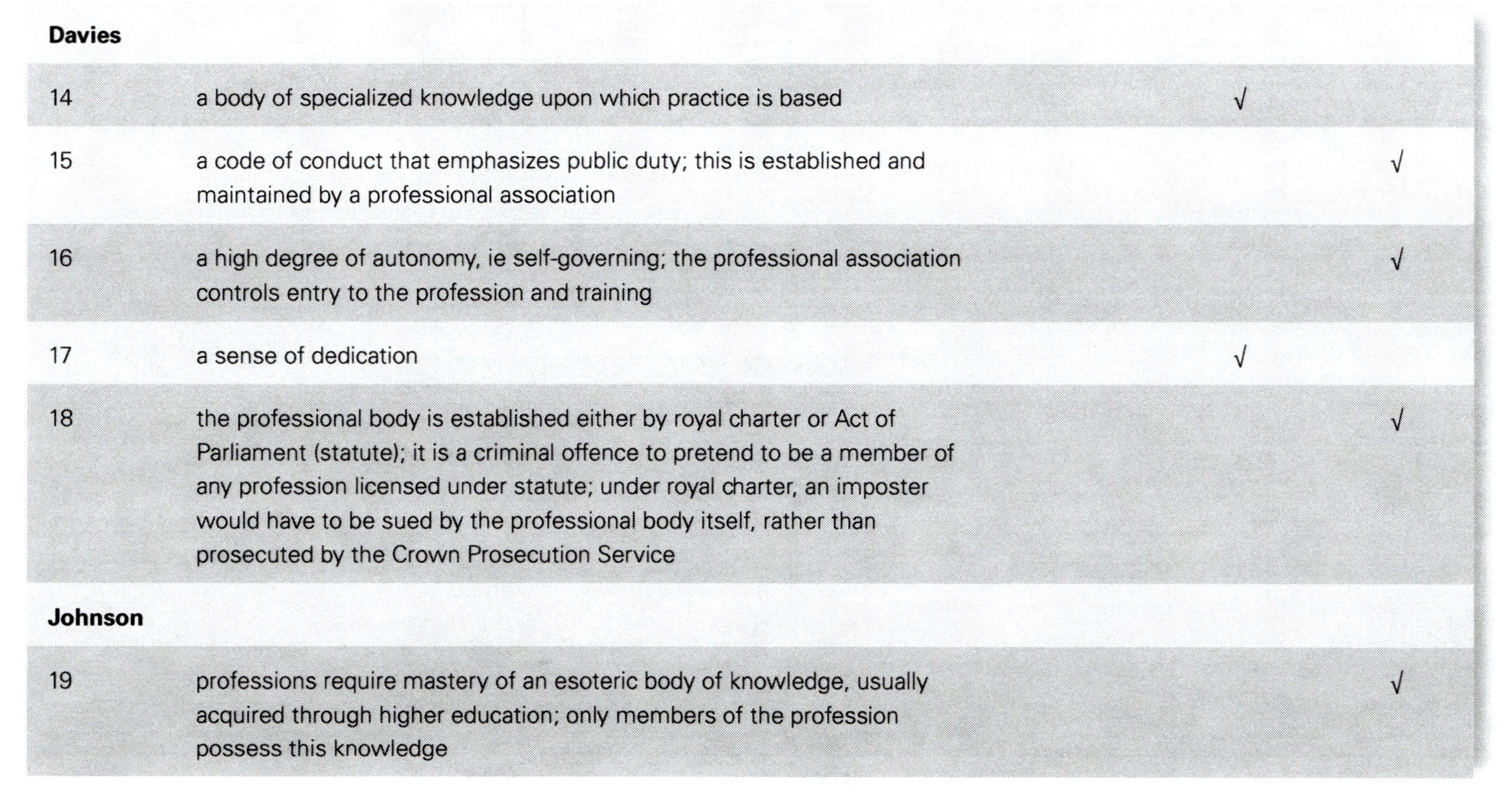

Davies			
14	a body of specialized knowledge upon which practice is based	√	
15	a code of conduct that emphasizes public duty; this is established and maintained by a professional association		√
16	a high degree of autonomy, ie self-governing; the professional association controls entry to the profession and training		√
17	a sense of dedication	√	
18	the professional body is established either by royal charter or Act of Parliament (statute); it is a criminal offence to pretend to be a member of any profession licensed under statute; under royal charter, an imposter would have to be sued by the professional body itself, rather than prosecuted by the Crown Prosecution Service		√
Johnson			
19	professions require mastery of an esoteric body of knowledge, usually acquired through higher education; only members of the profession possess this knowledge		√

(Continued)

TABLE 18.1 *(Continued)*

Writer	Feature	Essential	Desirable	Not Required
20	members of professions typically have a good deal of autonomy in their work compared to other occupations in which members simply act on orders given		√	
21	professions usually have a professional organization, recognized by state government, which controls admission to the profession and sets standards for practice			√
22	professions fulfil an important social function or are committed to a social good, for example, health as in the case of medicine			√
Total		1	9	12

The creative idea will be well rooted in a thorough understanding of the Positioning of the brand.

- When the research agency conducts a piece of market research on which key decisions are likely to be made it will follow well-developed standards of research design and explain the statistical significance of its findings.
- When a sales manager represents his or her firm they will conduct themselves at all times with integrity and decorum.
- When the PR adviser to a client represents a client to the press they will at all times put the client's interests first but never seek to mislead and thus corrupt the long-term reputation of the client.
- When the brand manager is redesigning Packaging he or she will seek to present the product in an attractive but honest way.
- When the marketing manager is training an assistant he or she will set a good example and not withhold trade secrets in the manner of the traditional master craftsman.

In these examples I have introduced the concepts of integrity and ethics because it seems to me that they are implied in all definitions of Professionalism. I will again return to this theme in the conclusion to this book, but for now suffice it to say that I believe that one reason why marketing has not been generally accepted as a Profession is that many people think it involves aspects of dishonesty as in misleading advertising, deceptive packaging, exaggerated claims etc.

Professionalism in sport

It is also important to understand what Professionalism is not. It is not just following a series of box-ticking exercises or a mantra delivered from on high. It is not excluding good judgement or individual expression. It is interesting to see what has happened in so-called Professional sport. Organized sport was largely introduced to the world by the British in the late 19th century. It offered two 'gifts'. First, a genius for codification, which meant that games of similar origin could be played between schools, then towns or regions, and finally nations. All kinds of football were played all over the world but the British codified a version of the rules as Association Football and now it is the world's most popular sport. The second gift was a love of sport for its own sake, ie you did not play for money but for the love of the game. Rugby was originally an amateur game only and when some players sought to take money they broke away to form a different version of the game called Rugby League. However, Rugby Union has now turned Professional, partly to legitimize existing underhand practice, partly to exploit its great popularity. I once discussed this with Will Carling, the former England captain, and suggested to him that the game would become more violent as a result, because once winning is the only objective then players will push the rules to their boundaries and beyond. He disagreed but it is a moot point as to which of us was right. However, a conference into the issue at the University of Glamorgan in October 2010 heard that the amount of injuries in rugby has risen from 67 per 1,000 playing hours in 1994 to 91 in 2009.

Ed Smith, a fine cricketer turned thoughtful journalist, wrote a fascinating article on the subject of Professionalism, 'Are we too Professional?', published in *Intelligent Life* in 2009. He starts by quoting a John Humphrys interview on the *Today* programme: Humphrys asked a young nurse what she considered the two most important qualities in her job. 'Being caring and being compassionate', she replied. 'Not being Professional?' Humphrys countered, emphasizing that her answer was very unusual. 'No, not being Professional', she confirmed. Smith asks how did the concept of Professionalism become so dominant and, further, why is it assumed to be innately desirable. He asserts that:

> In the space of a hundred years, the words 'Professional' and 'amateur' have virtually swapped places. At the end of the 19th century, an amateur meant someone who was motivated by the sheer love of doing something; Professional was a rare, pejorative term for grubby money-making. Now, amateurism is a byword for sloppiness, disorganisation and ineptitude, while Professionalism – as Humphreys suggested – is the default description of excellence.

Smith recalls from his 13 years as a cricketer that every captain under whom he played called for ever increasing Professionalism but with no obvious return: 'Professionalism wasn't so much a real process as a form of self-definition.' Only the occasional maverick would challenge the widely held assumption that Professionalism was the gold standard, by suggesting that actually it might inhibit natural flair. Smith believes that Mark Ramprakash, the most talented batsman of his generation, was held back by this and only late in his career threw it off and started to score freely, averaging 100 as a batsman.

Luis Felipe Scolari, the football coach who led Brazil to the 2002 World Cup said: 'My priority is to ensure that the players feel more amateur than Professional. Thirty to forty years ago, the effort was the other way. Now there is so much Professionalism, we have to revert to urging players to like the game, love it, do it with joy.' The issue is that if every team is using the same methods of hard work and extra coaching then it is necessary to find a new way to compete and that might be by appealing to the innate freshness and talent of the players.

Smith shows that over-Professionalism is everywhere. Teachers are instructed to plan their lessons weeks in advance and in three-minute segments thus eliminating any spontaneity. Journalists at several British national newspapers are encouraged to submit weekly workplans, even though the stories haven't happened yet. Diplomats are made to measure the inputs of their task, causing the distinguished ambassador Sir Ivor Roberts to write in his valedictory telegram when retiring as ambassador to Italy: 'Well conducted diplomacy cannot be properly measured. We manage or contain disputes; very rarely do we deliver a quantifiable solution. Indeed we should be sceptical of "permanent" solutions or models.' Lord Patten, the former Hong Kong governor, said 'it was sad to see experienced diplomats trained to draft brief and lucid telegrams ... terrorised into filling questionnaires by management consultants by the yard.'

Professionalism in business

John Kay in his book *Obliquity* (2010) covers similar ground and explains its links to the financial crisis headlined by the fall of Lehman Brothers in 2008. Kay's argument is that many goals are best pursued obliquely, and this includes Profit:

> If you emphasise Profit-orientation, what you are really doing is giving a local licence to individual greed. The history of the first decade of the 21st century is the history of the self-destruction of America's most aggressively Profit-oriented financial institutions.

Kay recites how ICI, for example, went from being Britain's largest and most successful manufacturing company for most of the 20th century to oblivion in a few short years. The rot set in when the predatory takeover specialist Hanson took a modest stake in ICI in 1991 and ICI responded by adopting a new mission statement: 'ICI's vision is to be the leader in creating value for customers and shareholders through market leadership, technological edge and a world competitive cost base.' After peaking in 1997, the share price declined remorselessly. By 2007, ICI ceased to exist as an independent company.

Applying this to the financial crisis Kay believes it was at least partly caused by excessive faith in the Professional expertise of the banks' quantitative analysts:

> Banks persuaded themselves that risk management could be treated as a problem that was closed, determinate and tractable. We, and they, learnt that they were wrong. We opened the door to much unscientific nonsense. The pursuit of a mistaken kind of rationality has in practice produced wide irrationality. It's a question of having the judgement to say 'This feels unstable.' The bogus Professionalism proved deceptive.

So the old-fashioned way of backing instinct might have averted a crisis that the modern methods caused. But that is a little simplistic as we had crises before when the old ways were being used.

In the search to rediscover flair and originality, attention to detail should not be regarded as undesirable. Lord Sainsbury of Preston Candover, who as John Sainsbury ran the eponymous supermarket chain for many years, is reputed to have said 'Retail is detail.' Attention to detail in location of stores, design of stores, selection of range, preparation of fresh foods, Pricing, Promotion and display of the merchandise, recruitment and training of staff, and a host of other details contributed to years of success and marked them out from many mediocre competitors, who at a superficial level might have appeared similar.

The balance between individuality and conformity to a set of standards is a vital part of the marketing mix. In Chapter 20 (Personality) I will return to this theme to look at encouraging self-expression and flair. But hard work is also required. As Stephen Leacock (1869–1944) said: 'I'm a great believer in luck. I find the harder I work, the more I have of it.'

> Shortly after Nick Faldo won the US Masters for the first time he came to open a golf course that Sony was sponsoring. I asked him how much he practised. He answered 'All the hours of daylight.' I knew then that I could never play golf like Nick Faldo.

There are many who argue that marketing is a Profession, quoting the numbers of people now taking marketing qualifications before starting their marketing careers. In fact, in the Higher Education Statistics Authority figures for 2008–09, out of 330,255 studying Business Studies at university just 23,710 were majoring in marketing, including postgraduate and undergraduate, full-time and part-time. These numbers include a substantial proportion from overseas. I would encourage continuous Professional development for marketers but the challenge is to apply the knowledge gained in the workplace.

And if I were to try to put the genie back in the bottle, what standards would I require of the newly minted Profession of marketing?

- A degree in any subject at all provided it tested and developed verbal reasoning, numeracy (including statistics), logic, social studies (including psychology), debate and presentation skills.
- Practical experience in a marketing-related discipline.
- The ability to analyse market trends and make intelligent forecasts based on robust business models.
- The ability to write (and read) a business plan.
- The ability to follow a repeatable process in executing a business plan.
- The ability to track performance in the market through research, consultation and listening.

Of all these, perhaps this last skill is the most important in being Professional, the art of listening. As Epictetus the Stoic said 2000 years ago, 'God gave man two ears but only one mouth, that he might hear twice as much as he speaks.'

Summary

In this chapter we have shown that:

- marketing does not meet the historical standards of a Profession;
- marketing does not meet the academic definitions of a Profession;
- Professionalism can be overrated and stifle imagination and flair;
- good marketing is characterized by operating to high standards, as is found in Professionalism.

Passion

19

It's like ham and eggs – the chicken's involved, the pig's committed.

MARTINA NAVRATILOVA

For many years *Marketing* magazine, for which I used to write, ran a regular feature interviewing young brand managers in which the first question was 'Describe yourself in three words'. Sometimes the brand manager would try to be witty saying 'Large, red-headed and clumsy' but usually they would say 'Hardworking, dedicated and Passionate'. This is as it should be because it is essential that a brand manager displays *Passion* in their work. As Henry Chester wrote: 'Enthusiasm is the greatest asset in the world. It beats money and power and influence.'

When I was in Chile I was privileged to receive a visit from Forrest Mars, one of the three children of Forrest Mars Sr, who now owned the business. For him this was a new flag on the map, the first Mars marketing unit in the whole of South America. I took him to Epoca, a Santiago advertising agency that had affiliated with Ted Bates following overtures I had made to Ted Bates in New York to get involved in South America. Forrest was keen to get his point over to the owners of Epoca as to the kind of marketing that Mars conducted. He spoke with such Passion that he was jumping up and down in his chair. The Epoca directors were fearful for their furniture but Forrest got his message across and Epoca gave us excellent support in developing strong brand awareness in Chile.

Louis Columbus, a *CRM Buyer* columnist, is a former senior analyst with AMR Research. He is the author of several books on making the most of analyst relationships, including *Best Practices in Analyst Relations* (2004). In an article in *CRM Buyer* in 2005, 'Passion: The Fifth P of Marketing' he wrote:

> Marketing must have a Passion to instil lasting change. Anything less is a waste of time and invites mediocrity and eventually a reputation in the market for doing 'just enough' to be in the industry rather than leading it.

As a commentator on CRM and channel management Columbus observes that what is important is not the size of budget that a company may allocate to marketing as much as a marketing department that has a Passion to execute and deliver results. He goes on to say:

> The traditional four Ps of marketing – Product, Price, Promotion and Place (or distribution) – are meaningless without Passion. The Passion for executing to a shared goal through channels, the Passion to launch Products that truly are on a mission, and the Passion to expel mediocrity from marketing departments and replace it with leadership who has the courage to change strategies and not just 'do what we have always done' to protect the status quo, are traits shared by companies who have discovered this fifth P of marketing and are busy turning it into a competitive advantage.

I fully agree with Louis and that is why I have included *Passion* in my 20 Ps of marketing, though as number 19, not number 5. Louis is specifically calling for Passion in the marketing of software and especially enterprise CRM, where he thinks the majority of marketing departments are not well enough coordinated with engineering, Product development, Product management, executive management and sales in order to understand fully what the latest concepts really mean to their companies. He says:

> Most likely one in twenty software companies have this level of integration – and where this comes from isn't a Six Sigma black belt but a culture of Passion for making change a competitive force for their companies. Marketing momentum comes from this Passion for delivering on what's real, and not just carelessly slinging around the latest industry buzzwords hoping for market traction. Sadly those companies with no Passion at all and only going through the motions of marketing don't even bother to sling the latest terms, they just do another data sheet and hope for the best.

Louis tests his ideas on the graduate classes he teaches and from these exercises he has gained the following insights:

- Products that market themselves on strong performance make for the most memorable Product launches.
- Enthusiasm reverberates through channels in strong launches.
- Marketers need to have the Passion to get away from talking to themselves in their own acronyms trying to communicate complex messages and instead talk to customers in their frame of reference – common sense but many companies don't do this.
- 'Me-too' marketing is worthless.
- Lack of credibility is the number one killer of Products.

While focused on the software industry Louis tests his hypothesis on the automobile industry and reaches similar conclusions. He observes that both markets are crowded with new Product introductions but only 20 per cent of these companies will ever become widely known, even to those prospects searching for them. That's because the top performing marketing departments are not just relying on themselves, but get the entire company behind their efforts and are Passionate about changing how prospects learn, consider, evaluate, purchase and use their Products. The clear winners, he believes, are those that turn Passion into a competitive weapon and get out of the blame game when a company doesn't reach its goals. There is a no-excuses mentality in these companies that have a Passion for marketing, and it's not coercive, it's driven by vision.

When I joined Pillsbury in 1984 the brief was to reinvigorate the Green's of Brighton brand while delivering its targeted profit contribution. Working with the Green's management team I set up a programme of New Product Development. Some projects were based on existing technology and some were based on new fruit-processing technology that we would need to adopt. We also sought to improve the ease of preparation as traditional mixes were no longer regarded as convenient by consumers now used to buying ready-to-eat Products. Some excellent Products were launched. One, Brownies, became the company's fourth highest selling Product in its first year. Company Profit contribution targets were met, market share increased and the brand's somewhat tired brand image revitalized. The key was to instil Passion in the whole team – the research chemists who developed the recipes, the manufacturing management who turned these recipes into mass Production, the marketing managers who developed the Packaging designs and marketing campaigns, the sales force who won the valuable listings from the major supermarket chains and everyone else who contributed in some way.

Another organization that has recognized the importance of adding Passion to the four Ps of marketing is 6P Marketing, a Winnipeg-based marketing communications agency. Their fifth P is People, which I included in Chapter 16. They offer a path to Passion as the client's roadmap to integrated brand excellence. They describe this as a journey of discovery that helps ensure that your brand looks at itself from the customer's point of view. What the customer believes and does with your brand defines your brand's journey from a market player to a market leader. They say:

> While there were originally just 4 Ps (Product, Price, Promotion and Place), service brands began adding 'People' to the marketing equation because poor customer service is a sure fire brand killer. When the People who present your Products or services to your customers are careless and or indifferent, they send a very powerful message to your customers: 'I don't care about you – or this Product.' Better yet, when a store tells customers that 'well, it's a great Product, but that one is $30.00 less', they are helping to train all customers to shop Price – not quality. People have become increasingly important as the odds of repatriating lost customers declines and the cost of doing so goes up.

I am not sure that the importance of People is confined to service businesses, as I explained in Chapter 16, but I certainly agree with 6P Marketing about Passion. They introduce Passion as the 6th P with the following explanation:

> Passion really matters. If you don't care, find someone who does to represent your precious brand. Syndicated and proprietary research studies have quantified what you already know to be true: customers who love the (Product or service) brands they use are more loyal, less Price sensitive, more forgiving when things go wrong (and you make them right), purchase more of your Products and services, and importantly, are much more likely to recommend your Products and services to friends and families.
>
> On the other hand – talk to someone who doesn't care about your Products and services and they'll tell you: 'I wouldn't use that stupid thing – even if you paid me!'

6P Marketing has understood a central truth here. By being Passionate in your marketing you can instil Passion in your consumers who become Passionate about the brand and want to buy them, own them and use them.

When Arun Sarin was chief executive of Vodafone I had the pleasure of having dinner with him at a major conference. After dinner he addressed the audience from the stage, holding a mobile phone high in the air. He had a clear vision as to how this device would increasingly become the central Product in everyone's everyday life. Today you do not leave the house without your keys, your wallet and your mobile phone. In the future the mobile phone will probably be all that you need as it will perform all the functions of the other items. And his company, Vodafone, would be at the heart of this with a range of services connecting the consumer to the community, his bank, his house, car and other possessions. Now, Mr Sarin is not the only one to profess this vision. A number of people have articulated it. But I was impressed with his singularity of focus – as throughout a 30-minute presentation without notes Arun Sarin held his phone high in the air so that we simply could not miss his point.

Kate Newlin is the author of *Passion Brands* (2009). In 2009 she wrote an article 'What Makes Consumers Passionate about Brands', which was published in *Chief Marketer Report*. She says:

> When the pressures mount on the bottom line, CMOs typically look to the expense side of Products, both R&D and marketing. However, one should not miss the opportunity that brand Passion creates to convince enthusiastic consumers to spend their financial and social currency... while exhorting friends and family to follow suit.

She went on to describe seven key ways to create Passion and develop a deep relationship with consumers. First you should 'Work the Worldview, Not Age, Race or Gender'. She picks out so-called 'Passion brands' such as Apple, Sony, American Express, Starbucks, Folger's, Target, Nordstrom, Craig's List, Whole Foods, Toys 'R' Us, Camel, Absolut, Kraft, Cadillac, BMW, Infiniti and Jeep, which she asserts rarely target consumers in a traditional way. Instead they identify shared values about the world and how it works and then illustrate how the brand shares that vision.

Second, she says that you should 'Differentiate on Design'. She believes that consumers respond to clever, intuitive Products. Great design engages. There's a joy in a well-designed idea that trumps other performance features. Third, Newlin calls for 'Passionistas as Brand Stewards'. Here the danger is taking your consumers or their Passion for your brand for granted. Your People must be genuine in their Passion, for only that will ensure that the brand continues to grow and evolve in relevant ways.

Her fourth point is to 'Know They Know You Need Them'. Everyone has become sensitive to the vocabulary of marketing and understands the rules of the game. So the imperative is to get out and watch consumers wherever they buy and consume. Engage with them. This is no more than an update of the great David Ogilvy's dictum, 'Never underestimate the consumer – she's your wife!' Fifth, you should 'democratize the brand'. The trick here is to engage People so that they own your brand, not just through purchase but through you allowing them in – so that the consumer believes that he or she is having it their way.

Newlin's sixth message is to 'Mine the Mythos'. Here she means that Passionate brand managers know what makes up the DNA, or heritage, of the brand and how far they can go to enable the brand to evolve without jeopardizing this.

And finally she talks about 'Brand the Buzz'. Passion can be a defining quality that can set your brand above the competition and provide a road-map to help keep you out in front.

When I joined NXT in March 2000 the culture was primarily oriented to research and development (R&D). The sales side was comparatively weak with inexperienced leadership. The R&D side, led by Henry Azima who really was a rocket scientist, was brilliant, and keen on future developments of the technology. There was a feeling that it was enough to have produced these great inventions. They would sell themselves.

I progressively oriented the organization to putting the customer first. Sector heads were given responsibility for driving the projects. Then the engineers on those projects were reporting directly to the sector heads. Then a marketing group of Product managers was formed, recruited from the engineers. I introduced an exercise to set out our 'Vision & Values'. All senior managers were involved together with representatives from all other groups of staff. The vision became 'To Help Our Customers Win through Superior Technology'. I wrote regularly in an internal newsletter to all staff on the Vision & Values and constantly gave good examples of how it was being implemented.

The culture changed to one where the interests of the customer were put first. Communication improved between customer-facing staff and other support staff. Eventually Products using NXT technology were introduced by customers in every one of our chosen business sectors. The brand came to express the Passion of the inventors and everyone associated with commercialization.

Jerry Smith is the co-founder of Marketing Action Club, focusing on small service-based businesses and independent professionals who want to grow but struggle to attract quality clients. In an article in *CRM Buyer* entitled 'Marketing with Passion' he observes that: 'Everyone wants to do business with someone who is Passionate about their Product or service.'

Smith thinks that it is easy to see through an insincere salesperson. What is needed to make the marketing message compelling is authenticity and personal quality. Authenticity means how you as a marketer want to serve your customers; personal quality is the sense that you understand the issues involved. I will return to this last point more in Chapter 20 (Personality).

Smith suggests that marketing messages without these two points – authenticity and personal quality – are likely to fall into one or two traps. For example, a clever tag line where the emphasis is on the humour. This may sound great but takes the audience away from what you actually do and instead focuses on the joke. A safer option is a list of services, but this relies on the hope that your customer will make all the necessary connections.

Instead Smith advocates engaging the emotions in order to make your message compelling. After all, you went into this kind of business to perform a service or supply a Product that solves a problem, alleviates a concern or simply makes the customer feel better. Since emotions are involved, why not show the love that you have for what you do. Again we see that by demonstrating our own Passion in the business we arouse Passion in our customers and they will become more loyal as a result.

To work this through Smith insists that you should first remember why you went into business for yourself. Then ask yourself:

- What service are you Passionate about?
- Who do you want to help?
- What problem do you solve?
- How does that feel to you?

Smith then links his previous message about being authentic and personal by saying:

> We talked about being authentic and personal. Take that feeling from a great client interaction. What sort of person do you care about Passionately enough to dedicate your business life to helping? That is the focus of your marketing effort. What pain were they suffering and how did working with you help them overcome that pain? That is the substance of your message.
>
> Staying connected with those two things will ensure you are authentic, and that your ideal client will recognize that the message is intended for them and react accordingly. That will give you longer lasting and more relevant attention than the amusement generated by a cute tag line.

While Jerry Smith focuses on the small service business his message should be relevant to those of us employed in corporate life. We will be much more successful if we are authentic in our marketing and understand the personal issues of our customers.

After returning from Chile to the UK I initially joined a young firm of food brokers set up by a friend of mine, John Eustace, a former colleague at both Procter & Gamble and Pedigree Petfoods. Another friend, Malcolm Hewitt, also a colleague at Pedigree, joined as Sales Director while I took the role of Marketing Director, but actually all three of us handled both clients and national account customers. I used my relationships with Mars Inc. to gain representation rights for ranges of Products that were difficult to get listed in the national chains. One, Thomas's of Halifax, had an extensive range of pet accessories and I convinced them to appoint Crombie Eustace to represent them. Another, Suzi Wan, was a range of oriental foods sourced via Holland and managed in the UK by Master Foods. To launch such complex propositions to the British grocery trade required enormous energy and enthusiasm – yes, *Passion* – and we had considerable success in building our distribution and awareness. I later returned to corporate life because it suited my personal circumstances better, but the opportunity to work in a small brokerage in which I was a director and shareholder gave me invaluable lessons in the importance of Passion in marketing.

Malcolm Ashworth (1925–78) was a British Army officer and a noted marketing and advertising executive. He is credited with saving the well-known Crawford's advertising agency from financial failure in the 1960s, and with helping to establish marketing as a professional discipline in the UK. He is also one of the first figures to talk openly about Passion in marketing. After military service in India, Burma and Malaya, he entered commerce in 1953 and made rapid progress, becoming Director of Marketing for Quaker Oats in 1957, Marketing Director of Revlon in 1961, and then returning to Quaker Oats in 1963. In 1965 he was appointed as Chairman and Chief Executive to the influential but financially ailing Crawford's advertising agency and in 1967 he masterminded the financial merger with Dorland. In 1970 he was appointed Deputy Managing Director of Overmark Smith Warden.

Ashworth was a leading figure in the growing recognition for marketing as a professional discipline, emerging from what he termed 'the marketing revolution' of the 1960s, which he compared to the Professional evolution of advertising in the 1950s. In his introduction to *A Consuming Passion* (1970), the first book ever published on marketing as a career, he noted that historically many people had 'become marketers as a result of happy chance, or had, in fact, been doing a marketing job for our companies without really knowing it'. He contrasted this to the new era of marketing, stating that while 'there are no recognised academic qualifications which ensure success in marketing... success in such a challenging situation demands intellectual ability, imagination and determination of a high order'.

Thus in Ashworth's words we can see that Passion is more than enthusiasm; it is an all-consuming Passion that demands very high qualities of the marketer if he or she is going to succeed. As I pointed out in Chapter 17 (Professionalism), a lack of Professional qualifications need not hold back the Passionate marketer. But he or she will get nowhere without dedication and commitment as well as superior rational and abstract intelligence.

In my career I have sold or marketed some Products that may not have immediately quickened the blood. They include deodorant, cat litter, breath freshener, baking powder, batteries and cardboard loudspeakers. But in every case I was Passionate about their success. This Passion was not artificial, because that cannot be effective. It was genuine. Tempo deodorant was a brand test-marketed by Procter & Gamble at the same time as Head & Shoulders shampoo. Unlike Head & Shoulders – which had very clear Positioning, with a unique formula that addressed the widespread problem of dandruff – Tempo was simply an effective deodorant with a pleasant perfume but no special qualities. Nevertheless I gave it as much endeavour as I did Head & Shoulders (although it was not a surprise when it was discontinued).

Thomas's brand of cat litter was a better class of cat litter, with absorbent quality that made its use more effective in the home. Cat litter allows many people to enjoy owning a cat in situations where access to the outdoors is limited – and so it does solve a problem. It might be hard to raise the emotions about cat litter but the volumes of sale were not insignificant and the Profit not inconsiderable.

Gold Spot was a brand of breath freshener marketed by Ashe Laboratories, a subsidiary of Akzo that Crombie Eustace represented to the grocery trade. It was highly Profitable and it gave me great pleasure to widen its distribution. Borwick's baking powder was a very venerable brand, probably the oldest with which I have been associated that was owned by Green's of Brighton. George Borwick's baking powder featured in a case at the Old Bailey in 1858 and it was claimed that it was the largest selling baking powder in the world. George's son was raised to the barony in 1916 and the peerage in 1922. While home baking was in decline it still was an important part of our brand heritage that we sold the most famous brand of baking powder, which allowed customers who want to bake good cakes to get a better result than relying on self-raising flour.

At Sony, the last Product most of us thought about was batteries. Our position in the batteries market was not strong and, of course, there were very well-established players such as Duracell. Nevertheless, we were asked by Tokyo to make a special effort and so we did and were able to gain significant distribution.

At NXT we developed a way of making a highly effective pair of loudspeakers with cardboard and a pair of NXT-patented exciters. Cardboard makes a surprisingly good radiator and we worked with a leading cardboard producer to fashion it into pyramids, but so that it would fold flat. The sound quality was remarkably good and the use value was infinite (I used them effectively at outdoor barbecues, for example, and still do to this day. We branded them SoundPax and I hired an experienced consumer electronics marketing manager to concentrate his efforts on building a business. Ultimately we were not able to get over the scepticism that most people had in thinking that cardboard speakers costing a few quid could not be as good as the bulky ones they had in wooden boxes, but for a couple of years our Passion for this invention was very strong.

These examples vary from Products such as Borwick's baking powder, which had enjoyed decades in the nation's larders but was now past its sell-by date, to Products like SoundPax and Tempo that never got off the ground. But in every case – and many more – my colleagues and I were always Passionate in our dealings with the Product at hand.

A highly successful Brazilian businessman called Ricardo Semler has written two best-sellers on his innovative way of doing business: *Maverick* (1993) and *The Seven-Day Weekend* (2003). In these he describes his unusual approach, but some of his central themes are close to the spirit of this chapter. He defines Passion as: 'Having a relentless desire individually and collectively to be the best in our business.' He describes his ideal workplace as a place 'where good enough is never good enough'. He makes a point of celebrating individual and team success and, above all, of 'Being excited about who we are and what we do'. Semler truly brings Passion to his business.

Business leaders like Semler know how to inspire their People. They know that enthusiastic employees produce better results. They understand that the best way to spark Passion in your people is to demonstrate your own Passion.

Here are three ways to authentically show your enthusiasm and inspire others:

- Focus on the Positive. Employees know when their leader truly cares about a company or a project. Passionate leaders can't help but talk about what's working well and try to find ways to fix what isn't.

- Don't suppress the negative. Passionate leaders aren't all about good news – they acknowledge negatives in a realistic way and help People to solve problems.
- Set high targets. This doesn't mean unreachable goals. Passionate leaders should inspire and challenge People to do their best, which is all you can ask for.

Summary

In this chapter we have seen that it is essential that marketing managers demonstrate Passion in their work:

- This should be a Passion to instil lasting change.
- It should also be a way of showing the customer that you care.
- This in turn will inspire Passion in the customer.

Personality

Personality is everything in art and poetry.

JOHANN WOLFGANG VON GOETHE

Twenty years from now you will be more disappointed by the things you didn't do, than by the ones you did do. So throw off the bow lines, sail away from the safe harbour. Catch the trade winds in your sails. Explore. Dream. Discover.

MARK TWAIN

As mentioned in Chapter 16, soon after I joined Sony in 1988 my managing director, Nobu Watanabe, invited me to spend an entire day with him at the company's flat in London to go through how he wanted me to work. I return to it here because Nobu taught me a particularly valuable lesson. He had drawn for me a diagram, quite complex in structure but essentially showing a circle that was divided into two equal parts. One half expressed the whole of the Sony Corporation with all its policies and procedures, its history and its reputation, its brands and its values, and yes, its *Personality*. The other half represented David Pearson, with my skills and experience, my intelligence and values, and yes, my *Personality*. The two together would be the result of my career in Sony. I was to accept Sony as it was and follow its policies and procedures, respect its history and its reputation, respect also its brands and its values and its Personality. But in return I should bring my skills and experience to Sony, use my intelligence and live up to my values and express my Personality.

Nobu was giving me a great gift. He was empowering me to express my Personality in my dealing with the Sony Corporation. I felt tremendously empowered and, far from being overawed by the immense Power of the Sony brand, I could see that it was mine to use. I was also blessed with an excellent marketing director, Satoshi Kakuda, known as Sam. He and I share a birthday, which seemed to bring us even closer together, and Sam accompanied me on my first Product line-up trips to Japan (I described line-up meetings in Chapter 7 on Persuasion). These trips to Tokyo were also an opportunity for Sam and I to meet with top management and discuss our market performance in the UK and perhaps seek support for some special project.

I thoroughly enjoyed the meetings with the great men who had built up Sony's fabulous business and its amazing brand. They metaphorically wore the medals of their famous campaigns on their chests. So Kozo Ohsone, who at this time was head of the audio group, had been the engineer responsible for launching Walkman. Minoru Morio, who was the head of the personal video or camcorder group, had been the engineer who had cracked the PAL code and so enabled Sony to sell its excellent Trinitron colour televisions in Europe. Hideo Nakamura had been one of the key engineers in the development of compact disc and was rewarded with the opportunity to build an in-car equipment business, which he called mobile electronics. And there were many more.

These men had clearly expressed their Personality in developing these marvellous Products and I was being invited to express my Personality in the marketing of them. It was a tremendously exciting opportunity for me, but then I realized that I had had this chance before. Mars too had encouraged me to express myself; it was perhaps the principal difference from Procter & Gamble, which tended more to enforce a single way of behaviour. Even at Pillsbury, with all its financial controls, I had been encouraged by my excellent boss, Bruce Noble, to radically overhaul the Product development plans and bring innovative Products to market. One I particularly enjoyed developing was Green's Fruit Whisk. There were well-established dessert mixes in the market, led by General Foods' Angel Delight. The customer simply whisked a flavoured powder with milk, set it in the fridge and served up a tasty dessert to the children, which because of the milk content could be described as nutritious even though the powder consisted of sugar and various chemicals, setting agents, flavourings and colourings. Green's could easily reproduce this Product and compete with General Foods on an own-label basis, for example, but we were looking to be more than a me-too manufacturer.

We had installed fruit-processing technology to support our range of cheesecake mixes and explored what more we could do with the capacity. Fruit Whisk was developed to compete with Angel Delight but to offer a more natural Product. It consisted of natural fruits such as strawberries, which with pectin could be mixed with milk and produce a delicious dessert almost instantly. Unfortunately, we did not have the marketing muscle of General Foods and the Product failed to gain sufficient volume, but it was a good example of how I had had the opportunity to express my Personality in an earlier incarnation before my Sony career.

At Sony there were many opportunities to express my Personality in the marketing of our great range of Products and I have described some of these in this book. However, there would be few examples of direct involvement in Product development other than our input at line-up meetings. Sam encouraged me to express my opinions even if I had no professional knowledge of the category. This went against the grain at first because I had been trained to do the opposite – that is, never to express a personal opinion of Products but rather trust the research to play back the consumer's view. Sony had a healthy disrespect for such research – for example, the conventional view is that Walkman would never have been launched if top management had listened to the research – but rather encouraged the expression of one's own views. This came from the top and is still the culture.

Norio Ohga, the president of Sony at this time, had been trained as a singer in Berlin under Herbert von Karajan and married a concert pianist. While still developing his career as a musician he became professionally interested in the tape recorders that Sony was trying to develop. He was quite critical of these pilot Products and was invited to come into the factory to give his comments directly. Eventually that turned into a full-time role and Ohga-san swiftly became one of the most important executives at Sony. He set up the Design Centre that concentrated the design efforts. Thus each Product group had its own design team but all the designers reported separately to Ohga–san so that he could control the design process and ensure consistency across the brand. His Product philosophy permeated all that Sony brought to market and was one of the principal reasons for its success. Steve Jobs, until his enforced sabbatical owing to ill health and subsequent untimely death, played a similar role for Apple in the recent past.

At Sony UK we did take one opportunity to influence Product development more directly. The world of high fidelity audio, hi-fi for short, is quite arcane. The physics are such that the high fidelity reproduction equipment that audiophiles are looking for should be relatively easy to develop. However, in practice there is a great deal of differing opinion on what makes good hi-fi. This is particularly the case with loudspeakers.

Loudspeakers were first developed for telephones and then for public address. The use of loudspeakers to listen to music at home, initially on the kitchen radio set, was based on 'moving coil' loudspeakers first invented in 1898 by Oliver Lodge, developed further by Peter Jensen and Edwin Pridham who established the Magnavox company, but it was the design of Edward Kellogg and Chester Rice, patented in 1924, that set the standard.

Loudspeakers typically combine different parts in an enclosure: a tweeter covers high frequencies, a conventional drive unit the mid-range and a woofer the bass frequencies. More sophisticated Products might add a super tweeter for very high frequencies and some favour a sub-woofer for very low frequencies, though many hi-fi enthusiasts frown on these. With so many different parts, the key to fidelity is the crossover between them and the quality of the components and wiring.

We imported a range of Sony loudspeakers but while our compact disc players were well received – after all we had co-invented the format – our loudspeakers always came up short. British audiophiles found them harsh and not sympathetic to British ears. The Japanese engineers could not understand this, but even in blind testing where the brand was not known the results were the same. I could understand the Japanese engineers' argument that the laws of physics are universal, but I also thought that music is not only about physics. After all, we grow up hearing different sounds, different languages and initially probably different music. Is it so surprising that we hear music in different ways?

Eventually we won the right to develop our own UK-designed loudspeaker. We gave them the sub-brand Brooklands, where our offices were

> The US-based Sony sales company had also developed its own idea, but in this case they persuaded Tokyo to take it up and introduce it into the worldwide line-up. The Americans thought it would be good if consumers could be introduced to Sony Products at a very early age. Thus 'My First Sony' was born, Products designed for use by toddlers. They were in rugged plastic with bright primary colours. Some were simplified versions of adult Products such as My First Sony Walkman, while others were specifically designed for children. One I particularly enjoyed playing with my daughter was a graphics tablet that hooked up to your TV allowing you to draw anything with a pallet of colours and see it on your screen. Of course, with such a range it gave us an opportunity to seek new outlets specializing in children's Products. One chain we approached was the Early Learning Centre; we told them that we had developed the range in tough plastic to stand up to children's abuse. 'Let's see,' said the buyer. He picked up one of the Products and threw it at the wall. He then tested if it was still working. It was. 'That seems to be OK.' And he moved on to the next issue. Not for the first time we silently thanked the professionalism of the engineers in Tokyo, but it was the American marketing team who had expressed their Personality in suggesting the idea.

based. The Products were developed by our own Product management in conjunction with UK specialist designers and were launched to a very positive response. It was a heartening demonstration of the principle that you should express your own Personality – in this case the Personality of British-based hi-fi.

Personality is a key element in developing leadership styles. In assessing performance, a useful mnemonic is MAP. This stands for Motivation, Ability, Personality + Vision in Leaders. In assessing a man or woman in business I want to know what they have made of themselves. As Erich Fromm said: 'Man's main task in life is to give birth to himself, to become what he potentially is. The most important Product of his effort is his own Personality.'

Corporate Personality

In marketing, a corporate identity is the 'persona' of a corporation, which is designed to accord with and facilitate the attainment of business objectives. It is visibly manifested by way of branding and the use of trademarks. Corporate identity exists when there is a common ownership of an organizational philosophy that is apparent in a distinct corporate culture – the corporate *Personality*. It is most powerful when the public feel that they have ownership of the philosophy. Corporate identity helps organizations to answer questions like 'who are we?' and 'where are we going?' Corporate identity also allows consumers to identify with particular human groupings.

In general, this amounts to a corporate title, logo and supporting devices commonly arranged within a set of rules. These rules regulate how the identity is applied and confirm approved colour palettes, typefaces, page layouts, exclusion zones and other such methods of maintaining visual continuity and brand recognition across all physical illustrations of the brand. These rules are generally catalogued into a package of tools called 'corporate identity manuals'.

Many companies have their own identity that runs through all of their Products and merchandise. The trademark 'Shell' logo, for example, and the red and yellow appear consistently throughout the Shell forecourts and advertising. Companies will pay handsomely for the research, design and execution involved in creating an identity that is distinctive and appealing to the company's target audience.

I once led a European-wide project to develop a common design identity for Sony Centres. At the time these were outlets owned and operated by independent retailers who committed to Sony to only sell our merchandise and in return received additional support, especially in Product supply. The existing design identity looked tired and needed a facelift. By getting this adopted as a European project, one of the first of its kind, I was able to spread the cost over the whole of the European sales organization. I worked with a UK-based design firm called XMPR and led a project team drawn from those sales companies that had expressed interest in developing the concept. We built a test store in the Sony Netherlands warehouse, which we could show discreetly to all interested parties. Then, once approval was gained, we wrote a book with all the guidelines about the use of the design, where the parts could be ordered and so on. Though this was done more than 20 years ago the design is still in use and still looks fresh. After this I was asked by Jack Schmuckli, the head of the European business, to be the first chairman of the Consumer Marketing Committee, looking for collaboration across all European sales companies and with the business groups.

Brand Personality

There has been considerable research and subsequent literature on the concept of brand Personality. This has been derived from Personality psychology and then applied to brands as symbols. Dimensions of Personality are described and even complex scales of measurement developed. Some of this research borrows from associative memory and others observe that humans have a natural tendency to anthropomorphize inanimate objects. Of course, in many cases the brand was designed, perhaps instinctively, to link to such tendencies. In others, the Personality was imposed at a later date by a smart advertising person.

Leo Burnett, who gave his name to the eponymous advertising agency, created the Personality of the Jolly Green Giant. I knew the Cosgrove family who originally owned this brand before it was sold to Pillsbury. Somehow the Personality of the Jolly Green Giant was an endorsement of quality for the vegetables that were inside the cans, or later in the frozen packages. Burnett also created the Pillsbury doughboy, which became an unavoidable expression of the brand Personality. Pillsbury dough is a convenient Product that is partially baked and will bake into a nice bread roll or croissant straight from the canister. The Product is good, but without the additional aspect of a distinctive Personality might appear a little anaemic.

The leading academic on brand Personality is Jennifer Aaker, General Atlantic Professor of Marketing at the Graduate School of Business, Stanford University. She is the daughter of David Aaker, vice-chairman of Prophet Consultancy and Emeritus Professor of Marketing at Haas Business School, University of California, Berkeley, and co-author of best-seller *Building Strong Brands*. Professor David Aaker and I both sat on the editorial board of *The Journal of Brand Management* for many years. Jennifer Aaker has a PhD in Marketing and a PhD minor in Psychology and combined these two disciplines to research brand Personality. In *The Personality Puzzle*, Helen Edwards of Passionbrand says: 'Aaker's central insight is that the dimensions of brand Personality must include some that humans desire but do not actually possess – which is one reason why interpreting brands as real people is misguided' (*Marketing* magazine, 12 January 2011).

Jennifer Aaker developed the brand Personality framework that plots five brand Personality dimensions: sincerity, excitement, competence, sophistication and ruggedness. Each of these is broken down into a set of facets: sincerity, for example, comprises down-to-earth, honest, wholesome and cheerful. Each of these, in turn, is divided into several traits, which can be gauged on a one-to-five scale. Thus her contribution is to have taken an area that previously was given highly subjective treatment and provide a basis for measurement.

Consumer Personality

Let us not forget that our consumers also have their own Personality and that this will determine how they relate to a brand. Again, the literature on this is copious and there has been extensive research into methods of testing how different Personality types will react to particular brands. The most successful brands are usually those that can appeal to a wide variety of Personalities but there are numerous successful niche brands that focus on a few or even one. Not every type of Personality is truly happy to see themselves behind the wheel of a Ferrari, though many might say that is what they aspire to. The people at Ferrari are interested in real money. They sell their brand to millions who buy the merchandise of a famous Formula One marque, while a few select individuals put up the six figures required to own one of their cars. Margaret Mead had the last word on consumer Personality when she said: 'Always remember that you are absolutely unique. Just like everyone else.'

Summary

In this chapter we have considered the importance of Personality in marketing as:

- an expression of individual contribution;
- corporate character;
- brand Personality dimensions and of consumer behaviour.

CONCLUSION

No man was ever yet so completely skilled in the conduct of his business so as not to receive new information from the experience of others. **TERRENCE 159BC**

I have made this letter longer than usual, only because I have not had the time to make it shorter. **BLAISE PASCAL**

In this book I have sought to set out a vision for marketing beyond the limitations of the original four Ps of marketing first delineated nearly 50 years ago. While it served countless students and practitioners reasonably well for a period of time I believe it is not only outdated but insufficient to describe the true role of marketing. I have based this model partly on some primary research, partly on secondary research, but mainly on my own extensive experience and observation during over more than 40 years in marketing roles.

It is not new to question whether the validity of the four Ps is still current, but I believe I am the first to go as far as 20, or even 10 Ps for that matter. I have not done this as some kind of marketing virility symbol – my list is longer than yours – but rather because I believe Passionately in the performance of marketing in the business process.

In an interesting article in the excellent *Market Leader*, the quarterly publication of the Marketing Society, of which I am a Fellow, Chekitan S Dev and Don E Schultz argued that it is time to kill off the four Ps (*Market Leader*, Summer 2005). They argue that the four Ps is a supply-side framework that assumes marketers are in control. As such, it is out of touch with 21st-century realities where the consumer is in control. Dev and Schultz describe a demand-side model that flips the emphasis from 'what marketers do' to 'what consumers want from marketing'. They call their model SIVA: solutions, information, value and access. They say:

> Interestingly, while the marketing concept presumes customers are paramount in any marketing plan, the four Ps approach ignores the primacy of customers, prospects, or even markets. Taking a four Ps viewpoint, the manager makes an

> assumption that commonly seems to follow this logic: if a manager successfully organises and implements the proper mix of the four Ps, customers and Profits will magically appear and the organisation will move successfully ahead. Moreover there are now generations of marketing academics and practitioners who seem to place unquestioning faith in this premise, even though it is antithetical to the ideal marketing concept of finding and filling customers' wants and needs.

I have some sympathy with this approach but have reached a different conclusion. The four Ps are out of date because they are insufficient to describe the job of marketing, not because they are not a part of it. It is right to be concerned about the Product, the Price, the Place and the Promotion. But there is a lot more to it than that, as I hope I have demonstrated in this book. Much of contemporary academic thinking about marketing has side-stepped the four Ps and argues that 21st-century marketing is a way of creating value through exchange. So it is. But as I have argued in this book it is really a strategic paradigm and very much more than a function. If the firm is organized around functions and the board is mainly concerned with historic results and governance procedures then it is likely that it is not managing its market and serving its customers well.

The great business thinker Peter Drucker said that innovation and marketing are the only two essential elements of a business. However, for the general public marketing is often discredited as something dishonourable. I think that as in any other Profession the need for a high standard of ethics is paramount. In some cases the public is justified. The financial information website Citywire has discovered at least nine ways in which companies mislead the public:

- Savings account names

  It might be expected that savings accounts with names like 'Halifax Liquid Gold' and 'NatWest Diamond Reserve' would be offering top interest rates but in reality they usually pay vanishingly small rates, according to a 2010 report by the Consumer Association. For example, the Newcastle Building Society's High/Extra High Interest Account was paying a rate of just 0.01 per cent. That would have given an annual return of just 10p on every £1,000 saved, not really 'extra high'.

- Supermarket deals

  Supermarkets tempt consumers with multipack offers implying that it works out cheaper than buying items individually. However, according to an investigation by the Consumer Association, this may not always be true. In September 2010 the Consumer Association accused Asda and Sainsbury's of 'illegally misleading' shoppers over the pricing of such offers and reported the pair to trading standards. On one occasion the Consumer Association found Sainsbury's was selling a triple pack of sweetcorn labelled 'bigger pack better value', when in fact it was cheaper to buy three individual tins. Both supermarkets put their mistakes down to human error.

- Broadband speed

  Broadband providers have come under scrutiny for failing to make it clear to consumers that the headline speed they advertise is not the actual speed they will get. Providers claim this is because your speed is affected by a whole range of factors such as where you live, how much you download and how often you go online. However, Ofcom has stated that this is unacceptable and has warned providers that they will face stricter regulation if the situation does not improve.

- Debt management companies

  Debt management companies are often guilty of misleading vulnerable and over-indebted customers into believing the service they provide is free, when it is not. In addition they do not always make it clear to the consumer that there are free government and charitable services available to them. In September 2010 the Office of Fair Trading said that the level of non-compliance with regulations across the sector was unacceptable and warned 129 debt management companies that they faced losing their consumer credit licences if they did not improve their standards substantially.

- Packaged current accounts

  Banks make strong efforts to sell their fee-paying packaged current accounts. The sales staff will point to all the 'free' Products that come with the account, such as travel insurance and mobile phone insurance, and ascribe high values to these wonderful extras. However, the fact is that unless the customer actually makes use of the Products they are worth nothing. Furthermore, on occasion bank staff have failed to explain clearly to the customer that they charge a fee for the account.

- Airlines

  So-called budget airlines are notorious for misleading consumers into believing they are getting a much better deal than they probably will, and have been severely criticized by the Advertising Standards Authority for advertising a low Price that excludes all the hidden charges. Airlines boost the ticket Price with extra charges such as booking fees, transaction charges, baggage charges, check-in charges, priority boarding fees etc. I have seen research that shows that in many cases the more established carriers are cheaper than the low-cost airlines when all the charges are taken into account.

- Energy companies

  Switching energy suppliers is supposed to save consumers a significant amount of money on their gas and electricity bills. However, in September 2010 Ofgem launched an investigation into four of the 'big six' energy companies over the mis-selling of energy contracts to consumers, which leave them worse off than if they hadn't switched deals. Meanwhile, a number of tariffs also have hidden fees tucked away in the small print of complicated contracts, which can mean consumers end up paying more for their energy than they originally anticipated.
- Insurance companies

  The terms and conditions of insurance policies can be confusing and consumers are often caught out by exclusions buried deep in the small print. For example, while a mobile phone insurance policy might claim the consumer is covered for loss, theft and damage, if they leave it in a public place or do not file the claim within the specified time limit the insurer is likely to refuse to pay out.
- Loan 'repayment holidays'

  Unfortunately a loan 'repayment holiday' is not quite as beneficial as it sounds. While some lenders sell the idea as a 'benefit', for the majority of people it will only make their loan more expensive. This is because they will be charged far more interest as a result and it will extend the length of their loans. This often isn't explained clearly at the time they take out their loan.

In this list, which is by no means exhaustive, I have referred to actual cases in which regulators have been involved. That we need so much regulation is dispiriting. In addition many industries seek to police themselves but often fall well short of the standards they claim to have set.

Early in the life of the Worshipful Company of Marketors, of which I am a Liveryman, Admiral Sir John Hamilton wrote a prayer for the use of the Marketors:

> Heavenly Father, we ask you that you give us a fresh vision of things we can do for you in our work-a-day lives; that as members of the Company of Marketors we may see our work as the rendering of service to others by providing them with goods and services to meet their needs; that we may never knowingly

> mislead them; that we may seek no more than fair reward for service honestly and thoroughly rendered.

I do not think you have to be religious to see the wisdom of such thoughts.

As a lifelong passionate marketer I am proud of the role that marketing has played in the world economy. Despite the ravages of two world wars, and totalitarianism prevailing for decades, more than half the world's population in the 20th century saw the greatest rise in prosperity in history. This was largely due to a combination of liberal democracy with free market (if not unbridled) capitalism. The engine of this was marketing, as marketing is about the search for innovative solutions to identified needs, the recruitment and retention of customers, the creation and building of value, the profitable development of the business proposition, the unifying theme of an enterprise, the response to competition and so much more.

In 1989 when the Berlin Wall fell it seemed as if all the issues had been resolved. Francis Fukuyama called it the end of history. Interestingly, on 29 December that year the Nikkei index peaked at 38,957.44 yen and has never seen such heights since. As I write this in May 2013 it is 13,694 yen having recently recovered from as low as 8,238.

At this point in the 21st century such triumphalism seems premature. The practice of mass production that led to mass consumption now looks short-sighted as we can see that we are consuming irreplaceable resources at an unsustainable rate. Wherever you stand on the climate change debate (and I am firmly on the side of the 98 per cent of scientists who believe that not only is the climate changing at an unusual pace but these changes are caused by mankind) it must be clear that fossil fuels are finite resources that took billions of years to develop and are being consumed in a few hundred years. Not only are fossil fuels finite, but many other critical materials are also scarce, including some of those that are required to develop replacement energy sources, as for example the lithium that is used in lithium ion batteries that will permit electric vehicles to replace internal combustion cars.

The fact is that any enterprise that uses resources faster than they can be replaced is not sustainable in the long run. Our success in marketing has been too complete. As we have learnt how to develop bigger and better business models built on Powerful brands and scalable franchises our need for constant growth has blinded us to the long-term problems that this will cause. Wherever one looks one sees the paradox of outstanding business success with unsustainable business practice. Supermarket chains gobbling up land banks and killing the high street and local farmers; fast-food companies targeting 'share of stomach' and cutting down forests to grow their beefburgers; financial institutions selling debt to those who can't afford to repay it; beverage companies using many litres of scarce fresh water to produce one litre of their processed Product; clothes manufacturers closing local factories to export production to sweat shops in developing countries exploiting child labour; food manufacturers encouraging obesity with the use of the wrong nutritional mix.

So am I some Johnny-Come-Lately getting on the logo-denying environmentalist bandwagon? Far from it. I did not subscribe to such views when they were first expressed because while I was concerned about their warnings I saw no hope in their alternatives. They seemed to be just advocating a cessation of marketing with a reversion to a long-lost alternative life. It is clear that the genie is out of the bottle and we can't put it back. Instead we need to use our marketing skills to develop new sustainable businesses that will both contribute to continued growth in prosperity but also adopt sustainable practice.

There will not only be opportunities in new forms of renewable energy but also in new practices to reduce our use of energy. The skills of marketing will be required to Persuade people to live and work in new ways. Greater density will be required in the design of new cities. New forms of ownership will be adopted so that our use of materials is infinitely more efficient. Recycling will be much more than car boot sales and eBay. There will be huge new industries in the recycling and reuse of valuable materials. New technologies will be developed that conserve rather than consume. Marketers will address the needs of conservers rather than consumers.

What I am calling for is a revolution. Not with blood in the streets but of business practice and consumer behaviour. I have lived through several revolutions and am confident that there will be at least one more. I have lived through the revolution of consumerism that has led to this situation. I lived through the revolution of civil rights. As an exchange student in the United States in the 1960s I met a Black Panther who told me that unless the black Power movement got what it demanded 'this country will burn, baby!' Then there has been the revolution of women's rights and in attitudes to various minorities. There was the overthrow of the Soviet Union and of its acolytes throughout Eastern Europe, which led to the liberation of countless millions. There has been the information technology revolution that has transformed ways of working and the organization of the firm. That has been succeeded by the internet revolution that is still going on and has further transformed many types of business and consumer behaviour.

So to paraphrase one of the greatest copywriters of all time, Karl Marx, the marketers have nothing to lose but their chains of consumerism. They have a world to conserve and sustain. Business men and women of the world, unite!

REFERENCES

Ambler, T (2000) *Marketing and the Bottom Line,* Pearson Education, Harlow

Ansoff, I (1965) *Corporate Strategy: An analytic approach to business policy for growth and expansion,* McGraw-Hill, New York

Ashworth, M (1970) *A Consuming Passion*, Educational Explorers, Reading

Bernays, E L (1945), *Public Relations*, University of Oklahoma

Birkman, R (1995, 1997) *True Colours: Get to know yourself with the highly acclaimed Birkman Method*, Thomas Nelson, Nashville

Chandler, A D Jnr (1962) *Strategy and Structure: Chapters in the history of the American industrial enterprise*, MIT Press, Cambridge, MA

Collins, J & Porras, J (1994) *Built to Last: Successful habits of visionary companies,* HarperCollins

Columbus, L (2004) *Best Practices in Industry Analyst Relations*, LWC Research, digital download

Davidson, H (1972) *Offensive Marketing*, Cassell, London

Davidson, H (1997) *Even More Offensive Marketing*, Penguin Business, London

Davidson, H (2002) *The Committed Enterprise,* Butterworth Heinemann, Oxford

Dibb, S, Simkin, L, Pride, W and Ferrell, O (2000) *Marketing Concepts and Strategies*, Houghton Mifflin, Boston

Dickens, C (1850) *David Copperfield,* Bradbury & Evans, London

Drucker, P (1954) *The Practice of Management,* Harper & Brothers, New York

Gilmore, F (1999) *Brand Warriors : Corporate leaders share their winning strategies,* HarperCollins, London

Harvey, C (1989) *Secrets of the World's Top Sales Performers,* Business Books, London

Harvey, C and Sykes, W(1988) *Your Pursuit of Profit,* Kogan Page, London

Heptonstall, N (1999) *The Will to Win*, NHA International, Henley-on-Thames

Kay, J (2010) *Obliquity: Why our goals are best achieved indirectly,* Profile Books, London

Kim, W C and Mauborgne, R (2005) *Blue Ocean Strategy: How to create uncontested market space,*Harvard Business School, Boston

Kotler, P (1967) *Marketing Management: Analysis, planning and control,* Prentice-Hall, Englewood Cliffs, NJ

Lancaster, G, Massingham, L and Ashford, R (2001) *Essentials Of Marketing,* McGraw-Hill, London

Levinson, J (1984) *Guerrilla Marketing,* Piatkus Books

McCarthy, E J (1960) *Basic Marketing: A managerial approach,* Richard D. Irwin, Homewood, IL

Meyer, C (2009) *Getting Our Way: 500 Years of Adventure and Intrigue: The inside story of British diplomacy*, Weidenfeld & Nicholson, London

Mintzberg, H, Ahlstrand, B and Lampel, J (2002) *Strategy Safari: A guided tour through the wilds of strategic management*, Prentice-Hall, Englewood Cliffs, N.J.

Moschella, D C (1997) *Waves of Power*, Amacom, New York

Newlin, K (2009) *Passion Brands: Why some brands are just gotta have, drive all night for, and tell all your friends about*, Prometheus Books, New York

Packard, V (1957) *The Hidden Persuaders*, David McKay Co, New York

Peale, N V (1952) *The Power of Positive Thinking*, Simon & Shuster, New York

Peebles, N (1999, 2012) *How to Sell Your Business the Easy Way!*, Amazon Kindle edition

Porter, M (1980) *Competitive Strategy: Techniques for analysing industries and competitors*, Free Press, New York

Reeves, R (1961) *Reality in Advertising*, Knopf, New York

Ries, A and Trout, J (1981, 2000) *Positioning: The battle for your mind* McGraw-Hill, New York

Ries, A and Trout, J (1993) *The 22 Immutable Laws of Marketing*, HarperCollins, New York

Semler, R (1993) *Maverick!* Century, London

Semler, R (2003) *The Seven-Day Weekend* Century, London

Slywotzky, A J and Morrison, D J (1998) *The Profit Zone*, John Wiley & Sons, Chichester

Thaler, R H and Sunstein, C R (2008) *Nudge: Improving decisions about health, wealth and happiness*, Caravan, New Haven

Tzu, S (tr Griffith, SB) (6th C BC; 1963) *The Art of War*, Oxford University Press, Oxford

von Clausewitz, C (tr Jolles OJM) (1832, 1943) *On War*, Random House, New York

FURTHER READING

Ahrens, T (1991) *Driving the Tiger: How to create and manage rapid growth*, Business Books, London

Brenner, J G (1999) *The Chocolate Wars: Inside the secret worlds of Mars and Hershey*, HarperCollins, London

Bullmore, J (2006) *Apples, Insights and Mad Inventions*, John Wiley & Sons, Chichester

Byham, W C and Cox, J (1988, 1998) *Zapp! The Lightning of Empowerment*, Fawcett Columbine,New York

Clancy, K J and Krieg, P C (2000) *Counter-Intuitive Marketing*, Free Press, New York

Clutterbuck, D and Kernaghan, S (1991) *Making Customers Count: A guide to excellence in customer care*, Mercury, London

Davis, S M (2009) *The Shift: The transformation of today's marketers into tomorrow's growth leaders*, Jossey Bass, San Francisco

Decker, C (1998) *P&G 99: 99 principles and practices of procter and gamble's Success* HarperCollins, London

Dunn, M and Halsall, C (2009) *The Marketing Accountability Imperative*, Jossey Bass, San Francisco

Falk, R(1961) *The Business of Management: Art or craft?*, Penguin, London

Geddes, K and Bussey, G (1991) *The Setmakers: A history of the radio and television industry*, BREMA, London

Gilmore, F (2001) *Warriors on the High Wire*, HarperCollins, London

Glasser, R (1964) *Planned Marketing*, Business Publications, London

Goold, M and Campbell, A (1987) *Strategies and Styles: The role of the centre in managing diversified corporations*, Blackwell, Oxford

Haig, M (2003) *Brand Failures*, Kogan Page, London

Hamel, G (2000) *Leading the Revolution*, Harvard Business School, Boston

Hamel, G and Prahalad, C K (1994) *Competing for the Future*, Harvard Business School, Boston

Hankinson, G and Cowking, P (1996) *The Reality of Global Brands*, McGraw-Hill, London

Hart, S & Murphy J et al (1998) *Brands: The new wealth creators*, Macmillan, London

Hastings, H et al (2004) *The New Marketing Mission*, Ana, New York

Hegarty, J (2011) *Hegarty on Advertising: Turning intelligence into magic*, Thames & Hudson, London

Jones, R (1974) *The Business of Advertising*, Longmans, London

Kashani, K and Turpin, D (ed) (1999) *Marketing Management: An international perspective,* Macmillan, Basingstoke

Kay, W (1987, 1989) *Battle for the High Street*, Judy Piatkus, London

Kochan, N (ed)(1996) *The World's Greatest Brands,* Macmillan, London

Kotler, J P and Heskett, J L (1992) *Corporate Culture and Performance,* Free Press, New York

Leaf, R (2012) *The Art of Perception; Memoirs of a life in PR*, Atlantic Books, London

Levitt, T (1983, 1986) *The Marketing Imagination,* Free Press, New York

Luh, S S (2003) *Business the Sony Way,* Capstone, Oxford

Lyons, N (1976) *The Sony Vision*, Crown Publishers, New York

Macrae, C (1996) *The Brand Chartering Handbook: How brand organizations learn living scripts,* Addison-Wesley, Harlow

Marx, E (1999) *Breaking Through Culture Shock: What you need to succeed in international business,* Nicholas Brealey, London

McIver, C (1959) *Marketing*, Business Publications, London

Morita, A, Reingold, E and Shimomura, M (1987) *Made in Japan: Akio Morita and Sony,* Collins, London

Nathan, J (1999) *Sony, The Private Life,* HarperCollins, London

Nayak, P R and Ketteringham, J M (1986), *Breakthroughs: How leadership and drive created commercial innovations that swept the world*, Mercury, London

Nilson, T H (1995), *Chaos Marketing: How to win in a turbulent world,* McGraw-Hill, London

Ogilvy, D (1963) *Confessions of an Advertising Man,* Longmans, London

Ohmae, K (1982) *The Mind of the Strategist*, McGraw-Hill, New York

Pavalko, R M (1971, 1988) *Sociology of Occupations and Professions,* F.E. Peacock, Itasca, Ill

Peppers, D and Rogers, M (1993) *The One-To-One Future: Building business relationships one customer at a time*, Judy Piatkus, London

Peters, T (1992) *Liberation Management*, Macmillan, London

Peters, T (1987) *Thriving on Chaos: Handbook for a management revolution,* Macmillan, London

Powell, W J (1985) *Pillsbury's Best: A company history from 1869*, Pillsbury, Minneapolis

Pringle, H and Gordon, W (2001) *Brand Manners: How to create the self-confident organisation to live the brand*, John Wiley & Sons, Chichester

Reddin, W (1970) *Managerial Effectiveness*, McGraw-Hill, New York

Schisgall, O (1981), *Eyes on Tomorrow: The evolution of Procter & Gamble,* JG Ferguson, Chicago

Schwartz, A, Gomes, J and McCarthy, C (2010) *The Way We're Working Isn't Working,* Free Press, New York

Smallbone, D W (1965) *The Practice of Marketing*, Staples Press, London

Toop, A (1966, 1978) *Choosing the Right Sales Promotion,* The Sales Machine, London

Toop, A (1991) *Cracking Jack! Sales promotion techniques and how to use them successfully,* Mazecity, Sandhurst

Webster, E (1964) *How to Win the Business Battle,* John Murray, London

Whiteley, RC (1991) *The Customer Driven Company,* Business Books, London

Woodward, R & Bernstein, C (1974) *All the President's Men,* Simon & Shuster, New York

INDEX

NB: page numbers in *italic* indicate figures or tables

CPSIA information can be obtained at www.ICGtesting.com
Printed in the USA
BVOW04s1015310714

361197BV00007B/260/P